Zacharias Topelius

Times of Gustaf Adolf

Zacharias Topelius

Times of Gustaf Adolf

ISBN/EAN: 9783743322455

Manufactured in Europe, USA, Canada, Australia, Japa

Cover: Foto ©ninafisch / pixelio.de

Manufactured and distributed by brebook publishing software (www.brebook.com)

Zacharias Topelius

Times of Gustaf Adolf

The Surgeon's Stories.

By Z. Topelius.

THE
SURGEON'S STORIES.

BY

Z. TOPELIUS,

PROFESSOR OF HISTORY, UNIVERSITY OF ÅBO, FINLAND.

A SERIES OF

Swedish Historical Romances,

IN SIX CYCLES.

(EACH CYCLE IN ONE VOLUME. PRICE $1.25.)

FIRST CYCLE — TIMES OF GUSTAF ADOLF.
SECOND CYCLE — TIMES OF QUEEN CHRISTINA.
THIRD CYCLE — TIMES OF CHARLES XII.
FOURTH CYCLE — TIMES OF FREDERICK ADOLF.
FIFTH CYCLE — TIMES OF PRINCESS OF WASA.
SIXTH CYCLE — TIMES OF GUSTAF III.

THE SURGEON'S STORIES.

TIMES OF GUSTAF ADOLF.

BY

Z. TOPELIUS.

TRANSLATED FROM THE ORIGINAL SWEDISH.

CHICAGO:
JANSEN, McCLURG, & COMPANY.
1883.

COPYRIGHT,
BY JANSEN, McCLURG & CO.,
A. D., 1882.

R R. Donnelley & Sons, Printers, Chicago.

INTRODUCTION:

TREATING OF THE SURGEON AND HIS LIFE.

HE was born in one of the smaller towns of East Bothnia, on the 15th of August, 1769—the same day as Napoleon. I remember the day also from the fact that the Surgeon was accustomed to celebrate it with a little social party, to which he always invited two or three of his old cousins (he called all his old aunts " cousins "), and two or three of his brothers (he called everyone brother who called him uncle). These people collected in his garret, and were treated with cakes and coffee. The apartment was necessarily rather dark, being lighted from the outside only through two dormer windows; but it was a large one, which was fortunate, as, besides the two or three cousins and the two or three brothers, the parties were attended by a dozen children—boisterous boys and chattering girls, who made a great deal of noise and tumbled everything about in disorder. For the Surgeon had an indescribable fondness for children, and allowed us to do as we liked, although our noise often deafened the older and more sedate guests. But we must return to the Surgeon's birthday—which is the first point in his claim to our interest; and he had more such points than have most people.

The fact that the Surgeon was born on the same day as Napoleon not only constituted the pride of his life but was the cause of several of his most important adventures, for he never ceased to see in this coincidence a very remarkable omen. Even if he had never become a great man, as perhaps in his youth he had dreamed he might, yet this omen urged him forward, to seek honor and fortune in various fields of life. His pride, like his ambition, was of that mild and genial kind which smiles silently at itself, and is unwilling to harm even a caterpillar. It was one of those innocent illusions which, born of the merest chance, are kept up through life as matters of the greatest weight and significance; which are never abandoned, though reality proves them a thousand times to be a dream. Anyone who understands human nature could easily have told the Surgeon that, with an ambition such as his, he would never be able to play a brilliant *rôle*, even were he a hundred times born on the same day as Napoleon. For altogether different is that ambition which, through a thousand hindrances, forces its way to the heights of human greatness; which, with the inexhaustible resources of genius, courage and energy, combines entire indifference to the means by which it seeks its end. When does the proud conqueror count the victims who, for his honor, bleed on the battle-field; all the tears, all the ruins of human happiness, over which he pushes his way toward that phantom of a greatness which gleams through the centuries?

Had the Surgeon, on his famous birthday, been brought into the world by Madame Lætitia Bonaparte, in Ajaccio, he might perhaps have become something else than a surgeon, but scarcely anything greater. It is true that Napoleon's celebrated cook once declared, in the consciousness of his greatness, that "one may *become* a cook, but one is *born* a turnspit." Yet he, a genius, forgot the predestination of genius; born a turnspit, one seldom becomes anything else in reality, even though he have gold on his collar or diplomas in his pocket. The Surgeon was not born to be a Napoleon; not because he had the burgher name, Andreas Bäck (he had studied Latin, and always signed himself Andreas, instead of the common form of Anders), nor because his father was a simple sergeant, who lost an arm in the Pomeranian War; but for the reason that one with such an inexhaustible fund of good humor and irresolution, even when possessing a more brilliant intellect than had fallen to the Surgeon's lot, may possibly become a bold partisan, but never a great general, in the battle of life.

The Surgeon was, in his childhood, as he himself used to say, a great rogue; but as he showed a quick understanding, he was sent by his uncle, a wealthy merchant, to a school in Wasa. At the age of eighteen, he had advanced so far that, with a firkin of butter in the wagon and seventeen dollars in his pocket, he went to Åbo, to pass his student's examination. He got through it without difficulty; and our newly-made student was now, according to the wish of his uncle and benefactor, going to strive with all his might for the gown and surplice. With secret sighs, he sat down to his Hebrew *Codex;* his thoughts flew all over the world, and his eyes strayed too frequently from *Bereschit bara elohim* to the parades in the square, where the fine-looking troops were reviewed before they left for the war. "Oh!" thought the future ecclesiastic, "if I were only a soldier, standing there so straight in the ranks, ready to fight, like my father, for king and country!" But there was one who put a decided stop to the matter: his mother had never been able to forget that his father lost his arm in the war, and she had exacted a sacred promise from her son that he would never become a soldier.

Young Bäck was a good son, so he returned from the parades to his *Codex;* but he had not gone more than half through Genesis before a bombshell scattered all his plans and thoughts. This bombshell was an advertisement in the Åbo newspaper, signed "Erik Gabriel Hartman," in behalf of the Medical Faculty, stating that students who wished to take service as surgeons in the hospitals and regiments during the war should present themselves without delay for private medical instruction; after which—quite soon, of course, for the war was in full progress—they could count upon being ordered out, with five or six dollars per month to begin with. Now our man was no longer to be held back: he wrote home that, as a surgeon, one is accustomed to take off other people's limbs, without losing any himself; and after much solicitation, he received the desired consent. In an instant the *Codex* stood upside down on the shelf. Bäck did not study—he swallowed—the art of surgery, and in a few months was as good a surgeon as many others: for in those times they were not so particular. Who does not remember how Franzén sings, in his excellent "Once and Now:"

> "Once, doctors cut off fingers, toes,
>   Whose uselessness was sure;
> Now, they quickly take off those
>   They know not how to cure."

It is very possible that the poet then thought of

Bäck. But our Surgeon did not allow himself to be disturbed.

He was in the campaigns of 1788 and 1789 on land, and of 1790 at sea; was in many a hard struggle, drank boldly (according to his own account), and cut off arms and legs in the most jubilant manner. At that time he knew nothing about Napoleon, nor the coincidence of his birth, and consequently did not yet consider himself destined for anything great. But he often related afterwards how, on the eventful 3d of July, in Wiborg Bay, with Stedingk on board the "Styrbjörn" at the head of the flotilla, he passed the enemy's batteries at Krosserort's Point, and had the splinter of a spar hit him in the right cheek, giving him a scar for the rest of his life. The same ball which caused the accident tore along the ship with great havoc, and whizzed by the commander's ear, making him completely deaf for a moment. Bäck was instantly on hand with his lancet and cordials, and in three minutes Stedingk had his hearing again. It was just at the time when the danger was greatest and the shower of balls hottest. Crash! The vessel was aground. "Boys, we are all lost!" shrieked a voice. "Oh, no!" answered another—Henrik Fågel, from Ahlais Village, in Ulfsby; "order all the men to the prow; it is the stern that has stuck." "All men to the prow!" commanded Stedingk. "Styrbjörn" was again afloat, and the whole Swedish fleet followed in its wake. Bäck used to say: "What the deuce would have become of the fleet if Stedingk had remained deaf?" and everybody understood the old man's meaning: he had saved the whole Swedish fleet, of course. But if one happened to smile at his innocent boast, then he laughed too, and added, good-naturedly: "Yes, yes; you see, brother, I was born on the 15th of August; that is the whole secret; it is no merit of mine."

When the war was over, Bäck began to feel uneasy at the hospitals, and as he (according to his own assertion) was in especial favor with Stedingk, he said good-by to the fleet and went with his patron to Stockholm—as family physician, I think he once said; but others assert that he was rather engaged as a scribe. Quick, energetic, and trustworthy, he understood many a side hint and received confidences, which he (according to his own account) honored perfectly. He stood at that time in extensive relation with valets, chambermaids, secretaries, and such people, who, in that time of political intrigue in high places, played an important part; nay, often were they apparently insignificant but in reality effective agencies in many an entangled cabal which spun its web in darkness until it had ensnared the highest personages in the kingdom and brought them to ruin. I have never been able to find out how much of a *rôle* the Surgeon really played in these celebrated cabals; it is possible that it was not so considerable as he sometimes made it appear. But that it was ever a low and perfidious one, I take it upon myself to deny. Bäck was too honest a fellow at heart for anything of that kind. I am more inclined to believe that he did others' errands without fully realizing their political import until he saw the results in open daylight. But one thing is certain: that in those times he was initiated into much gossip about prominent personages, both of his own and of past times, and picked up many curious items which were little known but yet were important and significant.

The Surgeon was a "Gustavian," in the same sense as a great part of the middle classes of Stockholm at that time. Dazzled by the brilliancy of the court, which was also reflected on the humbler circles in its vicinity, transported by the condescension with which Gustaf III. knew so well how to gain the favor of the masses when he needed it, the Surgeon became unconditionally devoted to his king. What did he care for the political dissatisfaction which had for a long time been lurking around the throne, and raising its head more and more threateningly? He was young; he needed no reason for his attachment. "Such a magnificent king!" was his only thought. He was at that time a thorough royalist; and if it happened that he executed others' commissions in the service of intrigue, it was because he, poor fellow, supposed he was doing the king a benefit.

One day in the beginning of March, 1792, the Surgeon, at that time a good-looking youth (to use his own words), had, through a chambermaid at Countess Lantingshausen's—who, in her turn (the chambermaid's of course), stood on a confidential footing with Count Klas Horn's favorite lackey—obtained a vague inkling of a murderous conspiracy against the king's life. The Surgeon resolved to play Providence in Sweden's fate, and reveal to the king all that he knew, and perhaps a little more. He sought an audience with his majesty, under the pretext of having a petition; but was flatly refused by the chamberlain on duty, De Besche. He renewed his request the second time, but with the result that he was turned out of doors. The third time, he placed himself in the road before the king's carriage, holding his written statement high in the air. "What does that fellow want?"

asked Gustaf III. of his attending chamberlain, as he alighted; and again, as ill-luck would have it, the chamberlain was De Besche.

"It is a discharged Surgeon," answered the courtier, ironically. "He humbly requests that your majesty may most graciously begin another war, to procure him something to do."

The king smiled, and the Surgeon remained standing in confusion at the gate.

Some days later, the king was shot. "It was not my fault," the Surgeon used to say, when he spoke of his valor on that occasion. "Had not that infernal De Besche been there . . But I won't say anything more."

Everyone understood what he meant. He had saved the Swedish fleet at Wiborg; he would also have saved the life of Gustaf III. had there not been an "if" in the way in the shape of a malicious chamberlain. There was already a little of the 15th of August in him; at least so he thought himself.

The Regency and Reuterholm were by no means to the Surgeon's taste. He had withdrawn from Stedingk's service, and began to practice his profession in Stockholm. More than ever was he drawn into the scandal of the day, himself a wandering chronicle from patient to patient. As such, he was used by the party of the old court to set certain reports in circulation. When there was anything wrong, he smelt it out before anyone else. He warned (so he insisted) the leaders of the movement of 1794; but none except the Alcibiades of the North believed him; and thus he had the satisfaction of having saved Armfelt, as he saved the Swedish fleet and Gustaf III. It was he who, with the state surgeon, Fröberg, represented the medical art at Lady Rudenschöld's execution. This cruel execution, where genius and beauty were trampled in the dust, where the people all around shed tears, and only the base partisan triumphed, stirred the Surgeon's honest heart. His tongue, unaccustomed to keep still, was sharpened by indignation more than was advisable; and he asked aloud, so that all heard it, why the lady was not allowed to *sit down*, when his excellence, Baron Reuterholm's uncle, *sat* on the scaffold? These words soon came to Reuterholm's ears; and, if we may believe the Surgeon, a scarcely milder fate than that of the unfortunate lady awaited him. The Surgeon, who had an ear in every lane, and an eye in every chamber-window, felt something unpleasant in the air, and decided to escape in time from the threatening storm. With his lancet in his pocket and his bandages under his arm, he fled on board a Pomeranian yacht, and in a few days was in Stralsund.

I no longer intend to be discursive about the Surgeon's experiences. After a little while he went afoot, as a wandering quack, on the road to Paris, where the Directory had just come into power. One army was raised after another. Every student took to the sword or the lancet. The Surgeon arrived at a lucky moment, received a little appointment in the Italian army, and stood by Napoleon's side when his sun of fortune rose beyond the Alps. Now first apprised of the significance of his birthday, the Surgeon felt an insatiable ambition awaken in his breast. One fine night he abandoned his hospital in Nizza, and hurried to Mantua. He wished to call on General Bonaparte in person; he wished to distinguish himself. In short, he wished to make of the 15th of August a ladder to immortality. I cannot comprehend how it was; but, in fact, he asserted that he obtained an audience with Bonaparte, and presented to him his request for a position as army physician. "But," sighed the Surgeon, whenever he described this remarkable day of his life, "Bonaparte was very busy; he did not understand me, and asked one of his adjutants what I wanted. 'Citizen General,' answered the adjutant, 'it is a surgeon, who requests the honor of sawing off your leg at the first opportunity.' Just then," added the Surgeon, "the cannon began to thunder, the Austrians advanced, and General Bonaparte told me to go to the devil!"

The Surgeon, who had saved so many great personages, was thus deprived of the opportunity of saving Napoleon. He got camp-fever instead, and lay sick half a year in Brescia. From there he followed the French army to Austria, ran away to Switzerland, and tarried for a time in Zürich. There he took charge of a drug-store, fell in love with a little red-cheeked Swiss girl, and was on the point of marrying her, when Prince Kosakoff, then Massena, and finally Suvaroff, overran the peaceful city with their hordes. In this confusion, the Surgeon's betrothed fled, and never came back.

He sat one day, sorrowfully looking out of the window of his shop, when two Cossacks approached, dismounted, seized him, in spite of his resistance, and hurried off at full speed. The Surgeon thought his last moment had come; he had not the slightest idea what this meant. But the Cossacks brought him, unharmed, to a simple hut. There sat some officers around a punch-bowl, and among them a stern man in large boots.

"Comrade," said the man, in a short and commanding tone, "out with your forceps; I have tooth-ache."

There was no help for it; the Surgeon had to take out his forceps. He ventured to ask what tooth it was that ached.

"You argue?" said the man, impatiently.

"No, I don't argue," answered the Surgeon, and pulled out the first tooth he got hold of.

"Good, my boy! March!" and the Surgeon was dismissed with ten ducats for his trouble. The list of his merits acquired an important addition; he had pulled out a tooth for—the hero Suvaroff.

Encouraged by this, the Surgeon resolved to seek his fortune in Russia. He went to St. Petersburg, and called upon the Swedish minister, General Stedingk, brother of his patron, the admiral. Here he obtained a situation as physician in a military hospital, where he got along nicely, and collected a little fortune.

Thus passed four or five years, when the intelligence came that Napoleon had mounted the Imperial throne. The Surgeon's old ambition now revived again; he resigned his place, and returned in 1804 to his fatherland. With his merits, he counted on a brilliant promotion; but no: the Medical Faculty had already become pretentious, and wished to see his diploma. In his vexation he renounced the medical profession, and, with the aid of his testimonials from Zürich, purchased a pharmacy in Stockholm.

The Surgeon was now thirty-five years of age. He looked back upon the life he had hitherto led, and found it rather boyish. He said to himself: "It is not sufficient to have saved the Swedish fleet, Gustaf III., and Armfelt; to have had an audience with Bonaparte, and pulled a tooth for

Suvaroff. One must also have an aim in life." And he began to realize that he had a fatherland.

The war of 1808 broke out. The Surgeon sold out his drug-store, came again in conflict with the Medical Faculty, and was not able to mount higher than to the position of an assistant physician in one of the Finnish regiments. It was just as well; he no longer fought for glory and the 15th of August. In the army were lieutenants with gray mustaches; why could not the Surgeon, with twenty years' experience, be an assistant physician? He took part in the campaigns of 1808 and 1809; his place in all engagements was close by the battle-field, in some hut by the roadside. There he fought, in his way, manfully and honestly, with misery, disease, and death; cut off arms and legs, dressed wounds, applied plasters, comforting the wounded soldiers, with whom he shared his flask, his bread, his purse, and, what was more, his continual good-humor, with a thousand diverting anecdotes of his wanderings in foreign lands. By half the army he was known as the *tupakka tohtori* (tobacco doctor)—probably because, through his business relations in Stockholm, he was constantly provided with the "excellent leaf," and was always ready to share with the soldier his pipe and quid. One can be Christian-like even in tobacco! The Surgeon was not so stuck-up that he, like Konow's corporal, went

"With two quids from sheer pride."

On the contrary, he rather went without any, when the need was great and a wounded comrade had got the last bit of the roll in the pocket of his yellow nankeen vest. Therefore the soldiers loved the "tobacco doctor," and Ficandt swore that he would promote him—for, next to bullets and gunpowder, there was nothing in the wide world so deserving of a man's respect as an honest quid and a package of smoking-tobacco.

The Surgeon's adventures during the war might easily fill a whole Christmas calendar; but I will leave them for the present, and only mention, in passing, that in 1808 he celebrated his birthday on the *seventeenth* of August, at Alavo. After the war, he resigned—without a pension, of course. When peace was concluded, in 1809, and so many Finns moved over to Sweden, the Surgeon considered it more honorable to share all vicissitudes with his fatherland, and therefore remained. His old roving disposition did not allow him to bind himself to any fixed place in the community; so he travelled around the country for a few years with his little medicine-chest, prescribing for and curing all diseases with lancet, cupping-horns, *essentia dulcis*, and *mixtura simplex*. From parish to parish and village to village, he drove around with his old horse and his medicine-chest, welcome everywhere, and just as much sought for as any Doctor Bolliger of modern times. The Surgeon was free as a bird on the wing. Voluble and amusing, he spiced his best rhubard with comical stories, sure to find in every farm-house a hospitable board and a talkative hostess. It was a happy season. I am perfectly convinced that the Surgeon then accomplished much good; but this, he never spoke of.

Still, the Surgeon did not long travel around the country as a practitioner among the peasantry. Since 1788 the medical art at the universities had advanced with seven-league boots. The medical

A   1

authorities began to take severe measures with quacks of all sorts, who still, in the beginning of this century, overran the country; often enough, it is true, to the detriment and shame of the medical profession, but as often to the benefit of suffering humanity: for regular physicians were extremely few, and apothecaries, likewise, far apart. Now, as the Surgeon had before been in open conflict with the Medical Faculty in Upsala and Åbo, it was only necessary for a zealous colleague to report his medical itineracies in the country. The Surgeon was called to Åbo, to undergo *colloquium familiare*, but did not choose to obey, which was really impolitic; for with his merits from the war, he would have been self-indorsed for the position of city physician. But he was stubborn, and too much in love with his independence, so he did not go to Åbo; and the result was that, under penalty of a heavy fine, he was forbidden to continue his practice.

The Surgeon now for the third time gave up medicine, settled down in his native place, and took to fishing. It was an interesting way of gaining a livelihood, but, alas, a very meagre support for a man who wished to have his daily cup of coffee and pipe of tobacco. In his days of prosperity, he might have accumulated a fine fortune; but he had been too liberal and too migratory. He now owned in this world scarcely more than his old brown cloak, his yellow nankeen vest, his cheerful disposition, and some hundred fish-hooks. He therefore let himself be persuaded to seek a situation as vaccinator, which he obtained through the influence of some former compatriots. The old marauder in the field of medical art was very well contented with his slight occupation, which still allowed him twice a year to roam around the country, chat with the old women, and live for the day according to his old habit. Nor was there anyone who knew better than he how to quiet the little children. When his needle punctured the fine, soft flesh of their arms, it went like play under kindly words; and before the little ones even noticed it, the pain was over. This gained for the Surgeon still more the good-will of all the mothers. They even forgave him his ugly habit of chewing tobacco: it was too late to cure it now.

And then the snow of old age stole mildly and imperceptibly over the Surgeon's head. He was one of the few fortunate ones who had gone through the storms of life without losing faith in humanity; always glad and free from sorrow, and without ever feeling his heart hardened under adversity or becoming puffed up when fortune smiled. He was really a good soul, who could smile at the follies of his youth; and yet they seemed to cling to him still. The Emperor Napoleon, "his natal brother,"—as he jokingly said, alluding to the 15th of August—had mounted the height of human greatness more quickly and descended from it again still more quickly; while the life of the Surgeon, like a pendulum in its even vibration, swung between the narrower degrees of a success which had never spoiled him, and an adversity which had never crushed him.

A bachelor all his life, since he happily escaped love's snares in Switzerland, he cherished, however, none of the prejudices which so often cause such men to undervalue the holiest impulses of the heart. He had left books too early to acquire a thorough education; but his rich experiences of life had not gone by without benefit, and I was astonished at his knowledge of human nature.

Often in our childhood and first youth we sat up there in the old garret chamber, around his leather-covered arm-chair, by the light of the crackling fire, and listened to his tales from the world of fiction and from life. His memory was inexhaustible; and as the old proverb says that even the wild stream does not let its waves flow by all at once, so had the Surgeon also a continually new stock of stories, partly from his own time, but still more from periods which had long since passed. He had not a wide historical knowledge; his tales were desultory character-sketches rather than coherent descriptions. More recently, I have found that one must exclude much that was merely gossip and party slander. There was also lacking those broad and elevated views which are only gained through the constant association of thought and feeling with that which is great in life; but what he had was fidelity, warm feeling, and, above all, a power of vivid delineation, such as I will not undertake to reproduce from memory.

When we had listened long to the old man, it sometimes happened that he took out a half-used-up electric battery, and drew from it spark after spark. "In that way the world sparkled when I was young," said he, laughing; "one had only to apply a finger, and, click! it flashed in all directions. But then it was our Lord who turned the machine."

But it was rare that he wrote out a story, as he did "The Duchess of Finland." The greater part of his tales were related orally. Many years have since rolled by; some of the stories I have forgotten, and some I have compared with traditions and books. If the reader finds a pleasure in it, the Surgeon will not have narrated his tales in vain during the winter evenings.

The Surgeon's Stories.

First Cycle:
Times of Gustaf Adolf.

Part I.—The King's Ring.
Part II.—The Sword and the Plough.
Part III.—Fire and Water.

CONTENTS.

PART I.—THE KING'S RING.

INTERLUDE		27
CHAPTER I.	The Battle of Breitenfeld	28
CHAPTER II.	The Nobleman without a Name	40
CHAPTER III.	Lady Regina	46
CHAPTER IV.	Lady Regina's Oath	63
CHAPTER V.	Judith and Holofernes	72
CHAPTER VI	The Finns at Lech	96
CHAPTER VII.	New Adventures	104
CHAPTER VIII	Nuremberg and Lützen	114

PART II—THE SWORD AND THE PLOUGH.

INTERLUDE		127
CHAPTER I.	A Man from the Club War	133
CHAPTER II.	Ashamed of the Peasant Name	146
CHAPTER III.	The Southerner in the North	158
CHAPTER IV.	Peasant, Burgher, and Soldier	167
CHAPTER V.	The Arrival at Korsholm	174
CHAPTER VI.	Loves of the South and North	183
CHAPTER VII.	The Siege of Korsholm	189

PART III.—FIRE AND WATER.

Interlude	. . . .	204
Chapter I.	Spoils from the Battle-field . .	212
Chapter II.	Two Old Acquaintances .	223
Chapter III.	The Treasure-Room . . .	228
Chapter IV.	The Duke and the Lieutenant .	240
Chapter V.	Reconciliation . . .	245
Chapter VI.	The Battle of Nördlingen . .	257
Chapter VII.	The Prodigal Son . . .	264
Chapter VIII.	The Fugitive	270
Chapter IX.	Don Quixote in the North . .	280
Chapter X.	Kajana Castle	289
Chapter XI.	The Prisoner of State . .	295
Chapter XII.	The Tempter . .	306
Chapter XIII.	*Abi, Male Spiritus*	312
Chapter XIV.	The Judgment of the Saints .	320
Chapter XV.	Bertel and Regina . . .	324
Chapter XVI.	The King's Ring — The Sword and the Plough — Fire and Water .	330

TIMES OF GUSTAF ADOLF.

PART I.—THE KING'S RING.

INTERLUDE.

AS you sit in your quiet home, surrounded by peace, comfort, and civilization, do you, reader, remember those memories, grand and tearful, which still, after hundreds of years, remain, now radiant with the brightness of sunlight, and now darkening, like indelible blood-stains, the variegated pages of history? Can your thoughts, torpid with repose, transport themselves back to the horrors and joys of the past, not straying indifferently from one thing to another which excites your curiosity, but taking a warm and vital interest, as if you yourself stood in the midst of those struggles, now long since fought out, bled in them, conquered or fell in them, and felt your heart beat with hope or apprehension, according as fortune smiled or betrayed? Standing on the heights of history, and looking far around on the wild arena of human destiny, can you transfer yourself into the vale of the past—the life physically buried and decayed, but spiritually immortal, which constitutes the essence and substance of history? Did you ever see history portrayed as an old man, with a wise brow and pulseless heart, weighing all things in the balance of reason? Is not, rather, the genius of history like an eternally blooming maiden, full of fire, with a burning heart and flaming soul, humanly warm and humanly beautiful?

Therefore, if you have the capacity to suffer or rejoice with the generations that have been; to hate with them, to love with them; to be transported, to admire, to despise, to curse, as they have done; in a word, to live among them with your whole heart, and not alone with your cold, reflecting judgment, —then follow me! I will lead you down into the vale. My hand is weak, and my sketch humble; but your heart will guide you better than I: upon that I rely—and begin.

CHAPTER I.

THE BATTLE OF BREITENFELD.

FOR centuries there has resounded through the history of Germany and Sweden a name, at the recollection of which the Swede raises his head higher and the freedom-loving German uncovers his head in admiration. It is Leipzig, Breitenfeld, and the 7th of September, 1631.

King Gustaf Adolf stood with his Swedes and Finns on German soil, to protect the holiest and highest interests in life—liberty and faith. Tilly, the terrible old corporal, had invaded Saxony, and the king followed. Twice already had they met; the tiger had challenged the lion to the contest, but the lion did not move. Now they stood for the third time in view of each other; the crushing blow must fall, and Germany trembled in anticipation of its fate.

Early in the morning, the united Swedish and Saxon armies crossed the Loder, *and marched toward the village of Breitenfeld, where they placed themselves in battle order. It was some new military tactics invented by the king: the foot-soldiers in brigades, the cavalry in small squadrons, between them the musketeers, and the whole in two lines; but the Saxons were by themselves.

The king rode along the lines, inspected everything with his keen glance, and spoke encouraging words. His eye rested with delight upon these brave men. There stood Gustaf Horn, with his troop of cavalry, on the left wing; in the centre the valiant Teuffel, and in front of him Torstenson, with his light but formidable leather cannon; Banér with his Livonians, and Hepburn with his Scots, occupied the second line.

Last of all, the king approached the right wing, which he himself commanded. There stood five regiments of cavalry: Tott, with his regiment; Soop, with his Westgoths; Stenbock, with his Smålanders; and, farthest of all, Stålhandske, with the Finns. The king's look brightened more and more as he slowly passed the saluting ranks.

"Stålhandske," said he, checking his colossal dark-brown steed at the last Finnish division, "I suppose you understand why I have placed you on the flank. Opposite us stands Pappenheim with his Wallachians. He longs to make my acquaintance," remarked the king, smiling; "and I expect that we will have a hard tussle if he throws the whole swarm upon us from this side. I rely upon you and your Finns to receive him energetically."

The king then raised his voice so as to be heard by the whole cavalry force, and added:

"See to it, boys, that you do not dull your swords on those iron-clad fellows; but rather beat down the horses first, and then you will have easy work with the heavy rider."

The Finnish cavalry realized full well both the danger and the honor of their position, and were proud of it. The king's confidence inspired all with courage and self-reliance. There was not a man who did not feel prepared to meet the dreaded Pappenheim himself. On seeing those short and thick-set figures on their small insignificant-looking horses, one would at the first glance have scarcely considered them equal to the attack of the stately Wallachians, on their large, fiery, strongly-built chargers. Tilly himself, in the speech he made to his troops directly before the battle, spoke with contempt of his starved-out naked enemies and their horses, which were meaner than the meanest pack-horses in the Imperial army.

"Ride straight upon them," added he, "and horse and rider will fall powerless under the hoofs of your snorting steeds."

But Tilly did not really know his enemy, or pretended not to know him. That which was lacking in the Finnish cavalry in outer bearing and appearance was more than compensated for by their iron muscles and their calm courage, indomitable in death; while their little horses had all that endurance of the Finnish race, which, during a prolonged and wearisome conflict, contributed not a little to the victory.

Followed by the glad hurrahs of the Finns, the king galloped away. Stålhandske turned to his men and repeated the king's words in Finnish. The faces of the eager soldiers shone with pride and joy.

"Well, Bertila," added Stålhandske, turning to a young man in the foremost ranks, who rode a handsome black horse and was distinguished from the rest by his height and bearing, "do you feel inclined to win the knight's spur to-day?"

The one addressed seemed surprised, saluted with his sword, and colored up to the brim of his helmet. "I have never dared to aspire to so great a distinction," answered he, while his glowing cheeks led one to suspect that just this had been the object of his most secret dreams. "I . . . a peasant's son!" he added, hesitatingly.

Stålhandske smiled.

"Thunder and lightning! the boy blushes like a bride at the altar! A peasant's son? What the deuce, then, have we others been from the beginning? Do you not furnish four fully-equipped horsemen for the war? Has not the Lord placed a heart in your breast and the king a weapon in your hand? That is a coat of arms in itself; you must attend to the rest."

A thousand swift thoughts flashed through the horseman's soul. He thought of his childhood away in Finland, in the distant East Bothnia. He remembered how his father, the old Bertila, who during the "Club War" had been one of Duke Carl's most prominent adherents, afterwards received from King Carl IX. four large homesteads, each of which furnished a horse and a man, and thus became one of the richest peasants in his country. He recalled his first youth in Stockholm, where his father had sent him with the ambitious hope that he might one day gain honor and favor at the king's side; and how he, still more ambitious, instead of acquiring peaceful knowledge, learned in secret to fence and to ride, until at last the stern father finally yielded, and allowed him to seek a place in the king's Finnish cavalry. All these recollections crossed the young warrior's mind in an instant; for now, now had come the time, the moment, when he, a youth from the people, could achieve for himself equal rank with this proud nobility which had hitherto looked down with contempt upon him and his class. It was this thought that drove the blood to his cheeks; he felt that it could impel him to face death.

Yet this was not all. His youthful heart expanded at the thought of fighting, under the eyes of the hero-king, a hard and decisive battle for his religious freedom, his country's glory, for all that is dearest and holiest in life; and this conviction, shared by the whole army, with the exception of some hired foreign troops, bore within it the certainty and foretaste of victory, even before the strife began.

Before the young horseman had time to reply to his noble-spirited chief, the king's high voice was heard in the distance calling to prayer. The chivalric hero took off his helmet as he lowered the point of his sword to the earth, and this motion was followed immediately by all the surrounding troops. And the king prayed in a sonorous voice:

"Thou all-merciful God, who bearest victory and defeat in Thy hand, turn Thy beneficent countenance to us, Thy servants! From distant lands and peaceful homes have we come, to fight for freedom, for truth, for Thy Gospel. Give us victory, for Thy holy name's sake! Amen."

At these words, a deep trust filled every breast.

The Swedish trumpeter rode forth to challenge the Imperial hosts, and Tilly answered proudly that the king well knew where to find him.

By noon the attacking Swedish army came within range of the Imperial artillery, which was stationed on the heights behind the ranks. The Swedish artillery responded, and the battle commenced. The sun shone right in the assailants' eyes; the south-west wind sent clouds of dust over them, and whirls of thick gunpowder smoke. The king wheeled his army to the right, so as to get the wind and sun on the flank. Pappenheim asked for orders to prevent this; and receiving leave, he hurried forward like a prairie fire, swung round, and took the Swedish right wing in the flank. In an instant the king threw the Rhine Count's regiment and Banér's cavalry in his way. The collision was terrible; horses and riders tumbled over each other. Pappenheim drew back, but only to throw himself the next moment upon the Finns. The Wallachians' long dark lines rushed forward in blind fury: in vain; they encountered a wall of iron. Their first rank was crushed, the next wheeled round; the second attack was repulsed. Pappenheim raged; for the third time he rushed to the assault. The Finns now had the Livonians and Courlanders at their side. Stålhandske received his enemy as coolly and resolutely as before. It was impossible to break through this living wall.

Stolid and slow to anger, the Finns had hitherto defended themselves with imperturbable calmness. But gradually they too became excited in the heat of the conflict. At the fourth attack the enemy's rage had communicated itself to them, and it was now scarcely possible to restrain them. Stålhandske's mighty tones sounded above the tumult of battle; once more the cavalry divisions closed up their ranks, once more the foe was thrown back. But Pappenheim, covered with wounds, urged on his Wallachians for the fifth time. And now the Finnish lines divided, but only to inclose the assailants in their iron embrace. It became a hand-to-hand struggle, and the Wallachians' horses began to tire. But their fury was as great as their defeat. For the fifth time repulsed, they made a sixth charge, equally bloody, equally futile. The seventh time Pappenheim was followed only by his most faithful men, and when this last desperate effort only covered the field with the bodies of the aggressors, his dreaded voice availed nothing more. The remaining Wallachians scattered themselves in the wildest flight toward Breitenfeld.

Covered with blood and dust, the Finns took breath. But scarcely had the smoke cleared away for an instant, before they discovered a cut-off remnant of the enemy's force. It was the Duke of Holstein, with his regiment of infantry, which had accompanied Pappenheim. The Finns were now warmed up at last, and not to be checked. Together with the East Goths, they surrounded the Holsteiners, crushed and annihilated them: these brave fellows defended themselves to the last man, and fell in the same order which they had held in the conflict.

While this occurred on the right wing, the left had fallen into the greatest peril. Fürstenberg, with his Croats, had attacked the Saxons, and these soon began to falter. Tilly saw his two wings engaged, and finally advanced with his sixteen large tertiers which formed the centre. Like a thunder-cloud his proud hosts spread themselves over the plain. Torstenson gave him a warm welcome. The cannon-balls swept terribly through the Imperial lines; Tilly drew aside, left Pappenheim, and threw himself upon the Saxons. An avalanche in its fall could not occasion greater destruction. Scattered at the first shock, the Saxons fled in all directions—their Elector leading in the flight—plundering all whom they met in the way. Tilly could now throw his masses against Horn and the left wing of the Swedes. Pressed by a formidable superior force, the latter withdrew slowly to the left, every moment ready to succumb in the unequal contest. The king hastened there, and cried to Callenbach, with the reserve, to close in, for God's sake! Callenbach did so, but fell in the first onslaught. Teuffel had the same fate. At last, Hepburn, with his Scots, and Soop, with the Smålanders, marched to Horn's assistance. The Croats rushed against Hepburn in thick swarms; then the Scots opened their ranks; the concealed cannon commenced firing, and strewed the field with corpses. Others of the enemy pressed on in their track. The Scots met them with a shower of bullets so terrible in its effect that whole ranks fell to the ground. The smoke and dust from all the rest of the field was driven here in dense clouds. Friends and enemies were mixed together in murderous confusion; they fought with swords and gunstocks, and victory inclined now to one side, now to the other.

Then began again unexpectedly the thunder of

cannon from the heights. The king, at the head of his cavalry, with the Finns in front, had conquered the Imperial artillery and turned their own cannon against them. This circumstance decided the issue of the battle. In vain had Pappenheim tried to regain the height; for the eighth time he was compelled to yield. The king, with his victorious right wing, bore down upon the enemy's flank. Everything was thrown into confusion. Tilly wept with rage. Pappenheim, who with his own hand had hewn down fourteen Swedes and Finns, was beside himself with fury. In vain were both threats and prayers; the Imperialists retreated in wild disorder. Tilly, whose famous gray steed was shot under him, barely escaped being taken prisoner; and the king's victory was complete.

But a bloody scene yet remained. Four regiments of infantry belonging to Tilly's veteran troops had withdrawn in good order from the field and placed themselves in the way of the pursuing Swedes. The king charged them with the right wing, Tott's cavalry, the Smålanders, and Finns. It was a hot skirmish: the Wallachians fought desperately; even while dying, they tried to pierce their enemies' horses as they rode over them. No quarter was asked, and none granted. At length the approaching darkness saved the remainder of this brave force, which retreated to Leipzig. The battle was ended.

The results of this victory were immeasurable. Gustaf Adolf, fearful of losing them through some imprudence, marshalled his troops at seven o'clock in the evening for the second time, and made them spend the night in order of battle. But first, the king rode from rank to rank, to thank his brave men.

"Stålhandske," said the king, when he came to the Finnish lines, "you and your men have all fought well, as I expected you would do. I thank you, my children! I am proud of you."

A jubilant cheer was the response of the troops.

"But," continued the king, "there was one among you who sprang from his horse, and, foremost of all, climbed the heights to take the Imperialists' cannon. Where is he?"

A young horseman rode from the ranks.

"Pardon, your majesty," stammered he. "I did it without orders, and therefore merit death."

The king smiled. "Your name?"

"Bertila."

"From East Bothnia?"

"Yes, your majesty."

"Good. To-morrow morning, at seven o'clock, you may present yourself, to hear your doom."

The king rode on, and the horseman returned to his place.

Night broke over the bloody field, covered with nine thousand mutilated corpses. The Finnish cavalry bivouacked on the heights where they had taken Tilly's cannon. The *debris* and the dead were quickly removed, and a fire of broken gun-carriages and musket-stocks spread its ruddy glow in the mild September night. The sky was clear, and through the thin smoke the eternal stars looked down upon this scene of carnage and strife.

The first care of the cavalry was to give their horses oats, and to water them at the Loder's muddy banks. Thereupon they had encamped around the fires upon the hillside, each man in his place, fully armed, and ready to spring up at the first alarm. The ground was slippery with dew and blood, but the fatigue was so great that many fell asleep on the spot where they had thrown themselves down. Others kept themselves in good spirits with food and drink; they had a good stock of ale, and let the tankard pass from hand to hand, as far even as the pickets, so long as there was a drop left; and drank, jokingly, the health of the Imperialists.

"And that they to-night may die of thirst!"

"Or drink to their own funeral!"

"Long live the king!"

At this moment was heard, quite near them, from a portion of the field dimly lighted by the fire, a woful voice, pitifully entreating help. The soldiers, accustomed to such things, knew by the foreign accent that the man was no comrade of theirs, and gave themselves no concern. But the piercing shrieks continued incessantly.

"Pekka, go there and give the Austrian dog a final thrust," cried some of the men, who felt annoyed at these wailing sounds.

Pekka, one of Bertila's four dragoons, short in stature, but strong as a bear, went reluctantly to stop the complainer's mouth. Superstitious, like all his comrades, he was not quite at ease among the dead on a dark night. Bertila, absorbed in thoughts of the next morning, did not notice this disturbance.

In a few minutes Pekka came back, dragging with him a dark body, which, to the astonishment of all, was found to be a monk, easily recognizable by his tonsure. Around his coarse gown he wore a rope of hemp, but to the rope hung the scabbard of a long sword.

"A monk! A Jesuit!" muttered the soldiers.

"Yes, what would you have me do?" rejoined

Pekka, in perplexity. "When I raised my arm to strike, he parried the blow with a crucifix."

"Slay him! He is one of the Devil's allies, who steal around in sheep's clothing to murder kings and burn faithful Christians at the stake."

"Down with him! When we stormed the heights, this same man stood with his crucifix among the Imperialists, and fired off a cannon."

"Let's see whether the precious object is of silver!" exclaimed one of the soldiers; and, sticking his hand inside the monk's gown, he drew forth, in spite of his resistance, a crucifix of silver, richly gilded.

"Just as I thought. Satan has plenty of gold."

"Let me see it," said an old cavalryman. "I know something about monks' tricks." He then examined the gilded image on all sides; and, behold! as he pressed a little spring in its breast, a sharp-edged dagger sprang from it.

As if stung by a serpent, the soldier flung the crucifix far from him. Horror and disgust had seized upon all the bystanders.

"Hang the viper by his own rope!" cried the soldiers.

"There is no tree here," objected one, "and none are allowed to leave the ranks."

"Drown him!"

"There is no water."

"Club him!"

No one would overcome his aversion so far as to touch the Jesuit.

"What shall we do with him?"

"*Misericordia! Gnade!*" exclaimed the captive, who, hitherto stunned by a wound in the head, began to regain speech and strength.

"Give him a kick, and let him go," proposed one. " We are Christian soldiers, and fear no deviltry."

"At least I will mark you first, highly reverend father, that we may know you if we meet you again," joined in one of the men, a Tavastlander by the name of Witikka, known for his strength and ferocity; and letting his long sword swing several times around the Jesuit's head, he cut off, before any one could prevent it, both his ears so skillfully that scarcely a hair was grazed. "Saint Peter could not have done it better!" exclaimed Witikka, laughing.

They who stood nearest turned away. Rude as they were, and accustomed to the cruelty of war, they considered this too gross a joke.

Bleeding, the Jesuit crept away on his hands and knees; but long was his voice heard from the surrounding darkness : "*Maledicti Fennones! maledicti! maledicti! Vos comburat ignis sempiternus!*" *

"Our Father who art in Heaven!" began a voice in the cavalry ranks. And all joined devoutly in the prayer.

CHAPTER II.

THE NOBLEMAN WITHOUT A NAME.

ON the morning of the 8th of September, at daybreak, the whole Swedish camp was in animation. Victory was certain; from all direc-

* Cursed Finns! May the eternal fire consume you!

tions came the intelligence of the total rout of the Imperial army. The king sent a part of the cavalry in pursuit of the enemy, while the remainder of the troops received the agreeable commission to plunder Tilly's camp, which was regularly apportioned among them. Great was the pillage; many here became rich for life. All was activity; the dead were tumbled into their graves in haste, the wounded forgot their pains. In the clear September morning, the whole broad plain swarmed with jubilant crowds on foot and horseback; and here, if ever, could one apply von Beskow's expression:

"The air was cooled by flags of victory."

The king had passed the night in a carriage. After he had offered prayer, and given the first orders of the day, he sent for several of those who had most distinguished themselves in the battle. Many a brave deed was there rewarded with honor and promotion. But higher than any other reward was their own inner satisfaction, and the approval of the hero whom all Europe had now learned to admire.

Among those summoned before the king, was a young man who plays a prominent part in this story. Gustaf Bertila was only twenty; his heart beat, at this moment, more quickly than it had done during the heat of the conflict. It is true, he expected that the king's magnanimity would not hold him blameworthy for disregarding orders in the hurry of battle; but he reddened and paled under the uncertainty of the king's purpose in this audience, which was in itself so great a distinction.

The king's tent had been raised under one of

the large elms at Gross Wetteritz; for all the buildings in the vicinity were partly burned down or demolished, by friend or foe. After a half-hour's waiting, Bertila was shown into the tent. Gustaf Adolf sat on a camp-stool, with his arm resting upon a table covered with charts and papers. He was tall and well built; the tight-fitting buff coat gave to his form a still more portly appearance. When Bertila entered, the king raised his mild, expressive eyes from a newly-signed order, and fixed a penetrating glance upon the young man. Gustaf Adolf was somewhat near-sighted; a certain effort to recognize a person, especially one with whom he was but little acquainted, gave his look a sharpness, which immediately afterwards disappeared.

"Your name is Bertila?" said the king, as if to assure himself that he had yesterday heard aright.

"Yes, your majesty."

"Your age?"

"Twenty years."

The king looked at him with a doubtful expression.

"His son, did you say?"

The young cavalier bowed, blushing.

"Strange!"

The king uttered this word as if unconsciously, and seemed thoughtful for a moment; then he resumed, with animation:

"Why have you not announced yourself to me before? Your father has rendered my father and the kingdom great services. I hope he is still living."

"He is living, and grateful for your majesty's goodness."

"Indeed!"

This word, like the former, resembled rather a secret thought than a question to the hearer. The young Bertila felt the blood rising more and more to his cheeks, and the king perceived it.

"Your father and I were once at variance," added the king, with a smile on his lips, while a slight cloud shadowed his brow. "Still," continued he, "all this is long since forgotten, and I am glad to find that such a deserving man has such a brave son. You were with the seventy Finns at Demmin?"

"Yes, your majesty."

"And you have not been mentioned for promotion?"

"My commander has promised to bear me in mind."

"Your king never forgets a faithful service. Gustaf Bertila, I have just issued your commission as ensign. Take it, and continue to serve with honor."

"Your majesty!" stammered the young cavalier.

"I have yet a word to say to you. Your conduct yesterday was contrary to orders."

"Yes, your majesty."

"I desire my soldiers to obey scrupulously. I am told, however, that you sprang from your horse at the foot of the steepest hill, in order to get up more quickly."

"That is true, your majesty."

"And that you, therefore, while the rest of the cavalry made a détour, arrived first on the hill, cut down two Austrians, and took the first cannon."

"Yes, your majesty."

"That is well. Ensign Bertila, I pardon your

disregard of orders, and appoint you lieutenant in my Finnish cavalry."

The young officer lacked words.

The king himself was moved. "Come nearer, young man," said he. "You ought to know that once, in my youth, I did your father a great wrong. Heaven, knowing my repentance, has at length sent me an opportunity of making amends to the son for the wrong done to the father. Lieutenant Bertila, you are brave and noble; you have received a military education. You have also brought into my service four fully-equipped horsemen. As an officer under my command, you are already a nobleman's equal. But in order that none of my officers, of however high birth, may consider you, a peasant's son, beneath them in standing, I will give you a name, a coat of arms, and a knight's spur. Go, young man . . . . . go, my son," repeated the king, with inexplicable emotion, "and show yourself worthy your king's favor."

"Unto death!" And, overpowered by his feelings, the young warrior bent a knee before Tilly's conqueror.

The king rose. The emotion which for a moment was reflected upon his manly and handsome face, quickly gave place to the majesty of the monarch and the commanding expression of the great conqueror. The young Bertila understood that the audience was ended.

Yet he still remained in his kneeling position, and handed the king a letter, which, until that morning, he had worn sewed in his coat.

"Deign to read this letter, your majesty! When, before I entered the field, I bade farewell to my old father, he presented me this, and said:

'My son, go; try to deserve your king's grace through faithfulness and manly courage. And if you succeed in one day winning his favor on your own account, and not merely because of your father's name, then give him this letter and tell him that it is my testament. His great heart will understand what I mean.'"

The king took the letter, broke the seal, and read. His features betrayed an intense but suppressed emotion; the violent dark flush, often in later years the only witness of the struggles of a soul which knew how to govern itself, rose like a slight cloud to the king's brow, crimsoned it a moment, and then disappeared again, leaving no trace. When he had finished the perusal, his eyes rested thoughtfully on the handsome fair young man, who still knelt at his feet.

"Rise!" said he, finally.

Bertila did so.

"Do you know the contents of this letter?"

"No, your majesty."

The king eyed him sharply, and seemed satisfied with the honest and frank expression in the youth's face.

"Your father, young man," continued he, after a short pause, "your father is a singular person. He has hated the nobility ever since the days of the Club War, when he fought many hard battles at the head of the peasants, and when the Flemming cavalry quartered themselves so rudely at his house. He forbids you ever to accept a noble name and escutcheon, if you wish to escape his paternal curse."

Bertila did not answer. A bolt from a clear sky had descended upon his young happiness; all his ambitious dreams of a coat of arms and a knight's spur were at once annihilated.

"A father's will must be obeyed," continued the king, with earnestness. "The noble name I intended to confer on you, you can not bear. Calm yourself, my young friend; you retain your sword and your lieutenant's rank; with them, and your brave arm, the path of honor will always stand open to you."

And, at a sign from the king, the young soldier withdrew.

CHAPTER III.

LADY REGINA.

IT was three or four weeks after the battle of Breitenfeld, when, one chilly October day, the beautiful Regina von Emmeritz, niece of the bishop, sat in a room in one of the turrets of the castle at Würtzburg, in company with three or four of her maidens, engaged in embroidering a picture of the Virgin Mary on a banner of white satin, intended to be presented, in token of their victories, to the garrison of the castle. The young girls were indulging in a lively conversation; for the master of the castle, the avaricious old bishop, had just started off, as he pretended, on a journey through the diocese, but, in reality, to escape Gustaf Adolf's approaching hosts. Fearing for his treasures, he had previously intrusted the defense of the town and castle to the bold cavalry commander, Keller, with fifteen hundred men; and

Keller, relying upon the castle's impregnable position on the banks of the Main, had assured his reverence that sooner should the heretic king crush his head against those walls than any of his godless followers gain an entrance.

The beautiful Regina was scarcely sixteen; she had locks dark as night, cheeks fresh as the dawn, and a pair of black eyes, deeply shining, like two stars which at midnight mirror themselves in a lonely lake. She was the old bishop's idol; he had left her as unwillingly as his treasures in the fortress. But Keller had assured him that solid walls, bristling with cannon, were, in such unquiet times, the best security for beauty; and Keller was a knight of faith and honor: with such a precious charge he would rather bury himself under the ruins of the castle than surrender.

Lady Regina raised her dark eyes from the embroidery and looked out through the little turret-window over the river, where a carriage, escorted by some horsemen, was crossing the bridge from the town to the castle.

"Who can the traveler be?" exclaimed she, with the rapt look which she rarely bestowed upon any object save the large and beautiful marble figure of the Madonna, in her sanctuary.

"Ah," exclaimed Kätchen, the youngest and most talkative of the maidens, "ah, Holy Virgin! how delightful it is to live in war times! Every day new faces, fine cavaliers, brave young squires, and now and then a jolly trip to town. It is quite a different thing from sitting here, shut up in a cloister, and hearing the monks chant *De Profundis* from morning till night. Yes," continued she, saucily, "may his grace, the bishop, only stay away a good long while!"

"Kätchen," chided Regina, "take care not to speak ill of the monks' masses! Remember that our confessor, Father Hieronymus, is a member of the holy Inquisition, and that the castle prison is both deep and dark."

Kätchen became mute for a moment. Then she answered, boldly:

"Were I in your place, my lady, I would rather think of the handsome Count of Lichtenstein than of that odious Father Hieronymus. He is a fine chevalier; God grant that he may return victorious from the war against the heretics!"

"And that they may all be exterminated with fire and sword!" joined in one of the maidens, with pious fervor.

"Poor heretics!" exclaimed Kätchen, smiling.

"Take care!" repeated Lady Regina, with naïve seriousness. "A heretic deserves no mercy. One who kills a heretic has seven sins pardoned; so Father Hieronymus has often told me. To hate the heretics is the eighth sacrament, and to love a single one of them is to consign your soul to the abyss."

As she spoke, Regina's black eyes flashed. One could see that the reverend father's teachings had taken deep root in her soul.

Kätchen did not lose courage.

"It is said that their king is mild and noble, that he shelters all the defenseless, and allows no excesses in his soldiers."

"Satan often disguises himself in an angel's shape."

"They say that his men are brave and humane. I, myself, heard an old Italian soldier describe to the garrison at the armory how seventy men, of a heretic people called Finns, for more than an hour defended their king against fifteen hundred Neapolitans. And when most of the heretics had fallen, the rest gained assistance and at last triumphed; but afterwards they bound up the wounds of their enemies, no less than of their comrades."

Lady Regina rose, and was about to give a stern answer, when at that instant a servant appeared at the door, and announced that the Count of Lichtenstein, sick and wounded, had arrived at the castle and asked hospitality. The young Regina, who, as the bishop's niece, was to be regarded as the mistress of the castle during his absence, immediately hastened down to welcome the new guest, who was a distant relative of hers.

The maidens exchanged glances, as if they considered this event especially significant. It had long been whispered among them, that the old bishop had chosen the count as the future spouse of the young lady; but in vain had they tried to discover a blush on her cheeks at the news of his coming. If Lady Regina cherished any tenderer feeling, she at least knew how to conceal it.

"Is it true," said one of the maidens, "that the heretic king has won a great victory over the true believers, and is approaching this place with his godless army?"

"So it is said," answered another. "But he can not come here. Our people have erected an image of the Swedish saint Brigitta in his way, in Thüringen Forest; and she will know how to check his progress."

In the meantime, Lady Regina had one of the bishop's own rooms put in order for her guest, and provided in every way for his comfort. The young Count of Lichtenstein was a proud and stately youth, dark as a Spaniard, and with eyes almost as flashing as Regina's. He approached his beautiful hostess with faltering steps, and yet with looks before which Regina cast down her eyes.

"How grateful am I not to Heaven," said he, "for these wounds, which have procured me the happiness of having so beautiful a nurse!"

The count's wounds were many, but not dangerous. Taken prisoner at Breitenfeld, he had shortly afterwards, still weak from his wounds, been exchanged, and immediately hastened here, to regain health and strength in the neighborhood of his heart's mistress.

"But," added he, after this account, "I learned with great uneasiness that the enemy, eager for prey, was rolling its masses hither like a devastating flood, to the rich valleys of Franconia. All the more quickly did I hurry to you, beautiful Regina, to share your vicissitudes and dangers. Be calm! Königshofen will make a stand against them; and Father Hieronymus, who, wounded like me, escaped from Breitenfeld, is stirring the country people to resistance all along the enemy's route."

"And so you think," replied Regina, anxiously, "that those godless heretics will venture so far as this?"

"The protection of the saints will be with beauty," answered the count, evasively. "Besides, we will soon receive more trusty news."

At these words, Regina looked out of the window, and saw a troop of horsemen hurrying at full speed toward the castle.

"I am not mistaken," exclaimed she; "there is Father Hieronymus himself!"

"Bad omen!" muttered the count, between his teeth.

Lady Regina had seen aright; it was Father Hieronymus who at that moment rode over the drawbridge. In appearance, the father was a little unpretending man, pale and thin, with sharp energetic features, and deep-set hollow eyes, whose restless glance flew spyingly from one object to another. Around the waist of his black gown he wore a rope of hemp, from which hung a long sword. But no longer did the tonsure gleam from the top of his crown. Wounded in the head, he wore over it a sort of skull-cap, or calotte of leather, whose black color made a ghastly contrast with his corpse-like face. Never had the dreaded Jesuit shown himself in such repulsive form. All the soldiers presented arms; all the servants of the castle hastened to receive his commands. A secret anxiety took possession of all the bystanders. It was as though death and disaster had in his person ridden through the portals of Castle Würtzburg.

The monk surveyed, with a hasty glance, the garrison drawn up in the court-yard, and then greeted Lady Regina with a smile, which was probably intended to modify the repulsiveness of his aspect, but which only made it still more hideous.

"Saint Patrick and all the saints protect you, gracious lady! The times are very bad, very bad! The Holy Virgin has permitted the heathen to penetrate to our very gates . . . on account of our sins," added he, crossing himself devoutly.

"And Königshofen?" inquired Count Fritz, who divined the answer.

"The faithless commander has surrendered."

"But the peasants, who were to oppose the enemy's march through the forest?"

"All are scattered like chaff . . . on account of our sins."

"And the holy Brigitta's image?"

"The godless heretics have placed it as a scarecrow in a grain-field. But," continued the father—and his voice acquired a commanding sharpness—"what is this I see, my daughter? You are still here, and the castle is filled with women and children, while the enemy is every instant expected at our gates?"

"Lady Regina shall never lack protection so long as this arm is able to wield a sword," interposed Count Fritz.

"The castle is provisioned for a whole year," said Regina, timidly. "But, worthy father, you are fatigued; you are wounded, and need rest. Let me dress your wounds; you are injured in the head!"

"A trifle, my daughter, a mere nothing. Who now should think of me? You must go instantly . . . to the stronghold of Aschaffenburg."

"I fear it is too late," exclaimed Count Fritz, who was looking out upon the river and town.

"Holy Mary! are they here already?"

The Jesuit and Lady Regina flew to the window. The afternoon sun cast its last rays over Würtzburg and the surrounding country. Horsemen were seen riding at full speed through the streets, and a large crowd of fleeing inhabitants were already moving toward the castle: monks and nuns, women and children, who hurriedly dragged with them hand-carts loaded with their valuables. Beyond the town, in the direction of Schweinfurt, on the east side of the Main, appeared a troop of cavalry, from whose threatening but cautious advance one could without difficulty recognize the vanguard of the Swedish army.

"*Maledicti Fennones!*" burst out the Jesuit, with an indescribable expression of hate on his pale countenance. "These heretics have wings! May the earth swallow them!" And he hurried out with fanatic zeal, to place himself at the head of the defenders of the castle.

The bishop's castle, also called Marienburg, raises its old walls from a height on the right bank of the Main. Toward the river side of the town the heights are steep and rocky, but on the opposite side sloping and easily accessible. A rampart, crescent-shaped, formed a strong outwork before the gates; if the enemy overcame this obstacle, a deep moat, cut in the rock, awaited him on the other side; and should he succeed in crossing this, then he would find in his way the inner and highest castle-wall, swarming with iron-clad warriors, ready to shoot down with their heavy muskets all who approached; or, if he came nearer, to cut him down with their long halberds, or crush him with the large stones collected on the walls. When we add to this, that the only passage over the river was a narrow bridge, and that the castle's forty-eight cannon commanded the whole town and the region far around, it will be seen that Keller, at the head of fifteen hundred brave men, and richly provided with all necessaries, had good grounds for bidding the departing bishop to be of good cheer.

But Gustaf Adolf had also an important reason for making himself master of this fortress, cost what it would. Tilly had drawn reinforcements from all directions; and, a few weeks after the battle of Breitenfeld, fully prepared, and eager for revenge, was on the march from Hessen, with thirty thousand men to assist Würtzburg.

The king challenged the town, and forced an entrance into the suburbs; but it was already late in the evening, and the attack had to be postponed The next morning the town surrendered. But Keller had profited by the darkness of the night to transfer his whole force, a large number of fugitives, and the portable property of the town, to the castle, after which he blew up two arches of the bridge across the Main, and thus blocked the enemy's way.

But to return to the fortress.

That night none but the little children had slept in the bishop's castle. New crowds of soldiers, monks and women were constantly arriving; one baggage-wagon after another rattled in through the castle gates; the echo of the archways repeated the cries of the sentinels, the commands of the officers, and the weeping of the children; and in the midst of all this noise and confusion, were plainly heard the masses of the monks, who in the chapel invoked the protection of the Holy Virgin and all the saints in behalf of the threatened fortress, the strongest Catholic bulwark in all Franconia.

To make room for all the fleeing crowds, Lady Regina had not only thrown open the bishop's private apartments, but also the two magnificent rooms set apart for her own use in the interior of the castle, and, with her maids, moved up into the small chambers in the east turret. In vain was it represented to her that this point was exposed to the enemy's fire. She had here the best and most extensive prospect in the whole castle, and this position she was not willing to exchange.

"Hinder me not!" said she to the warning

Jesuit. "I wish to see the heretics bleed and fall before our cannon. It will be a glorious sight."

"Amen!" answered Father Hieronymus. "You know, my daughter, that this castle is protected by two miraculous images of the Virgin, one of pure gold, the other of gilded wood. I will hang up the latter in your room; it will avert the enemy's bullets, like so many puff-balls, from your turret."

At daybreak, Lady Regina was on the lookout at her little turret-window. It was a glorious sight, as the sun rose over the autumn hills, with their still verdant vineyards, among which the river Main wound like a band of silver and gold, glittering in the morning sunlight. Yonder in the town all was activity: four Swedish infantry regiments marched in with flags flying and bands playing; their armor shone in the sunlight, and the officers' plumes waved in the wind. At this sight, the hearts of the young girls alternated between emotions of fear and curiosity.

"Do you see," said Lady Regina to Kätchen, "the two horsemen in the yellow jackets, who ride at the head of the heretic troop?"

"What a fine bearing they have! Now they turn round a street corner . . . . there they are again. See how all make way for them!"

"Send for Count Fritz. He has been in the Swedish camp more than two weeks, and knows all their chief men."

The count, who was prevented by his wounds from taking part in the defense of the castle, willingly obeyed the beautiful Regina's call.

In the meantime the Swedes had taken possession of the town, and began to show themselves in scattered groups at the shore and by the exploded bridge. At that instant the castle cannon opened fire. Now here, now there, a ball fell among the Swedes, who sought shelter as well as they could behind the houses by the river.

"Holy Mary! a man falls! He rises no more!" exclaimed Kätchen, unable to conceal her compassion.

"Saint Francis be praised, there is one heretic less in the world!" rejoined old Dorthe, Lady Regina's duenna, who was appointed by Father Hieronymus to watch all her steps.

"But it is terrible to shoot down a human being!"

Count Fritz smiled.

"You should have seen the battle-field at Breitenfeld! Nine thousand killed!"

"It is horrifying!"

"Can you tell me, count, who those horsemen are, who, in the midst of the shower of balls, keep by the bank, and seem to be examining the situation of the castle?"

"Pardon me, my beautiful cousin; the smoke begins to obscure the view. Those horsemen . . upon my honor, it is the king himself and the Count Per Brahe. I pity them, if Father Hieronymus recognizes them. He would then direct all the cannon of the castle toward this one point."

At these words, old Dorthe stole from the room.

"How is that, my cousin? You pity the heretic prince?"

"Why do your eyes flash so darkly, beautiful Regina, at these words? You, so noble and tender-hearted, do you not understand that one can feel compassion for a brave and chivalrous enemy? The king of Sweden is a hero, worthy our admiration in as high a degree as our hatred."

"I do not understand you. A heretic!"

"Heaven prevent you from one day seeing him within these walls! you would then understand me better. . . . Ha! they are preparing to storm the bridge . . . they throw planks over the bare arches. Heavens! that is daring!"

"There fell four at once!" screamed Kätchen.

"I know them," exclaimed Count Fritz, more and more excited by the tumult of strife and the increasing cannonade, which caused the castle walls to tremble. "I know them; they are the Scots. There are no braver troops to be found in the whole Swedish army; the Scots and the Finns are always first where the danger is greatest."

"Ah, my cousin, do you see your Scots draw back? They dare not take the dangerous leap."

"That requires more than human courage. Twenty-four feet below the narrow plank roars the flood."

"Two slender officers spring out on the plank."

"They are the brothers Ramsay, both quite young. I know them by their blue scarfs. They both love the same lady; and both wear her colors, without therefore loving each other the less."

"O Heaven, protect them! . . . Ah, Holy Mary, this is frightful!" And Kätchen hid her face in her apron. The intrepid Scots had not reached the middle of the plank before they were seen to reel, lose their balance, and fall headlong into the river. For a moment they struggled with the waves, but, pierced by the enemy's bullets, they felt their strength fail them; the heavy armor drew them down. A second more, and these chivalric youths disappeared beneath the surface.

"You rejoiced a while ago at war," said Lady Regina, with a calmness which was contradicted by her loudly beating heart.

"Ah, yes, at the handsome cavaliers—at the music and the banquets—but not at this!" exclaimed Kätchen, weeping.

"The Scots turn back!" cried one of the maidens.

"Yes," said the count, hesitatingly; "but the Swedes are beginning to cross the river in boats."

"The Scots again try the planks."

"Just as I expected," answered the count, coldly.

"Heaven help us! They come over; they take their stand on this side. Our men attack them."

"Take care, Lady Regina, do not lean so far out of the window. The Swedes direct their artillery toward the turret."

"Are you afraid, count?" Regina smiled as she uttered these words.

Lichtenstein colored.

"I believe I have sufficiently proven the contrary. Listen, and you will every other minute distinguish a whizzing, whose cause you do not know, and a rattling, as of pebbles. I will tell you what it is. It is cannon-balls, my lady; you would understand their music better did not the noise out there deafen you. For the last half-hour they have torn piece after piece from the walls of the turret, and almost always at the same point. They are not sugar-plums, my cousin. These Swedes have learned their art from the wild huntsman himself."

"Do you actually believe . . ."

"That the Swedes intend to shoot down this turret, in order to fill the castle-moat with its ruins? Yes, my cousin, and I believe they will succeed.

You are not safe here for an instant; you must go away."

"Directly, gracious count, directly! Come, my lady," exclaimed Kätchen, trying with friendly force to take her young mistress with her. But Regina was in an excited frame of mind. The habit of commanding, and perhaps still more the willfulness which lay at the bottom of this strangely contradictory character, was blended with the burning fanaticism which the Jesuit had so well understood how to inspire in her from childhood. . . . She took a step back, seized the gilded image of the Virgin, which Father Hieronymus had sent for her protection, and placed it before her on the window-sill.

"Go!" said she, "if you are so weak in the faith as to doubt the protection of the saints. I remain here, and the heretics' bullets will avail nothing against . . ."

Lady Regina had not time to finish the sentence before a ball struck the wall at an oblique angle, loosening a piece of the outer edge of the facing. A shower of stones and mortar swept in through the window, knocking down the image of the Virgin, and covering Lady Regina with dust.

"Away from here! You now see for yourself!" exclaimed the count.

"Let us go!" repeated the maidens, beside themselves with terror.

But Regina, for a moment confused, regained her self-possession immediately, bent down to pick up the image, and said confidently:

"They will avail nothing against the Holy Virgin."

She was mistaken. The Holy Virgin of wood had broken into three or four pieces. On the count's lips played a satirical smile of unbelief, as he led his terror-stricken cousin unresistingly from the dangerous room.

While these events were going on in the turret, Keller had quickly and intelligently arranged the castle's defense. He could not hinder the Swedes from crossing the river, but every step nearer the castle brought them also nearer his cannon. Terribly did they decimate the ranks of the brave assailants. That whole day the Swedes could accomplish nothing.

Father Hieronymus and his monks moved around on the walls, sprinkled the cannon with holy water, and made the sign of the cross over them. The old Dorthe had whispered something in his ear, and the Jesuit's whole attention was turned toward the spot where the two horsemen in buff jackets had just been seen. The reverend father now undertook himself to direct one of the castle's heaviest cannon toward this point; but, before he fired it off, he fell on his knees and repeated four *pater nosters* and four *ave Marias*. Then thundered the discharge; but in vain did the Jesuit seek to discover any effect from it. Unharmed, immovable as before, the figures of the two horsemen were seen through the dissolving smoke. Hieronymus now supposed that four *paters* and four *aves* were too little, and accordingly repeated eight of each kind, after which he let the cannon thunder for the second time. Impossible! The balls seemed to avoid the chosen victims. Not yet had Providence appointed Gustaf Adolf's death-hour; and Per Brahe was to be spared for Finland. Who can calculate what would have become of Sweden's victories and Finland's civilization if the Jesuit's murderous balls had hit their aim!

Father Hieronymus raged. Once more he determined to try his luck with twelve *paters* and *aves*, when some one touched him on the shoulder, and behind him stood an old soldier, who, with Count Lichtenstein, had returned from Swedish captivity.

"Let it alone," said the old man, in a warning tone; "it wastes our powder uselessly. The man at whom you are aiming is not to be hit: *he is invulnerable*."

The Jesuit's superstition was in such cases greater than his craftiness. He turned round hastily, and muttered under his breath:

"I ought to have guessed that. But how do you know that he is invulnerable, my son?" added he, raising his voice.

"I heard it in the Swedes' own camp. The king wears on the forefinger of his right hand a little ring of copper, scratched all over with magic signs. He received it in his youth from a sorceress in Finland; and, so long as he wears this ring, neither iron nor lead, neither fire nor water, has any effect on him."

"Nothing affects him, you say? Oh, *maledicti Fennones!* why do ye pursue me everywhere?"

"Neither iron nor lead," continued the soldier, in a whisper; "but if I dared to disclose another means . . ."

"Speak, my son; you have absolution beforehand."

"But, worthy father, it is a sinful means."

"For the welfare of the holy cause, all means are sanctified. Speak out, my son."

"Gold from a saint's image . . ."

"No, my son, no; we certainly dare not employ that. Had it been a dagger of glass, a subtle poison, it might have been done; but gold from the image of a saint—no, my son; let us think of it no more."

In the meantime, darkness had descended, and the work of death for the day was over. The tired warriors refreshed themselves with food and drink, Keller dispensing noble wines to strengthen their courage.

Lady Regina had descended into one of the inner rooms of the castle; Count Fritz had retired to rest. Soon was heard through the castle only the call of the sentinels, mingled with the coarse songs of drunken soldiers, and the sounds of the banquet which Keller gave his officers in the large armory. But in the magnificent chapel, where uppermost on the altar stood the images of the Virgin Mary and the Savior, of pure gold, surrounded by images of the Apostles, in the finest silver, the midnight mass was already over, and the monks had one after one stolen away to rest, or to the wine-cup. Only one solitary figure was seen still kneeling at the altar; and the ever-burning lamp cast its faint glimmer over the deadly-pale features of the praying Jesuit.

"Holy Mary," prayed he, "forgive thy unworthy servant for daring to stretch out his hand to pilfer a scrap of thy golden mantle. Thou knowest, O *sanctissima!* that it is done for a good and sacred object, in order to destroy thy sworn enemy and that of the holy church, the heretic prince whom the heathen Finns, with their godless witchcraft, have rendered impervious to the swords and bullets of the true-believing Catholics. Grant that this gold, which I, to thy honor, cut from thy glorious mantle, may pierce the sinful heart of the heretic king; and I promise thee, Holy Mary, to give thee, in place of what thou hast lost, a costly robe of velvet and true pearls. Three gilded candles shall also be kept burning night and day before thy image. *Amen.*"

When Father Hieronymus had finished this prayer, he looked up tremblingly; and it seemed to him that the image, in the rays of the eternal lamp, nodded its approval to his fanatical petition.

CHAPTER IV.

LADY REGINA'S OATH.

THE events last described were succeeded by a hot and sanguinary day. The castle was vigorously bombarded by the Swedes, who now began to approach the walls under cover of skilfully-constructed earthworks. The Imperialists defended themselves bravely. Time was precious to both parties: in a few days more, Tilly would stand at Gustaf Adolf's back, a probable disaster to the Swedes, a sure deliverance for the beleagured.

Lady Regina and her maids were now confined to the inner regions of the castle, and could no longer enjoy their interesting view. There was all the more to do inside. The number of the wounded increased, and these had to be cared for. The young girl went like an angel of mercy from couch to couch in the armory, where the wounded were now quartered; her gentle hand poured balsam on their wounds, her mild words poured consolation into their hearts. She spoke of the holy cause for which they bled; she promised gold and honor to those who survived, eternal salvation to those who fell in the strife.

The cannonade was so heavy that the old walls trembled. Regina remembered that she had left her rosary up in the turret, and it was now needed for the prayers of the wounded. She already stood on the threshold of the armory, when a fearful crash shook the castle to its very foundations. Pale with terror, she stopped, and, at the same instant, the Count of Lichtenstein rushed in.

"What has happened?" asked the young girl.

"Thank the saints, my lady, that you yesterday obeyed a friend's advice. The turret has fallen."

"And we are lost!"

"Not yet. The Swedes calculated that it would fill the moat with its ruins, but it has fallen inside. The enemy seem inclined to attempt a storm. Come here to the window; this overlooks the castle walls. Do you see? Father Hieronymus is on his knees by the large cannon. I wager he has caught sight of the Swedish king."

The count had guessed rightly. The Jesuit's falcon glance was steadily directed toward a single point, and his thin lips mumbled with anxious haste one prayer after another. His spying eyes had discovered Gustaf Adolf on horseback, as yesterday, at Per Brahe's side. The two riders kept quite near the outworks; a pile of *débris* protected them from the musket shots, but was evidently no shield against a ball from heavy artillery. Father Hieronymus relied upon the massive lead ball, into which, amidst fasting and vigils, he had poured the gold from the Holy Virgin's mantle. He bent down to aim the cannon; the pupils of his eyes contracted, his nostrils dilated, while a stream of Latin orisons continued to flow from his lips; then he rose quickly, swung the burning linstock in the form of a cross, and fired.

Flame and smoke burst from the mouth of the cannon. Oh, revenge and fury! When the smoke cleared away, the two horsemen, still unharmed, were seen to ride a little aside. But this time Gustaf Adolf had been near death; for the ball struck the heap of rubbish and covered him and Brahe with a cloud of dust.

Tired out and furious, the Jesuit hurried from the wall.

"Wait, you King of Belial!" he muttered to himself; "I will yet succeed in stealing the ring which protects you, and then, woe be unto you!"

The king now gave orders to storm the outworks. Axel Lilje, Jacob Ramsay and Hamilton hurried forward with their men. The difficulties which they had to encounter were incredible. They were obliged, under a shower of balls and blows, to climb the precipitous rock, then to leap over the moat, and finally scale the ramparts. First of all, went the East Bothnians and the Scots, unchecked, irresistible. The foremost were seen to fall, with crushed heads; others, with their swords between their teeth, immediately climbed up the ramparts in their places. The king himself rode as near as he could, in order to encourage his men. A musket ball tore away a piece of his buff gauntlet, without injuring him. The belief was general that Gustaf Adolf was invulnerable.

At last, after two hours bloody strife, the Scots and the Finns had decided the struggle. The important outworks were taken, and the defenders drew back within the castle walls. It was then about four o'clock in the afternoon.

After the advantage they had gained, the Swedes took a few hours' rest. A council of war was held, and it was decided that the following morning at daybreak the famous yellow-and-blue brigade should storm the castle. The East Bothnians were selected by the king to head this perilous undertaking; and the Scots, who had lost many men, were this time to rest. Accounts add, that the brave Hamilton regarded this tenderness as involving such a disgrace that he requested a discharge on the spot, and quit the army.

The situation of the besieged was yet far from desperate. They still had about a thousand able men, whom, since the loss of the outworks, they could the better concentrate upon a single point. But they had lost belief in victory; and this loss counted more than that of an outwork. In vain did Keller try to exhort them to courage; in vain did the monks go in procession around the walls, with the golden image of the Virgin. When night came, all was confusion; the soldiers no longer obeyed orders, and a part of the most faint-hearted discussed among themselves whether they ought not to make use of the darkness, in order to escape unseen.

At midnight Lady Regina was on her knees before the altar in the chapel, praying with burning fervor to the image of the Virgin.

"Holy Mary," said she, "protect this castle, protect thy Catholic faith, against the heretics! And if it is thy will that this stronghold shall fall, then let it bury under its ruins our enemies, who are also thine; and first of all, the godless king, their prince, as well as his heathen Finns, who to-day, and many times before, have fought most bitterly against thy holy cause."

"Amen!" said a voice; and when she looked around, Father Hieronymus stood behind her. His bearing was darkly solemn, and a grim smile played over his pale features. "Do you know what you are praying for, my daughter?"

"Victory to the Catholic faith; death to the heretics!"

"You are young, and the human mind changes. Have you the strength to hate the enemies of your faith, even if you ever, as a woman, felt tempted to love one of them?"

"I have, my father; yes, most surely!"

"I am your confessor, and I would not see your soul lost for all eternity. Have you courage to sacrifice yourself for the holy cause, and thereby gain an imperishable martyr-crown?"

"Yes, my father."

"Very well; then know that the castle can not hold out. I foresee that it will, within a short time, fall into Swedish hands. They will take you prisoner. You are young and beautiful; you will win the favor of the heretic king. You must avail yourself of it to approach his person; he will not distrust you, and when the Holy Virgin grants you a good opportunity, you must . . ." The Jesuit took out a crucifix of silver and pressing a spring in the breast of the image, a flashing dagger sprang out.

"Grace, my father; this charge is terrible!"

"No grace. The holy church demands a blind obedience. *Perinde ac cadaver* — like a dead body—without will. Do you love the Mother of God?"

"You know that I do."

"Do you see this piece of her golden robe she has lost during the night? It is a sign which portends her anger. Do you love me also, my daughter?"

"I revere you more highly than any other, my father."

"Then look at this mutilated head." So saying, the Jesuit removed his black leather calotte, and exposed the repulsive stumps of his two amputated ears. "Thus have the blasphemous king's miscreants, the Finns, treated your friend, your confessor. Do you still hesitate to avenge the Mother of God, to avenge me?"

"What do you ask of me, my father?"

"Listen! The heretic king wears on his right forefinger a little ring of copper; in it consists his security against death and danger. This ring you must gain possession of through artifice; and, if you then feel your arm too weak, call upon me. We will reach his heart, even were it coated with a dragon's scales."

"If it is the will of the saints . . . so be it."

"Lay two fingers on this crucifix, and repeat the oath I dictate to you: 'I swear by this cross, and by all the saints, to accomplish what I now vow before the image of the Holy Virgin. And if I ever break this oath, then may the curse rest upon me and my posterity to the seventh generation.'"

"'I swear by this cross, and by all the saints, to accomplish what I now vow before the image of the Holy Virgin. And if I ever break this oath, then may the curse rest upon me and my posterity to the seventh generation.'"

"*Fiat voluntas tua, ut in cælis, sic etiam in terra.* Amen!"*

And the night's silence sealed this dreadful oath, which chained with copper fetters, the coming generations to the wavering decision of a girl of sixteen.

At the same hour of the night, the East Bothnians, with the other troops chosen for the assault, assembled in the lately-conquered outworks. The wine-cup circled round, but this time very moderately; for the king's vigilance permitted no imprudence. A number of volunteers from several regiments had asked and obtained leave to take part in the adventurous expedition. All were in good spirits in the expectation of victory and pillage.

Last among the volunteers appeared a tall, fair-complexioned youth, of a cheerful and jovial appearance.

"Thunder and lightning! is that you, Bertel?" exclaimed a short and thick man, Lieutenant Larsson, of the East Bothnians.

"As you see," said the youth, shaking his hand cordially.

"Well, I declare, the good boy wishes to season his new lieutenant's commission! It is not my fault, my dear fellow, but may I be tossed by a buffalo bull if there is a single drop left in the flask. But tell me, what is the matter with you, that you have changed your name, Bertel? What sort of a mixture is it? neither Swedish nor Finnish."

"It was done at Breitenfeld," said Bertel, coloring slightly. "My comrades have long called me so, and . . . it is shorter."

* Thy will be done on earth, as it is in heaven.

"Nonsense! I hope you don't feel too good to bear a peasant's name, now that you have become an officer?"

"Have the lots already been cast?" rejoined the youth, without answering the other's question.

"You came just in time to try your luck."

The younger officers, all of whom sought the honor of commanding the first dangerous reconnoissance, had determined to draw lots, as the difficulty could not be settled in any other way. The lots were shaken up in a helmet; fourteen hands were stretched out to seize the slips, and the lucky one who read his name on the slip was Bertel.

"Look out for yourself, my boy," cried the little Larsson. "Thunder and lightning! remember that the castle is full of Jesuits. At every step a trap-door under your feet, in every crucifix a dagger, and even in the moment of victory, a mine which blows the conqueror into the air."

It was after four o'clock in the morning, and they had yet a half hour before dawn. Bertel, with seven men under his command, was ordered to reconnoitre the fort, approaching it as near as possible. In the meantime, the troops held themselves in the captured outworks, ready for the first signal.

The night was coal black. Bertel and his men approached the drawbridge with cautious steps, and without being observed by the sentinels. Who can picture his astonishment when he found it down!*

He stopped for an instant, doubtful and un-

---
* Some authors assert that the drawbridge could not be drawn up, on account of the weight of the many dead bodies left there after the strife.

decided, recollecting Larsson's words. Could this be a snare?

All was still. Bertel and his men advanced, boldly but slowly and cautiously over the bridge.

"Who goes there?" thundered an Imperial sentinel, in the darkness.

"Swede!" cried Bertel, cleaving with one blow the man's skull. "Comrades, the castle is taken!" And the seven pushed on resolutely in his footsteps.

Inside the drawbridge stood two hundred Imperialists on guard. Appalled and dumbfounded, they believed that the whole Swedish force were storming in over the drawbridge. They hastened to regain the sally-port; but the bold lieutenant and his seven men stood their ground. To Bertel's good fortune, the darkness in the arched gateway was impenetrable; no one could distinguish either friend or enemy, and the Imperialists struck their own men as often as the foe. The press soon became so great that no sword could be raised to strike, and the rash assailants narrowly escaped being jammed to death against the walls by the rushing mass of mail-clad men.

Bertel's cry and the tumult of strife had been heard in good time by those in the outworks. The whole Swedish force now stormed against the fortress. Keller, with his followers, seized their weapons, and hastened out to defend the entrance; but the Finns had got breathing space, and pressed forward: in a short time they stood inside the castle yard. Keller and his men fought with the courage of despair: many valiant Swedes and Finns fell in the very moment of victory. Their fall incited their countrymen to revenge. They began to cry, "*Magdeburger pardon;*" and this cry meant death without mercy to all Imperialists. The carnage became fearful. Many monks threw themselves fanatically into the strife, some with torches, some with sword in hand. Most of them were hewn down; others cast themselves on the ground, feigning death. Day began to dawn over the sanguinary scene.

Then Lennart Torstenson started forward, seized the madly-struggling Keller around the waist, and took him prisoner, thus saving him from the fury of the soldiers. The Imperialists, or the few of them who yet lived, laid down their arms, and the castle was taken.

CHAPTER V.

JUDITH AND HOLOFERNES.

AS the first rays of the sun shimmered on the waves of the river Main, Castle Marienburg was in the possession of the Swedes. The king rode into the court-yard, which was covered with his fallen enemies; more than twenty monks were counted among the dead. But some of these seemed to the king to have altogether too blooming cheeks to resemble corpses. "Stand up!" said he to them; "you shall suffer no harm." And immediately many of the pretended dead sprang up, sound and well, on their two feet, and bowed, full of joy and gratitude, to the magnanimous heretic prince.

As the castle was taken by storm, the soldiers were allowed to plunder. Grand was the booty of silver and gold, weapons, and all sorts of precious things. The king reserved to himself the armory, with complete equipments for seven thousand infantry and four thousand cavalry, forty-eight cannon, four mortars, the stables with the choicest horses, and the wine-cellar, filled with the purest wines. The library was taken as a donation to the Upsala University; the sacred images of gold and silver found their way to the treasury. Notwithstanding that many of the residents of the town recovered the property they had brought there, the soldiers' booty was so great that, at the division, they measured the clinking coin with full helmets. Finally, Keller was obliged to disclose the vault, which, cut in the rock itself, deep below the cellar, preserved the bishop's treasure. Fryxell relates, that, when the soldiers carried up the heavy chests, the bottom of one fell out, and a quantity of shining ducats rolled out on the ground. The men threw themselves down to pick them up, leaving some to the king, for decency's sake, but stuffing the most part into their own pockets. Gustaf Adolf noticed this, and said, laughing:

"Never mind, boys; as it has once fallen into your hands, you may as well keep it."

After that day, scarcely a soldier was to be found in the whole Swedish army who did not have a new suit of clothes. In the camp a cow was sold for a dollar, a sheep for a few pennies; and the learned Salvius writes: "Our Finnish boys, who are now accustomed to the vineyards down there, are not likely to come back to Savolax very soon. In the Livonian war, they were often obliged to put up with ale-soup made of water and mouldy bread; now, the Finn makes it in his helmet, with wine and cakes."

Among the prisoners were the Count of Lichtenstein and Lady Regina. The king commanded that both should be treated with chivalrous courtesy. To the young lady he offered safe-conduct to the bishop, her uncle. Regina declined this offer, on account of the insecurity of the times, and begged as a favor to be allowed to remain under the king's protection for the present. Gustaf Adolf consented.

"I do it unwillingly," said he, smiling, to the Margrave of Baden Durlach, who rode by his side. "Young girls are a superfluity in the field, and confuse the heads of my young officers. However, she can go with me to Frankfort, as a hostage, to bind the bishop's hands."

"Your majesty knows how to capture all through your magnanimity," replied the Margrave, with a courtier's politeness.

"Lieutenant Bertel," added the king, as he turned to the officer who, close behind him, commanded a troop of Finnish cavalry, "I confide Lady von Emmeritz to your protection. She has permission to take with her an old woman attendant, one maiden, and her father confessor. See to it that you do not fall in love, lieutenant; and, above all, give close heed to the monk: that sort are not to be trusted."

Bertel silently saluted with his sword.

"One thing more," continued the king. "I have not forgotten that you were the first who pressed through the sally-port. After you have placed the young girl in safety, you can commence service in my body guard. Have you understood me?"

"Yes, your majesty."

"Good;" and the king again turned to the Margrave, as he merrily added: "Believe me, it would have been risky to intrust the beautiful black-eyed girl to one of my warm-blooded Swedes. The boy there is a Finn; they are the most phlegmatic people I know of; they are bad love-makers; it takes them a year to get on fire; one girl can put twenty of them to flight in a ballroom; but if it is a question of grappling with Pappenheim, then your grace knows what they are capable of."

Far into the autumn, Gustaf Adolf flew from victory to victory. Tilly, who had come too late to save Würtzburg, did not dare attack him, and, irritated by ill-luck and constant small defeats, turned back to the Bavarian frontier. Gustaf Adolf marched along the Main, entered Aschaffenburg, and compelled the cautious city of Frankfort to open its gates. On the 6th of December, he forced a passage across the Rhine at Oppenheim, and on the 9th took possession of Mayence, which the Spaniard De Sylva defiantly promised to defend against three kings of Sweden. The Swedish arms had now gained the ascendency over the whole north and west of Germany, and the conqueror chose as his winter quarters Frankfort-on-the-Main. Here a brilliant court gathered around the hero; it was here that flattery hastened to adorn his head with the German Imperial crown; it was here that Maria Eleonora hastened on the wings of longing to embrace her consort; in Hanau, where the king had ridden to meet her, she clasped him in her arms, as she exclaimed: "Now, at last, is the great Gustaf Adolf captured!"

One day, at the end of December, 1631, the king gave a large banquet in Frankfort, in honor of the queen's arrival. Immense throngs pressed outside the castle, whose high Gothic windows at night diffused a radiance like that of day. Ale and wine ran continually from large casks, for the regalement of the people; around the spigots workmen and soldiers jostled each other, holding out tankards and cups, which, quickly filled, were as quickly emptied again. The good citizens of Frankfort were beside themselves with admiration of the great king. Gossip of his justice and clemency was freely circulated: now he had had a soldier hung for stealing a burgher's hen; now he had stopped in the street and spoken familiarly with those he met. They imagined that they saw his shadow pass by the small window-panes, and wondered whether the German crown would not be placed upon the mighty brow that very evening.

In the halls of the castle a princely magnificence prevailed. Gustaf Adolf knew his consort's weakness for outward grandeur, and probably wished also to produce an imposing effect upon the assembled German nobility. The floor was covered with rich Flemish carpets; over the windows hung drapery of purple satin, with tassels of gold; and costly chandeliers, heavy with a thousand wax-lights, were suspended from the ceiling, decorated with arabesques. They had just finished one of those measured and stately Spanish dances at that time in vogue, in which the heavy-footed northerner tried in vain to compete with the German and French nobility. The king had offered his arm to his wife, and was promenading the brilliant rooms with her. His tall and portly figure, with the simple dignity which at once inspired reverence and love, seemed even more tall and manly by the side of the slender and delicate queen, who, with sincere devotion, leaned upon his arm. Maria Eleonora was at that time thirty-two years of age, and had retained a great part of the beauty which in her first youth had gained her so many admirers. Upon her black hair, arranged in short curls around the snow-white temples, flashed a diadem of immense value, just presented to her by the king; her expressive blue eyes rested with indescribable affection upon her royal escort; she seemed to forget herself, to enjoy only the admiration which surrounded her husband. In the train of the royal pair, followed a numerous throng of all the illustrious personages which Protestant Germany at that time could boast. One saw there the deposed King Frederick of Bohemia, the Dukes of Weimar and Würtemberg, the Landgraves of Hesse, the Margrave of Baden Durlach, the Counts of Wetterau, as well as other distinguished chevaliers. Not less than twelve ambassadors from foreign courts had assembled there around the hero feared by all Europe. Of the king's own people, Tott, Banér, and Gustaf Horn were elsewhere occupied with affairs of war; but there at Gustaf Adolf's side, great as he in stature as in intellect, was the gifted Oxenstjerna; and behind him, the man with the bloodless and insignificant aspect, and the calm, penetrating, and commanding glance, Lennart Torstenson, as well as the proud Finn, Wittenberg, then lieutenant colonel. Many of the Swedish and almost all the Finnish generals—Stålhandske, Ruuth, Forbus, and others—did not thrive well in the stillness of the royal halls, among this haughty nobility, whose court ceremonials appeared to the stern warriors unendurably tedious; they therefore had withdrawn in good time to one of the smaller rooms, where pages, in gold-embroidered velvet suits, poured the choicest Rhine wines freely into silver goblets.

Among this brilliant assemblage must be mentioned the members of the common council of the city of Frankfort, and many of the most prominent citizens, with their wives and daughters, as well as a large number of ladies, from the high-born duchess down to the scarcely less proud councillor's wife. Yes, one saw there even a small number of Catholic prelates, easily recognizable by their bald heads: for the king wished to proclaim religious freedom by word and deed; and the prelates, although in their hearts cursing the mean *rôle* they played there, when once invited did not dare to remain away.

Doubly gorgeous became this scene through a magnificence, a luxury of attire, of which one now-a-days can scarcely form a conception. The king himself wore a simple tight-fitting suit of black velvet stitched with silver, a short Spanish cape of white satin embroidered by the queen's own hand, short top-boots of yellow leather, and the well-known broad lace collar which one sees in all his portraits, together with the close cut hair and long goatee. The luxury-loving queen wore a richly jeweled dress of silver brocade with a short waist and half-sleeves; even the little white satin slippers glittered with brilliants. The ladies of the higher aristocracy and the rich burgher wives vied among themselves and with the queen in display. Here were seen both silver and gold fabrics, velvet, satin, and costly Brabant laces; especially had the good dames an inexplicable taste in decking themselves with bright ribbons in all possible colors, buckles, rosettes, and long sashes, which, fluttering in the current of air, gave everything an aspect of gaiety. Princes and chevaliers, some in the loose German costume, others in the closer-fitting Spanish, with their plumed hats under their arms, and the attendant pages in velvet and silver, completed this bright picture of a time when uniforms were not yet known.

Wherever the king went, flattery and admiration offered their incense.

"Sire," said the insinuating King of Bohemia to him, "your majesty can only be compared to Alexander of Macedon."

"My cousin," answered Gustaf Adolf, smiling, "you do not mean to liken the good city of Frankfort to Babylon?"

"No, sire," joined in the French ambassador, Brezé, who walked by their side; "his Bohemian majesty only wishes to liken the Rhine to Granicus, and hopes that the new Alexander's Hyphasis may lie beyond the frontiers of Bohemia."

"Confess, Count Brezé," said the king, changing the subject, "that our northern and your French beauties have to-day been vanquished by a German."

"Sire, I share your opinion, that her majesty the queen, in order to vanquish, does not need the enviable place at your side," responded the polite Frenchman.

"My consort will be grateful for your compliment, Sir Ambassador; but she yields to Lady von Emmeritz the preference which belongs to youth."

"Your majesty over-flatters our national pride," said the Duke of Würtemburg, with a bow.

"Beauty is cosmopolitan, your grace. It was in truth a precious spoil my warriors took at Würtzburg."

The king thereupon approached Lady Regina, whose radiant beauty was enhanced by a tightly-fitting robe of black velvet, strewn with stars of pale silver.

"My lady," said he, courteously, "I should count myself happy if the mourning attire you wear covered a heart which was able to forget all sad memories, and to live in the hope of a happier time, when war and feuds shall no longer frighten the color from your beautiful cheeks. Believe me, my lady, that time will come; I, no less than you, desire it with all my heart; and let this hope call joy to your lips, where it ought always to dwell."

"At your majesty's side, one forgets everything," replied Regina, as she respectfully rose from the high purple-covered arm-chair. But her cheeks paled still more at these words, and betrayed too vivid a recollection of the past and of her present captivity.

"Are you not well, my lady?"

"Perfectly well, your majesty."

"You have perhaps something to complain of? Confide in me . . . as in a friend."

"Your majesty is very good. . . ."

Regina struggled with herself. Finally she added, with downcast eyes, "Your majesty's kindness leaves me nothing to desire."

"We shall see each other again." And the king continued his promenade through the hall.

Lady Regina drew back into the deep window-niche of an adjoining room, and burst into tears. "Holy Virgin," prayed she, "forgive me that my heart does not belong to thee alone! Thou, who seest my inmost thoughts, thou knowest that I have not the strength to hate this heretic king as thou demandest of me. He is so great, so beautiful! Woe unto me that I tremble at the thought of the holy work thou hast laid upon me!"

"Courage, my daughter!" whispered a voice quite near, and Regina's evil demon, the pale Jesuit, stood behind her. "The moment approaches," continued he, in a low tone. "The godless prince is captivated by your beauty; rejoice, my child; the Holy Virgin has doomed him to destruction. This night shall he die."

"O my father, my father! what do you ask of me?"

"Listen to me, my daughter. When Holofernes, the Assyrian chief, laid siege to Bethulia, there was a widow, Judith, the daughter of Merari, beautiful as you, my child, and as pious. She fasted three days, then went out and found favor in the eyes of the enemy of her people and her faith; and the saints gave his life into her hands. She drew his sword, cut off his head, and delivered her people."

"Grace, my father!"

"For this deed, great glory was accounted her, and eternal salvation, and her name became mentioned among the greatest in Israel. So shall they one day mention your name, my daughter, among the blessed saints of the Catholic Church. Know that last night the holy Saint Franciscus appeared at my couch and said: 'The hour has come: go, say to Judith that I will give the head of Holofernes into her hands.'"

"What shall I do, my father?"

"Mark well how you should act. This very

F

evening you must request of the king a secret meeting."

"Impossible!"

"You will reveal to him a fictitious plot against his life. He will listen to you. You will entice the ring from him. Once in possession of it, I will be ready to assist you. But if he refuses you the ring, then . . . take this paper; it contains an irremediable poison; Saint Franciscus himself gave it to me. You shall mix it in the beverage which the king drinks at night. . . ."

Lady Regina took the dangerous paper, leaned her head against the window-frame, and scarcely seemed to hear the Jesuit's foreboding words. An entirely new thought had seized this ardent soul, and was working itself to clearness. The Jesuit, however, misunderstood her; he supposed that her silence proceeded from submission to his despotism, from fanatic ecstacy over the martyr-crown he held up to her.

"Have you understood me, my daughter?" asked he.

"Yes, my father."

"You will then this evening ask the king for a private audience? You will . . ."

"Yes, my father."

"*Benedicta, ter benedicta*, thou thrice-blessed chosen instrument, go to thy heavenly glory!" And the Jesuit disappeared in the throng.

The large clock in the coronation chamber pointed to the hour of midnight. By means of an ingenious mechanism, invented by a Nuremberger, two immense tables, set with elegant silver service, rolled out from an adjoining room at the twelfth stroke, and stood at once, as if risen from the floor, in the centre of the hall. Upon a sign

THE KING'S RING.

from the master of ceremonies, the king and queen placed themselves before two purple chairs at the middle of the upper table; and all the guests took their places in rows according to rank and dignity, around the festive board. One of the prelates present said grace in a loud voice, after which the king himself recited a short psalm, and the rest joined in with familiar voices. All now seated themselves, with considerable bustle, and did not allow themselves to be incommoded by much further ceremony. The dishes were both numerous and substantial. Richelieu had sent Gustaf Adolf a French cook; but the king, who indulged little in high living, employed the fine Frenchman only for ornamental dishes, on such occasions as this; nor did he, perhaps, trust fully the cardinal's gift, as it was said that Richelieu's dinners were scarcely less dangerous than those of the famous Borgias. Besides, the cooking of the Netherlands and of Germany was at that time in higher favor than that of the French. The chief ornaments of the table at this banquet were a wild boar roasted whole, embellished with flowers and laurel leaves; and a piece of pastry, presented by the Frankfort bakers, representing the triumphal march of a Roman emperor. The guests fancied that they recognized, in this six-inch victor of dough, the features of Gustaf Adolf; and many jesting words passed from one to another, as they pretended to discover resemblances between their neighbors and the doughty Roman warriors.

The queen, whose delicate hand was first to break this masterpiece of the baker's art, smilingly transferred to her silver plate one of the last slaves in the triumphal procession; but the king, who was above superstition, and generally blessed

with a good appetite, when he had time to gratify
it, seized the great pastry hero rather ungently
with his warrior hand, and placed a considerable
portion of it on his own plate. In the meanwhile,
the silver goblets were filled with the choicest
Rhine and Spanish wines; the king quietly drank to
the queen, and all the guests followed his example.
The retainers and pages, who stood in glittering
rows, one behind each chair at the upper table,
while at the lower table one stood behind every
other chair, refilled the empty goblets; the king
drank to the prosperity of the city of Frankfort, and
then rose hastily, offered the queen his arm, and
repaired to his own apartments. Gustaf Adolf's
mode of life was frugal, as behooved a warrior; his
meals were usually despatched quickly, although
on more joyful occasions, when time permitted, he
was easily prevailed upon to linger an hour at the
table. Still, he did not require that all should
follow his habits, and, when he himself departed,
delegated the office of host to one of those nearest
him.

This time it was the jovial old Scot, Patrick
Ruthven, who received this trust; and he discharged it with tried ability. Oxenstjerna had left
the room at the king's side. The ladies also rose
and left the hall; but the male guests remained
sitting, regaling themselves with the wine-cup, and
with the nuts, passed around in silver bowls,
among which were a number of stone nuts, painted
so skillfully that they could not immediately be
distinguished from the real. From the witticisms
which these suggested, arose the saying, "a hard
nut to crack." For the rest, the heroes of the
Thirty Years War were pretty hard drinkers; to

empty a full beaker of Rhine wine at a draught, upon their knightly oath, was for them an ordinary matter. But they did not carry their drinking to the same wild excess here as at many private drinking-matches: they knew the king's stern principles, and did not dare to see the bottom of the cup too often. Still, they sat there far into the night; and some of the officers treated each other to a delicacy, hitherto quite scarce, but then imported from the Netherlands: a black, stringy substance, which was carried in boxes, and circulated from man to man, so that each one had a morsel, which some, with grimaces, spat out again, and others kept in their mouths with evident satisfaction. This substance was, as the reader has probably guessed, tobacco.

While the carousal in the hall continued, the queen, attended by her maids of honor, had retired to rest; but the king conversed a while longer confidentially with Axel Oxenstjerna. What these two powerful men, the general and the statesman, talked about, can rather be conjectured than related. Perhaps it was Sweden's poverty, the resources of the emperor, and of God, still greater; the victory of the right, the Roman Imperial crown, and a future German Protestant empire. No one knows with certainty, for after the king's death his confidence went with Oxenstjerna to the grave.

It was now very late, and Oxenstjerna was on the point of retiring, when the officer on guard, Bertel, announced that a veiled lady persistently demanded an audience with the king. This unusual request, at such an hour, astonished both Gustaf Adolf and his companion; but, supposing some important reason under so secret a visit, the king commanded Bertel to usher in the stranger, and requested Oxenstjerna to remain.

Bertel went out, and returned in a moment with a tall and slender lady dressed in black and closely veiled. She seemed frightened, and surprised not to find the king alone; no word passed her lips.

"Madam," said the king, rather brusquely,— for he was but little pleased at this nocturnal visit, which, if it became known, might excite gossip among the courtiers, and perhaps cause jealousy in his sensitive wife—"madam, a call at this time must have a weighty cause, and I desire in the first place to know who you are."

The veiled lady made no reply. The king thought that he guessed the reason of her silence, and continued, pointing to his neighbor:

"This is Chancellor Oxenstjerna, *my friend;* and from him I have no secrets."

The lady in black threw herself at the king's feet, and raised her veil. The king started as he recognized Lady Regina von Emmeritz, whose dark eyes flashed with ecstatic fire, while a marble paleness overspread her delicate and transparent features.

"Stand up, my lady," said Gustaf Adolf, gently, as he reached the kneeling woman his hand and raised her. "Why do you come to me at this hour? Speak, I beg of you! Reveal without fear that which oppresses your heart, as I have already asked you to do."

Regina breathed deeply, and began in a voice which, at first scarcely audible, soon, through her burning enthusiasm, became clear and strong.

"Your majesty, I come to you because you asked me to. I come to you because I have hated you, sire; because I have for a long time prayed daily to the Holy Virgin that she might destroy you and your whole army. Your majesty, I am a weak girl, but a faithful Catholic. You have persecuted our Church, you have allowed our cloisters to be plundered, expelled our holy fathers, and melted the images of the saints; you have slain our troops, and done our cause irreparable harm. Therefore I have sworn with a sacred oath to destroy you; and in reliance upon the Holy Virgin's help, I have followed you from Würtzburg with the design of killing you."

The king exchanged a glance with Oxenstjerna, which expressed a doubt of the fanatical girl's sanity. Regina noticed this, and continued with a firmer bearing:

"Sire, you believe me insane, because I say such things to you, the conqueror of Germany. But hear me to the end! When I saw you for the first time in Würtzburg Castle, and witnessed the humane mildness with which you protected the weak and granted life to your subjugated enemies, then I said to myself: It is the evil power which simulates the mercy of Heaven. But when I followed you here, and, close by you, saw your greatness as an individual, and added it to your greatness as a hero . . . sire, then my resolution wavered, my hatred began to abate; I struggled with myself, and this evening your kindness has overcome my before unalterable purpose. Sire, I now love you, as I have hitherto hated you . . . I admire you, revere you . . ."

And the beautiful girl cast down her eyes to the floor.

"Well, then?" said the king, hesitatingly, and with some emotion.

"Your majesty, I have made this confession because you are sufficiently noble and high-minded not to misunderstand me. But I have not come to you at such an hour merely to disclose the feelings of an unhappy girl. I have come here to save you, sire . . ."

"Explain yourself!"

"Hear me, your majesty! I am disarmed, but others, who are more dangerous, remain. Six Jesuits in Augsburg have sworn to kill you . . . Oh, you know not of what these men are capable! They have drawn lots for your life, and the most dangerous among them steals around your person every day. Your majesty cannot escape them. Some day — perhaps to-morrow — you will be reached by the dagger or by poison. Your death is certain."

"My life is in God's hands, and not in those of a miserable secret assassin," answered Gustaf Adolf, calmly. "The evil have not power proportioned to their will. Be not alarmed, Lady von Emmeritz; I fear them not."

"Nay, sire, the saints have decreed your death. I know you trust in this ring,"—Regina seized the king's hand,—"but it will not help you. Sire, I tell you that your death is sure; and I have not come here to save your life, and thus betray the cause of our holy Church."

"And wherefore, my lady, do you now stand here?"

Regina again threw herself devotedly at the king's feet.

"Sire, I have come *to save your soul*. I cannot endure the thought that a hero like you, so noble, so great, shall be lost for all eternity. Hear me, I entreat! I conjure your majesty, by your hope of salvation, not to persist in your heretic belief, the fruit of which is damnation, when you have certain death before your eyes. Be persuaded! turn while it is yet time; turn to the only saving Catholic Church; abjure your heretic faith; go to the holy father in Rome, confess your sins to him, and use your victorious arms in the service of the Church, instead of employing them to her ruin. She will receive you with open arms, and then, whether your majesty lives or dies, you will always be sure of a place among the chosen saints in heaven."

The king for a second time lifted up the excited girl, looked steadily and calmly into her flashing eyes, and answered seriously:

"When I was young, like you, Lady von Emmeritz, my teacher, the old Skytte, brought me up in the same burning zeal for the evangelical doctrines which you now entertain for the Catholic. I hated the pope, at that time, with all my soul, as you now hate Luther: and I prayed God that the day might come when I could dethrone Antichrist, and convert all his followers to the true faith. Since then I have not changed my conviction, but I have learned that the ways are many, if the spirit is one. I stand firm by the evangelical faith I profess, for which I am prepared to die on the field, if God so wills. But I respect a Christian's belief, even if it differs in some points from mine; and I know that God's mercy is able to bring a heart to salvation, although the way may be beset with error and danger. Go, Lady von Emmeritz; I forgive you that, deluded by the monks' fanatical teachings, you have tried to turn the Lord's champion from his struggle for the light. Go, poor child, and let God's word and your own experience teach you

4*

not to place reliance upon the saints, who are
nothing else but sinners like ourselves, or upon
images and rings, which are not able to avert
the judgment of the Supreme. I thank you; for
you have meant well, although in childish ignor-
ance. Be not concerned for my life; it is in the
hands of One who knows to what end He wishes
to use me."

King Gustaf Adolf was grand as he uttered
these words.

Lady Regina was at once depressed and elevated by the king's sublime tolerance. She perhaps remembered his answer to the citizens of
Frankfort, when they asked to be allowed to
remain neutral: "Neutrality is a word which I
cannot possibly endure, least of all in the strife
between light and darkness, between freedom and
slavery." Educated in hatred of a different faith,
she could not comprehend how it was possible that
the same sword which destroyed the worldly
supremacy of the Church, mercifully lowered its
point before its spiritual power over the heart and
conscience.

The impassioned girl raised her tearful eyes to
the king; then her cheeks paled which had so
lately burned with the flush of enthusiasm, and
she stared with horror at the scarlet hangings of
the king's bed.

Oxenstjerna, who, more suspicious than Gustaf
Adolf, had constantly, with watchful eyes, followed the strange girl's motions, immediately perceived her frightened glance.

"Your majesty," said he, in Swedish, to the
king, "be on your guard; there are owls in the
swamp."

And without awaiting an answer, he drew his

sword and advanced resolutely to the sumptuous bed—a gift of the citizens of Frankfort, the swelling eider-down cushions of which the royal hero had had exchanged for a simple hair mattress and a coarse blanket of Saxony wool, such as his soldiers used in their winter quarters.

"Hold!" exclaimed Regina, almost involuntarily. But it was too late. Oxenstjerna had, with a quick motion, thrown back the hangings; and behind them appeared a corpse-like face, with dark, burning eyes, and a head covered by a black leather calotte. Another fold of the scarlet was removed, disclosing the full figure of a monk, with hands clasped over a crucifix of silver.

"Step forth, reverend father," said Oxenstjerna, mockingly. "So modest a position does not befit such a reverend man. Your reverence has chosen an unusual place to perform your evening devotions. If his majesty permits me, I will procure you several hearers."

And, at the sound of the bell, Lieutenant Bertel entered, with two of the body-guard, who, with their long halberds, were posted on each side of the entrance.

The king fastened upon Lady Regina a look in which was reflected more of sorrow than anger. It grieved him that so young and beautiful a girl could be an accomplice in such black treason.

"Mercy, your majesty! mercy for my father confessor! He is innocent!" exclaimed the young girl, beseechingly.

"Will your majesty allow me to put some questions in your place?" asked Oxenstjerna.

"Do as seems best to you, chancellor!" said the king.

"Well, then, what has your reverence to do here?"

"To restore a great sinner to the arms of the only saving church!" replied the monk cunningly, with a pious glance toward heaven.

"Indeed! One must acknowledge that your zeal is great. And for so holy an object you bring with you the image of the crucified Savior?"

The monk bowed, and made the sign of the cross devoutly.

"Your reverence is very pious. Hand me the crucifix, that I may admire so precious a treasure."

The monk reluctantly handed him the image.

"A fine piece of work! It must have been a skillful artist who ornamented this sacred image." And with this the chancelior's hands felt carefully all over the crucifix. Finally, at a pressure on the breast of the image, a sharp-edged dagger appeared.

"Ah! your reverence is also familiar with innocent playthings. Such a well-sharpened dagger, just suitable to pierce the heart of a noble king! ... Miserable monk!" continued Oxenstjerna, in crushing tones, "do you not know that your abominable crime becomes a hundred-fold more abominable through the impious means you employ?"

Like all the kings of the Wasa branch, Gustaf Adolf was in his youth a person of hot temper, which more than once led him to hasty deeds. The ripening influence of manhood, and a rich life-experience, had somewhat cooled his fiery disposition; but occasionally the Wasa blood boiled over. This occurred now. He was great enough to regard with the composure of majesty a base treason against his life, upon which, however, Germany's weal or woe depended at that moment;

THE KING'S RING. 93

and he looked down with calm contempt upon the convicted traitor, who stood there trembling before his judge. But the base misuse of the Savior's holy image, in turning it as a murderous weapon against one who, for the pure evangelical faith of Jesus Christ, was prepared to sacrifice his life, this seemed to him so frightful a profanation of all that he considered sacred and precious in life, that his calmness in an instant changed to the most violent anger. Large and powerful, like a lion in a rage, he stood before the deathly pale Jesuit, who was unable to endure his fiery glance.

"On your knees!" cried the king, in thundering tones, and stamping his foot on the floor so violently that the palace walls echoed the sound.

The Jesuit fell down, as if struck by lightning, and crept in deadly anguish to the king's feet, like a venomous serpent, which, charmed by the conjuror's gaze, impotently crawls in the dust at the feet of its conqueror.

"Ye brood of vipers!" continued the king, beside himself with rage, "how long do ye expect that the Almighty will tolerate your shameful mockery? God knows I have seen much. I have seen your Antichrist and Rome, the Babylonian harlot, prevail over the world with all the deeds of darkness; I have seen you, monks and Jesuits, poison the frightened conscience with your devilish doctrines of murder and villainy committed for the glory of heaven; but a deed so black as this, a blasphemy so opposed to all that is most sacred in heaven and on earth, I have never before been able to imagine. I have forgiven you everything. You have conspired against my life at Demmin and elsewhere; I have not taken revenge. You have behaved worse than Turks and heathen toward the innocent Lutherans; wherever you have had power, there you have laid waste and desecrated their churches, burnt them alive at your heretic stakes, driven them away from house and home, and, what is more, you have tried with persuasions and threats to draw them over to your idolatrous faith, which worships deeds and miserable images, instead of the living God and His only begotten Son. All this I have not revisited upon your cloisters and churches and consciences. You have gone free in your belief, and no one has on that score harmed a hair of your heads. But now at last I know you, ye servants of the Devil! The Lord God has given you into my hand. I will scatter you like chaff; I will chastise you, ye profaners of sanctuaries, and pursue you to the world's end, so long as this arm is able to wield the sword of the Lord God. You have hitherto beheld me merciful and mild; you shall henceforth behold me hard and formidable. I shall, with God's power, uproot you and your cursed doctrines from the earth; and there will be a new order of things, such as the world has not seen since the fall of Rome."

And the king paced the floor excitedly, without honoring with a look the Jesuit lying at his feet, or the trembling Regina, who, standing apart in the recess of a window, buried her face in her hands. Oxenstjerna, always calm and self-possessed, feared some imprudent step from the king's hastiness, and tried to avert the storm.

"Will your majesty be pleased," said he, "to order Lieutenant Bertel to place this monk in safe custody, and let the court-martial make a terrifying example of him?"

"Grace, your majesty!" exclaimed Regina, who

cherished a blind affection for her father confessor. "Grace! I am the only criminal. It is I who persuaded him to this unfortunate step; I alone deserve to be punished for it."

At this noble self-sacrifice, a ray of hope passed over the Jesuit's pale features, but he did not dare to rise. The king paid no heed to the suppliant. Instead, his wrath turned upon the guard.

"Lieutenant Bertel," said he, sharply, "you have had command over my body-guard to-night; through your neglect has this scoundrel stolen in. Take him to jail immediately, and answer with your head that he does not escape. After that, you can resume your place in the ranks. You are from this moment degraded to be a common soldier."

Bertel gave the salute, and answered not a word. The loss of his master's good-will grieved him more than the loss of his position; all the more because he had kept his post with the utmost vigilance. How the Jesuit got in was to him a complete enigma.

In the meantime the latter had embraced the king's knees, and begged for mercy; but in vain. Gustaf Adolf pushed him back, and he was carried off, gnashing his teeth, and with revengeful heart.

The king then turned to the trembling girl at the window, took her hand, and looked her sharply in the eyes.

"Lady," said he, sternly, "it is said that when the prince of darkness wishes to accomplish some especially atrocious work on the earth, he sends out his emissaries disguised as angels of light. What do you expect me to think of you?"

Regina had sufficient courage to lift her eyes

to her formidable questioner. "I have nothing more to say. Kill me, sire, but spare my father confessor!" repeated she, with the inflexible resolution of fanaticism.

The king gave her a dark glance, and his scarcely subdued anger fermented again in his breast.

"If your father, lady, had been a righteous man, he would have taught his daughter to fear God, honor the king, and speak the truth before all persons. You have tried to convert me; I shall, in return, educate you, for you seem to need it. Go! you remain my prisoner until you have learned truthfulness. Oxenstjerna, is the old stern Märtha of Korsholm still alive?"

"Yes, your majesty."

"She shall have a pupil to educate. At the first opportunity send this girl to Finland."

Regina left the room, mute and proud.

"Your majesty!" said Oxenstjerna, with mild reproachfulness.

CHAPTER VI.

THE FINNS AT LECH.

IT is necessary, before going farther in our story, to cast a hurried glance back at Frankfort.

After Regina's unfortunate attempt to convert the king, she was strictly guarded, and later in the spring, when the waters were free from ice, sent to Finland, where our story may one day find her again. No religious hatred, still less revenge, occasioned the anger of the usually magnanimous Gustaf Adolf toward this young girl. Abused confidence wounds a noble heart deeply, and Regina did nothing to remove the conviction of her guilt from the king's mind. She strengthened it more and more through her fanaticism; and hate still struggled in her young heart for the place which should have belonged to love alone.

An inexplicable event increased the king's resentment. The same night that the Jesuit Father Hieronymus was taken by Bertel to the state prison, to be hung the next day, this dangerous monk escaped, no one knew how. These men of darkness had everywhere their allies and their secret passages. That very night a hitherto unknown secret door was discovered to the king's bedchamber. Bertel's innocence of course thus came to light; but his new offence, in allowing his prisoner to escape, again excited the king's anger; and the young lieutenant retained his place in the ranks as a common soldier.

In the middle of February, 1632, the king began to prepare for decampment. He captured the stronghold at Kreutznach in March, after a two weeks' seige, and left the queen, as well as Axel Oxenstjerna, in Mayence. But Tilly had in the meantime surprised Gustaf Horn at Bamberg, and done great damage. The king marched after Tilly down the Danube, and tried to invade Bavaria by crossing the Lech. In vain did his generals object that the stream was too deep and rapid, and that the elector, with Tilly, Altringer, and twenty-two thousand men, awaited him on the opposite shore. The king spoke Alexander's words at Granicus: "Shall we, who have crossed the Elbe, Oder, and Rhine, nay, even the Baltic itself, stop disheartened at the river Lech?" And the passage was decided.

Long did the king ride along the bank to seek a suitable place. Finally he found it at the bend of the stream. One of his dragoons disguised himself as a peasant, pretended that he wished to go over, and lured the information from the credulous Bavarians that the Lech was twenty-two feet deep. Some peasant huts were torn down, and of the timber trestles were constructed of just the right height for a bridge; four batteries, with seventy cannon in all, were erected on the bank, and breastworks thrown up for the sharpshooters; while a thick smoke of green wood and damp straw obscured the whole vicinity.

But Tilly was old and sagacious. In a short time he stood, with his whole army, in the woods on the other shore, where he built strong fortifications, and dug deep trenches in the loose soil, from which his musketeers directed a murderous fire. On the 3d of April, the Swedish cannon began to retort, and swept clean the opposite tongue of land. By the 5th of April the trestles had been laid right under the fire of the enemy. Planks were now thrown across, and, as usual, the Finns were sent to the front. Three hundred of their foot-soldiers, all volunteers—the little dumpy Larsson and the daring Savolaxen, Paavo Lyydikäin, at the head—were ordered to cross the planks and throw up works on the opposite shore for the defence of the bridge; and to each and all was promised a handsome reward. It was a solemn and decisive moment, upon which Bavaria's fate depended; for Tilly's balls might at any moment strike the bridge and prevent the crossing.

The Finns laid aside their arms, took up spades and pickaxes, and cheering as they went, rushed at full speed over the planks. The most terrific cross-fire from all Tilly's batteries was immediately directed upon this single point. Every instant a ball fell in the water, spun round in a seething foam, and whizzed against the frail bridge; another fell short of its aim and buried itself in the sands of its own shore; others swept in high circles over the swiftly advancing Finns, dropping among them and scattering in the way their mutilated limbs. It is not stated how many of the three hundred got over; for, in fact, those who came had no time either to look back or to count their number. They went vigorously to work with their spades and picks, and in a short time had thrown up an earthwork which in some measure protected their front, while the flanks continued to be exposed to the fire from the batteries.

Tilly realized too well the importance of this position and redoubled his fire. The Swedes likewise understood the exigency of the moment, and riddled the opposite wood with a hail of balls, which at one instant struck against the stones, making the sparks fly, then mowed down the tree-tops far around, and whirled the branches and fragments over the ranks of the Bavarians, who stood underneath, awaiting the order to advance. The king himself, in order to encourage his men, hurried to the batteries, and directed with his own hand no less than sixty shots. The noise of the cannon was so great that it was heard several miles in the interior of the terrified Bavaria.

The ranks of the advancing Finns had now fearfully withered; but not until the entrenchment was finished did those who survived look about them, and become aware that their number had melted to less than half; a hundred or more lay bleeding on the ground, and many the flood had swallowed up. But at that moment the king commanded the young Karl Gustaf Wrangel, afterwards so celebrated, to hasten to the relief. The Finns, beside themselves with pride at their countrymen's courage and anxiety for their fate, clamored to be led into the fight; and in a trice Wrangel was surrounded by three hundred Finnish volunteers, with whom he heroically sprang over the shaking planks. They were greeted with loud hurrahs from those on the other side. The gallant Duke Bernhard, who, like the king, had a partiality for the Finns, requested and received permission to make a diversion for their benefit. Followed by a troop of Finnish cavalry, he found, at a little distance, a fording-place in the river, passed over successfully, and, with boundless courage, closed in upon the enemy's right flank. The Bavarians, whose attention was fastened upon the bridge, were completely surprised, fell into disorder, notwithstanding their great superiority of numbers, and offered a weak defence. Terribly did Duke Bernhard's little band ravage the broken lines; and before the enemy had time to recover their senses, he and his cavalry had cut their way to the other Finns at the end of the bridge.

It was through these bold and crushing cavalry charges that the Finns obtained the dreaded name, *Hackapeliter*, from the words "*Hakka päälle!*" ("Hew down!") with which they encouraged each other in the onslaught against the enemy.

Stimulated by the Finns' success, one detachment after another of both Swedish and German infantry, now commenced to cross the bridge.

Tilly, who had avoided exposing his men to the murderous fire of the Swedes until the very last moment, now sent Altringer, with a strong force of infantry, to take the fortification at the end of the bridge, and drive back the new-comers. The Bavarians advanced at full speed, but had not gone far before whole ranks fell to the ground under the shower of bullets. Still, their country was at stake; and all who had life and strength dashed with fury against the Finnish entrenchment. Wrangel's young and heroic heart beat violently; his men stood immovable. The crisis was at hand. Like a dark cloud stormed the enemy's host, momently decreasing, but yet four or five thousand strong, against the outwork. The Finns gave them a warm welcome: at fifty paces their long muskets were discharged; every shot felled its man. The Bavarians faltered for a moment; most of them were new recruits. They wavered. The Finns had time to reload; again a volley, and the whole body of the assailants dispersed in wild flight along the shore. Altringer hurried forward, collected them again, and led them for the second time to the onset; at that instant a cannon-ball whizzed so close by his ear that he fell senseless to the earth. For the second time the Bavarians gave way; Tilly saw this from his entrenchments, and sent his prime favorites, the old Wallachians, down to the shore. Even the Wallachians could not maintain their ground, so scathing was the fire. Then Tilly himself seized a standard, and flew at the head of his warriors toward the Finnish works. He had taken but a few steps before he sank down, struck by a falconet-ball, which crushed one leg. The old general was carried senseless from

the field, and died two weeks afterwards, the 20th
of April, in Ingolstadt.

The Bavarian army, which had now lost its
best commander, became utterly disorganized.
The elector, present in person, retreated under
cover of the darkness, leaving two thousand dead
on the battlefield, and the way open for the Swedes
to the heart of Bavaria.

The following day the whole Swedish army
crossed the Lech. The king, with a liberal hand,
distributed rewards to his brave men. Among
these was a horseman who had accompanied Duke
Bernhard, and who was spoken of by him in the
highest terms. This horseman was Bertel; three
wounds — all fortunately slight — confirmed the
duke's account. Bertel regained his rank, but not
what he most valued, the king's favor and confidence. Yet he resolved to win this back, even at
the cost of his life.

Then Gustaf Adolf marched to Augsburg, which
took the oath of allegiance, and gave brilliant
festivals in his honor. Rumor, which joined the
names Gustafva Augusta, whispered that the king,
here, in the capital of his future German empire,
another Hannibal in Capua, abandoned himself to
effeminacy and pleasure. But rumor was mistaken. Gustaf Adolf was only taking a breathing
spell, and revolving still more daring projects in
his brain. But from this time shadows hung about
the pathway of the king. The death-angel went
before him with drawn sword, and aimed, now
here, now there, a blow, as if constantly to cry in
his ear, " Mortal, remember thou art not a god!"

One could almost believe, now that ambition
began to gain ascendency over the king's mind,
and he was no longer actuated solely by the sacred

struggle for faith, that the powers of evil had redoubled their dark designs upon him. A secret but formidable enemy went everywhere in his road and meted to him death, but as yet always in vain. At the daring though unsuccessful attack on Ingolstadt, there was, so Fryxell relates, a cannon on the ramparts, called "Fikonet," celebrated for shooting both far and sure. The cannoneer on the ramparts saw, out on the field, a man with a waving plume, riding on a proud charger, and surrounded by attentive followers. "There," said he, "rides a fine lord; but I shall soon put an end to his career;" with which he aimed and discharged "Fikonet." The ball threw down horse and rider: the rest hastened to the spot in alarm; but the king, for it was he, raised himself up, covered with blood and dust, but unharmed, from under the crushed horse, as he exclaimed: "Not yet is the apple ripe!" The citizens of Ingolstadt afterwards exhumed the dead horse, and stuffed his skin, as a perpetual remembrance. Shortly afterwards the king was riding at the side of the young Margrave of Baden Durlach, who had so lately been one of the most brilliant cavaliers at the balls in Augsburg. A cannon-ball went whizzing quite near the king; and, when he looked around, he saw the margrave sink headless from the saddle.

CHAPTER VII.

NEW ADVENTURES.

THE king turned from Ingolstadt to Landshut, in the interior of Bavaria. The farther he penetrated into this land, which had never before seen a heretic army within its borders, the darker became the fanaticism of the inhabitants, the wilder their resistance. Great masses of country people collected, commanded by their monks, and lay in wait everywhere for the Swedes, pouncing on all they came across, and torturing their prisoners in all conceivable ways. The king's people, on their side, arrogant from success, and irritated by these cruelties, began to do discredit to their honorable reputation for military discipline, and visited with bloody revenge the regions they marched through. Far and wide, in the Swedish army's track, raged murder and violence; and woe unto the troops who, not sufficiently strong in numbers, ventured any distance from the main force!

Arriving still deeper in the country, the king one day wished to send important orders to Banér, who, in slower marches, covered the retreat from Ingolstadt. Owing to the insecurity of the country, such a mission was extremely dangerous; and the king did not care to employ a large force for it. A young Finnish officer volunteered to execute the charge, accompanied by but two horsemen. The king consented; and the rash troopers started off, late one evening in May, on the perilous undertaking.

The young officer was none other than our old acquaintance, Bertel, attended by the East Bothnian, Pekka, and the Tavastlander, Witikka. The night was dark and cloudy; the three horsemen rode cautiously in the middle of the road, as much afraid of getting lost in a strange country as of being struck by the balls of lurking Bavarians in the edge of the woods. A fine rain made the roads, already cut up by the advancing baggage-wagons, nearly impassable; and at every step they were in dread of stumbling over a stone or of sinking into the deep ruts.

"See here!" said Witikka, jokingly, to the companion at his side; "you are a Pohjalaine, and consequently can practice sorcery?"

"I would n't be much of a man if I could n't do that," responded Pekka, in the same tone.

"Then transport us in a flash to Hattimala Heights, and manage so that we may there, beneath the hill, see the light glimmer from Hämeenlinna Castle. There sits a gypsy girl that I used to love; and I would rather be at her side to-night than here in the mud-puddles of this cursed wood."

"That is a small matter for me," answered Pekka, laughing loudly. "Look! there you see the light shine from Hämeenlinna."

His comrade strained his eyes, uncertain whether the East Bothnian spoke jest or earnest, for the latter he considered fully as possible as the former. In reality, a gleam of light was seen in the valley below; but the Tavastlander well knew that he was still two hundred miles from his native village. The horses stopped suddenly, and could not be induced to go further. A close barricade of felled trees directly across the road made an insuperable obstacle to their progress.

"Be still!" whispered Bertel, "I heard a noise in the underbrush."

The horsemen turned off a little, stopped, and bent down on the horses' backs in breathless silence. On the opposite side of the road were heard footsteps and the rustling of broken twigs.

"They must be here within a quarter of an hour," said a voice with the well-known Bavarian accent.

"How many are there?"

"Thirty horsemen, with ten or twelve pack-horses. They started at twilight from Geisenfeld, and bring with them a girl prisoner."

"And how many are we?"

"About fifty with guns, and seventy or eighty with axes and pitchforks."

"Good! No shot must be fired before they are within three steps."

At this moment Bertel's horse neighed. He was a little beast, but lively and strong, called Lappen, and brought from Rovaniemi.

"Who goes there?" cried a voice from the road.

"Swede!" answered Bertel, boldly, as at Würtzburg's sally-port; he fired off a pistol in the direction of the voice, and by the flash perceived a large body of peasants, stationed inside the barricade. Then he turned his horse, urged his comrades to follow, and galloped rapidly back towards Landshut.

But the flash had also revealed the three horsemen to the peasants; and they hastened to stop their flight. Bertel, with Lappen, succeeded in getting away; but Witikka's horse stumbled over a tree-stump, and Pekka's fat farm-horse, struggling to get out of the mud, received a pike-thrust in the breast.

Bertel, who saw the danger of his comrades, and could not persuade himself to abandon them, swung round, cut down the nearest peasant, seized Pekka's horse by the bridle, and tried to drag him up, at the same time calling to Witikka to leave his horse and jump on Lappen's back. This bold attempt almost succeeded. The three were already on their way again, when suddenly something whistled through the air; a lasso descended around Bertel's shoulders and pulled him violently from his horse. Witikka fell at the same moment. Lappen, freed from his double burden, galloped away with loose reins; and, whether willingly or unwillingly, Pekka also followed. Bertel and Witikka were in a twinkling overpowered and pinioned.

"Hang the dogs before the others come!" cried one.

"With the head down!" proposed another.

"And a little fire underneath!" joined in a third.

"No fire! No noise!" commanded a fourth, who seemed to have most authority. "Hark, comrades," whispered he to the prisoners lying on the ground, "was it Finnish you spoke together?"

"Go to the devil!" growled Witikka.

"*Maledicti, maledicti Fennones!*" exclaimed the former voice in the darkness. "You belong to me!"

"They are coming now!" exclaimed one of the gang; and, indeed, horses' hoofs were heard on the road to Ingolstadt. The peasants kept still, and, for greater security, gagged their prisoners' mouths. Those approaching bore torches, and appeared to be a troop of German marauders returning from a foraging expedition. In consequence of their rapid pace they did not become aware of the barricade until they were close upon it, and at that instant a destructive volley thundered over the hewn trunks of the trees. Ten or twelve of the foremost dropped to the ground; the horses reared, and dragged the fallen men by the stirrups; the whole troop fell into confusion. A part wheeled round immediately, riding over each other and the pack-horses; others discharged their pistols, hap-hazard, at the concealed enemy. The peasants rushed forth from their ambush, threw themselves with fury upon those who remained, and with their nooses jerked them from the horses' backs. The men defended themselves with the courage of desperation, but in vain. In a very few minutes the whole band were scattered; eight or ten had escaped, fifteen lay bleeding on the road, and six or seven were captured, as well as most of the spoils they had with them. Only four of the peasants had fallen. The revenge of the Bavarians was inhuman. They discharged powder in their prisoners' faces, blackening them past recognition, buried them half-way in the wet ground, and stoned them slowly to death.

When this cruel work was finished, they started to take the plunder to a safe place. Bertel and his companion were cast, bound, on one of the captured horses; and they began the march into the woods. After a while a halt was made at a solitary house. The prisoners were dragged in, and laid on the floor of a chamber, while the peasants, in the large room adjoining, wild with exultation over their conquest, refreshed themselves with the wine they had captured. Into the chamber now entered a monk, deadly pale, wearing at his side a sword in a rope of hemp. With delight he placed the torch near the prisoners' heads, took away the gags from their mouths, and regarded their features in silence.

"If I see aright," said he, at last, with a smile of scorn, "it is Lieutenant Bertel, of the king's body-guard?"

Bertel looked up, and recognized the Jesuit Hieronymus.

"Welcome, lieutenant; and thanks for the last time we met! So rare a guest must be treated in the best manner. It seems to me that I have also seen your comrade before," continued he, pointing to Witikka.

The wild Tavastlander looked him steadily in the eyes, and twisted his mouth into a defiant grin.

"What have you done with your ears, monk?" cried he, mockingly. "Away with the calotte, henthief, and let us see whether any asses' ears have grown there!"

At this reckless reminder of the battlefield at Breitenfeld, the Jesuit's brow was shadowed by a dark cloud; a flush passed over his livid features, and his lips were drawn in with rage.

"Think of your own ears, comrade!" said he. "*Anathema maranatha!* they will soon have heard enough in this world."

At these words the Jesuit clapped his hands twice; when in came a blacksmith, with his leather apron, carrying a red-hot pair of tongs, which he kept aglow in the furnace close at hand.

"Well, comrade, are your ears getting hot?" taunted the monk, grimly.

Witikka answered defiantly:

"You fancy yourself very smart; and yet you are nothing compared to the devil. Your lord and master doesn't need any tongs, only claws."

"The right ear," said the Jesuit, laconically. The smith put the tongs to the Tavastlander's head. Witikka smiled contemptuously. A hasty flush colored his brown cheeks, but only for an instant. He had now but one ear.

"If you will adjure your faith, acknowledge the pope, and curse Luther, then you may keep your other ear."

"Niggard!" burst out the Tavastlander. "Your lord and master used to offer lands and kingdoms, and you only offer me a miserable ear!"

"The left ear!" continued the Jesuit, coolly.

The smith did as commanded. The tortured soldier smiled.

"Monk, this is infamous!" exclaimed Bertel, lying bound at the side of Witikka. "Kill us, if you will, but do it quickly!"

"Who has said that I intend to kill you?" responded Father Hieronymus, smiling. "On the contrary, it depends upon yourself whether you regain freedom, unharmed, this very night."

"And what do you ask of me?"

"You are a brave young man, Lieutenant Bertel. It pains me that the king has so shamefully and unjustly deprived you of the rank you earned with your blood."

"Ah, indeed! it pains you! Well, what then?"

"In your place, I would take revenge."

"Revenge? Oh, yes! I have thought of it."

"You belong to Gustaf Adolf's body-guard. Do you know, young friend, what the true-believing Catholic princes would give the one who delivered the king, dead or living, into their hands?"

"How should I know, reverend father?"

"A prince's domain, if he were a nobleman; fifty thousand ducats if he were a commoner."

"Reverend father, that is very little for so great a service."

"Choose between death and a princely recompense!"

"It was this, then, that you sought, reverend father?"

"Do as you choose; when you have reflected upon the matter, we can talk further together. This time you can purchase life and liberty at a lower rate—for a trifle."

"What may it be, reverend father?"

"Listen to me. I demand only a sacred oath that you will do me an insignificant service. King Gustaf Adolf wears on his right forefinger a little copper ring. It is to him of slight value; but for me, young friend, it has higher importance. I am . . . a curiosity-seeker; I would like to possess a memento of a king whom I must hate as an enemy but admire as a man."

"And the ring?"

"The ring you must swear to put into my hand, by some means or other, before the next new moon. Do this, and you are free!"

"Oh—only a little sin against the seventh commandment? And you have absolution all ready—is it not so? Go, miserable thief! and thank your good fortune that my arm is bound. By Heaven! otherwise it would teach you respect for a soldier's honor!"

"Be quiet, young man; remember that your

life is in my hands. When I have finished with your companion, I shall begin with you."

Bertel only gave him a contemptuous look.

"Smith, to work!" muttered the Jesuit, under his breath. And the smith again drew his white-hot tongs from the fire.

At that instant a confused uproar arose among the peasants in the outer room. Cries of, "To arms! The Swedes are upon us!" were heard, and just then the door was thrown open. Part of the peasants seized their guns; others lay asleep and drunk on the floor; but without was plainly heard the Swedish officer's command:

"Set fire to the house, boys; we have them all in a trap!"

At these words the Jesuit jumped out of the window.

A hot but brief struggle now ensued at the door. The peasants soon yielded, and begged for quarter. In answer, the foremost were knocked down with halberds, the rest bound, the cabin was plundered of the pillage just brought there, and Bertel and his maltreated comrade were loosed from their bonds.

"Is that you, Larsson?" exclaimed the freed prisoner, gladly.

"Thunder and lightning! Is it you, Bertel? Is this where you wished to deliver the king's orders?"

"And you yourself?"

"Why, you know that I am a child of fortune. I am sent to guard a train; I meet on the road some rascally marauders, who speak of an ambuscade here in the woods; I hurry in the direction from whence they came, deliver a brave comrade, and gain a pretty girl. Look at her—cheeks like a tulip, eyes to buy fish with!"

Bertel turned round, and saw at his side a trembling girl, half fainting with fright.

"It is Kätchen, Lady Regina's maid!" exclaimed Bertel, who had many times seen the light-hearted girl with her gloomy mistress.

"Save me, lieutenant! save me!" cried the girl, seizing his arm violently. "They have snatched me by force from my aunt's house."

"Larsson, I beg of you, give me the girl!"

"Does the devil ride you? Do you mean to take my girl from me?"

"Let her go, I beg you!"

"In a few weeks certainly I will; but release her, I tell you, or . . ." The hot-blooded little champion raised his long sword, upon which he had so lately impaled peasants.

"The cabin is on fire!" was cried at that instant, in all directions; and a thick, stifling smoke proved the reality of the danger. Bertel started out with the girl, Larsson after him; and the heat of anger passed off before that of the fire. Not until they saw the cabin in a blaze from outside, did it enter Bertel's mind that the house was full of people—about thirty peasants, bound hand and foot.

"Come, make haste; let us save the poor creatures!" exclaimed he.

"Are you crazy?" retorted Larsson, laughing. "It is only some of the lubbers who have just taken the lives of so many of our brave fellows. Come! fire up, boys, that the ale-drinkers may not freeze from good cheer."

It was now too late to afford any help. The unfortunate Bavarians fell victims to the barbarous war-system of the time which so often permitted one cruelty to outdo another. With abhorrence we turn away from the wild scenes of those times, and hasten to the grander and more inspiring picture of the Swedish lion's last struggle.

CHAPTER VIII.

NUREMBERG AND LÜTZEN.

LIKE wave heaped upon wave in a roaring rapid, events now crowded themselves; and our narrative, pressed within narrow limits, is forced to hurry forward with the rapid's swiftness. We must hasten over the most remarkable events in a remarkable time, to find again the thread of our story, slender, but running through many generations and vicissitudes—the king's ring.

Wallenstein the Terrible had become reconciled with the emperor, collected a formidable army, and turned like a dark thunder-cloud toward the wealthy city of Nuremberg. Gustaf Adolf broke off his victorious career in Bavaria, to hurry to meet him; and there, in two strongly-fortified encampments, both armies stood motionless, opposite each other, for eleven weeks—the panther and the lion, crouching ready for a spring, and watching sharply each other's slightest movement. The whole region was drained for the subsistence of these armies, and provisions were constantly brought in from a distance by foraging parties. Among the Imperialists, Isolani's Croats distinguished themselves in this work; among the

Swedes, Taupadel's dragoons and Stålhandske's Finnish cavalry.

Famine, the heat of summer, disease, and the depredations of the German soldiers, spread want and misery everywhere. Gustaf Adolf, who, after joining Oxenstjerna's and Banér's combined armies, had a force of fifty thousand men, marched, on the 24th of August, 1632, against Wallenstein, who, with sixty thousand men, stood behind impregnable fortifications. Long before day, Torstenson's artillery commenced to thunder against Alte Veste. In the darkness of night, five hundred German musketeers of the White Brigade climbed up the steep heights, and, in spite of the terrible shower of balls, mounted the ramparts. For a moment victory seemed to reward their contempt of death; the drowsy foes' bewilderment, the shrieks of the women, and the Swedish balls, which threw down tents and people, favored the attack. But Wallenstein maintained sense and composure, sent away the women, and turned mass upon mass against the besiegers. The gallant brigade was driven back with loss. The king did not give way; once more the White Brigade stormed—in vain. Then Gustaf Adolf called his Finns, "in order," as Schiller says, "to put the German cowards to the blush with their northern courage."

These were the East Bothnians, in the ranks of the Swedish brigade. They saw death before their eyes in the shape of a hundred fiery mouths; but resolutely, with unshaken courage, they clambered up the precipice, slippery with rain and blood. But against these solid ramparts, against this murderous shower of balls, all their valor rebounded; in the midst of fire and death, they tried once more to gain a foothold on the rampart, but in vain; the few who had escaped the bullets and pikes were hurled violently back. For the first time, Gustaf Adolf's Finns were seen to retreat; and equally futile were all attempts of succeeding troops. The Imperialists hastened out in pursuit, but were driven back. With great loss of life, the strife raged all day; many of the bravest leaders fell; and the death-angel again aimed a bullet at the king, but without harming more than the sole of his boot.

On the left wing, the Imperial cavalry came in collision with the Swedes. Cronenberg, with his cuirassiers, clad in mail from head to foot, and widely celebrated as the "Invincibles," bore the Hessians to the ground. The Landgrave of Hesse remarked, resentfully, that the king wished to spare his own troops at the expense of the Germans. "Well, then," said Gustaf Adolf, "I will send my Finns; and I hope that the change of men will give a change of luck." Stålhandske, with the Finns, were now sent against Cronenberg and the "Invincibles." Between these superb troops ensued a proud, a glorious struggle, of imperishable memory. On the shore of the Regnitz River, thickly overgrown with bushes, the two detachments encountered each other, man to man, horse to horse; sword-blades were dulled against helmets, long pistols flashed, and many valiant horsemen were driven down in the whirl of the river. It is probable that the Finnish horses here also held out better than the beautiful and swift Hungarian chargers; and this contributed to the victory. The brave Cronenberg fell; his "Invincibles" fled before the Finns. In his place, Fugger, with a formidable force, charged the Finns, and drove them, under constant fighting, with breast toward the enemy, slowly to the underbrush. But here the Imperialists were met by the fire of the Swedish infantry. Fugger fell, and his cavalry were again repulsed by the fatigued Finns.

At nightfall, more than three thousand dead covered the heights and plain. " In the battle of Alte Veste," says Schiller, " Gustaf Adolf was considered conquered because he did not himself conquer." The next day he withdrew to Bavaria. Forty-four thousand persons—friends and enemies —had pest and war swallowed up during these fatal weeks in and around Nuremberg.

The darkness of autumn increased; its fogs covered Germany's blood-stained soil; and yet there seemed to be no end to the struggle. But a great spirit was destined here, after many storms, to find a peaceful haven, and to go from life's autumnal evening to the eternal light. Nearer and nearer hovered the death-angel over Gustaf Adolf's noble head, shedding upon it the halo of a higher world, which is often seen to beam around the noble of earth in their last moments. The multitude about them misunderstand it, but the departing ones divine the meaning. Two days before his death, the people of Naumberg paid homage to Gustaf Adolf as to a god; but through his soul flew a presentiment of the end of his career, and he said to the court minister, Fabricius:

" Perhaps God will soon punish both their idolatrous folly, and me, who am the object of it, and show that I also am a weak and mortal person."

The king had gone up to Saxony, to follow in the track of the ravaging Wallenstein. At Arnstadt he took farewell of Axel Oxenstjerna; at Erfurt, of Queen Maria Eleonora. There and at

Nuremberg it was perceived, from many of his arrangements, that he was prepared for what was coming. Wallenstein, who believed that the king had gone into winter quarters, sent Pappenheim, with twelve thousand men, to Halle; he remained at Lützen, with twenty-eight thousand men, and the king in Naumburg with twenty thousand.

But on the 4th of November, when Gustaf Adolf learned of Pappenheim's departure, he hastily broke camp to surprise his weakened enemy, and would have succeeded had he come to the attack on the 5th. But Providence threw in his triumphant path a slight obstacle—the little stream Rippach, which, together with freshly-ploughed fields, hindered his progress. Not until late on the afternoon of the 5th did the king approach Lützen. Wallenstein had gained time, and knew how to use it. Along the high-road to Leipzig he had had ditches dug and breastworks thrown up on both sides of the way, and filled them with his best sharpshooters, intending to destroy with their cross-fire the advancing Swedes. The king's council of war dissuaded from the attack. Only Duke Bernhard advised it, and the king was of the same opinion: "For," said he, "it is best to wash one's self thoroughly clean when one is once in the bath."

The night was dark and dreary. The king spent it in an old carriage, together with Kniephausen and Duke Bernhard. His restless soul had time to think of everything; and then, says the tradition, he drew from his right forefinger a little ring of copper, and handed it to Duke Bernhard, with instruction that, if anything should happen to him, he should deliver it to a young officer of the Finnish cavalry.

Early in the morning, Gustaf Adolf rode out to inspect the order of battle. He was clad in a jacket of elk-skin, with a gray cloak. When exhorted to wear armor on such a day, he answered: "God is my armor."

A thick mist delayed the attack. At dawn the whole army joined in singing, "A mighty fortress is our God;" and as the fog continued, the king began, with his own voice, "God, be to us gracious and kind," as well as, "Be not dismayed, thou little flock," which latter he had shortly before composed. Then he rode along the ranks, crying:

"To-day, boys, we will put an end to all our troubles;" and his horse stumbled twice.

It was eleven o'clock in the forenoon before the mist was dispelled by a slight gust of wind. The Swedish army immediately advanced to the assault. On the right wing, which was commanded by the king, again stood Stålhandske with the Finns, and behind them the Swedish troops; in the centre, the Swedish Yellow and Green Brigades, under Nils Brahe; on the left wing, the German cavalry, under Duke Bernhard. Opposite the Duke stood Colloredo, with the flower of the cavalry; in the centre, Wallenstein himself, with close masses of infantry in four large tertiers, and seven cannon in their front; opposite Stålhandske stood Isolani, with his ferocious but brave Croats. The battle-cry was on both sides the same as at Breitenfeld. When the king gave the order to attack, he clasped his hands and exclaimed:

"Jesu, Jesu, help me to fight to-day for the glory of Thy holy name!"

Lützen was now set on fire by the Imperialists; the artillery began to thunder, and the Swedish army advanced, but suffered great losses at the very outset. At last the Swedish centre crossed the trenches, took the seven cannon, and routed the enemy's first two brigades. The third had already turned to flee, when Wallenstein succeeded in rallying them; the Swedes were taken in the flank by the cavalry, and the Finns, who had put the Croats and Polanders to flight, had not yet crossed the trenches. Then the king rushed forward at the head of the Smålanders, only a few of whom had sufficiently good horses to follow him. It is said that an Imperial musketeer aimed at the king with a silver bullet; the certainty is, that his left arm was crushed, and that he endeavored to conceal his wound, but soon, weakened by the loss of blood, begged the Duke of Lauenburg, who rode at his side, to lead him, unobserved, from the strife. But in the midst of the tumult, Götz's cuirassiers came up, led by Moritz von Falkenberg, who recognized the king, and shot him through the body, with the exclamation:

"Thee have I long sought!" and directly afterwards Falkenberg himself fell, struck by a ball.

Now the king has reeled in his saddle, and entreated the duke to save his own life; the duke has seized him around the waist to support him, but at that instant a whole swarm of enemies have rushed upon them and separated them. A pistol-shot has singed the duke's hair; the king's horse has been shot through the neck, and has reared; Gustaf Adolf has sunk from the saddle, has been dragged a little way by the stirrups, and then left on the ground. The young page, Leubelfingen, from Nuremberg, has offered him his horse, but has not been able to lift up the fallen man. Some Imperial cavalrymen have come to the spot, and asked who the wounded person was; and when

Leubelfingen has not been willing to answer, one of them has run a sword through his body, another has shot the king through the head; after this, others have discharged several shots at them, and the two have been left under a pile of corpses. But Leubelfingen lived a few days after, to relate to after-times the sad and never-to-be-forgotten story of Gustaf Adolf's heroic death.

In the meantime, the Swedish centre had been compelled to retire, a thousand mutilated corpses covered the battle-field, and yet not a foot of soil had been gained. Both armies occupied nearly the same position as at the beginning of the battle.

Then the king's wounded horse, with the empty saddle covered with blood, galloped in among the ranks. "The king has fallen!" And, as Schiller beautifully says, "Life fell in value when the most sacred of all lives was no more; death had no longer any terror for the humblest, since it had not spared the crowned head."

Duke Bernhard galloped from rank to rank:

"Ye Swedes, Finns and Germans," said he, "liberty's defender, your defender, and ours, has fallen! Every man who holds the king dear will hasten forward to avenge his death!"

The first to respond to this appeal was Stålhandske and the Finns. With incredible exertion they leaped the trenches, and drove before them swarms of scattered enemies; all fell before their blows. Isolani, put to flight, wheeled round and attacked the Swedish wagon-trains, but was again repulsed. With like fury, Brahe, with the centre, pressed across the trenches; while Duke Bernhard, without heeding the ball which had crushed his arm, took one of the enemy's batteries. The whole Imperial army faltered, staggered and broke before this fearful assault; their powder-carts were blown into the air. Wallenstein's word of command and Piccolomini's brilliant valor were no longer able to stay the reckless flight.

But at that instant there resounded far over the plain the jubilant cry, "Pappenheim is here!" And Pappenheim, the bravest of the brave, was there with his cavalry, and his first question was: "Where is the King of Sweden?" They pointed to Stålhandske's lines, and he started there. The hottest, the most infuriate contest now took place. The Imperialists, regaining courage, turned back and attacked from three sides at once. No one yielded ground. Brahe, and with him the Yellow Brigade, fell almost to the last man. Winckel, with the Blue, fell in like beautiful order, man by man, just as they stood in the ranks. The rest of the Swedish foot-soldiers drew slowly back, and victory seemed to smile upon the all-powerful Pappenheim.

But he, the Ajax of his time, the man with a hundred scars, was not destined to see the day of triumph. Already, in the first attack against the Finns, a falconet-ball had struck his hip; two musket-balls had pierced his scarred breast; it is said that Stålhandske's own hand had reached him. He fell, even in his last moments rejoicing over Gustaf Adolf's death; and the news of his fall spread terror through the Imperial ranks. "Pappenheim is dead; all is lost!" Once more the Swedes advanced. Duke Bernhard, Kniephausen, Stålhandske, performed miracles; but Piccolomini also, who, with six wounds, mounted his seventh horse, fought with more than mortal courage. The Imperial centre stood firm, and only darkness suspended the conflict. Wallenstein withdrew, and the exhausted Swedish army encamped on the battlefield. Nine thousand dead covered the plain of Lützen.

The results of this battle were severely felt by the Imperialists. They had lost all their artillery — Pappenheim's and Wallenstein's reputation for invincibility. The great Friedlander raged with fury; his hard hand dispensed the gallows to the cowardly as liberally as ducats to the brave. Sick and gloomy, he retired with the remainder of his army, about ten thousand men, back to Bohemia, where the stars became his nightly companions, treasonable plans his daily relaxation, and death, by Butler's hand, the end of his brilliant career.

But over the whole Catholic world went a great jubilee of victory, for Lutherism and the Swedes had lost infinitely more than their foes. Paralyzed was the arm that had so powerfully wielded the victorious sword of light and liberty. The grief of the Protestants was general and deep, mingled with fear for the future. Not without ground was the *Te Deum* sung in the cathedrals of Vienna, Brussels, and Madrid; twelve days' brilliant bullfights celebrated in Madrid the fall of the dreaded hero; but Emperor Ferdinand, greater than his contemporaries, is said to have shed tears at the sight of his slain enemy's bloody jacket.

Many stories were circulated about the great Gustaf Adolf's death; now it was the Duke Franz Albert of Lauenburg, now Richelieu, now Duke Bernhard, whom popular belief accused of participation in the king's fall; but none of these suspicions have been confirmed by the impartial historian. A recent German author communicates the following popular version: "Gustaf Adolf, King of Sweden, received, while he was yet very young, from a lady whom he much loved, a ring of iron, which he never afterwards allowed to be taken from his hand. The ring consisted of seven circles, which formed the letters of both his names. Seven days before his death, this ring was taken from him without his being aware, at the time, of the singular theft."

The reader knows that our story joins its thread to the same ring; but several reasons entitle us to the supposition that the ring was of copper.

The evening after the battle, Duke Bernhard sent his soldiers with lighted torches to look for the king's dead body; and they found it, plundered, disfigured, under a heap of corpses. Brought to the village of Meuchen, it was there embalmed, and the soldiers received permission to behold the remains of their king and hero. Bitter tears were there shed, but tears full of pride; for even the most humble considered himself great through the honor of having fought by the side of so heroic a king.

"See," said a veteran of Stålhandske's Finns, sobbing aloud, "they have robbed him of his gold chain and his copper ring. I still see the white mark left by the ring on his right forefinger."

"What would they care for a ring of copper?" asked a Scot, who had just come to the army, and knew nothing of the story which circulated among the people.

"His ring!" exclaimed a Pomeranian, mysteriously. "You may rely upon it that the Jesuits knew what it was good for. The ring was enchanted by a Finnish witch, and, as long as the king wore it, neither iron nor lead had any effect upon him."

"But, you see, to-day he lost it," joined in a third; "and therefore . . . do you comprehend?"

"What is that the Pomeranian pear-eater says?" burst out the Finn, bitterly. "God's power, and no other, has protected our great king; but the ring was given him, a long while ago, by a Finnish girl whom he held very dear in his youth. I know something more about it than you, apple-muncher!"

Duke Bernhard, who, sombre and thoughtful, contemplated the king's pale features, looked around at these words, put his unhurt hand within his unbuttoned jacket, and turned to the Finn, saying:

"Comrade, do you know one of Stålhandske's officers named Bertel?"

"Yes, certainly, your highness."

"Is he alive?"

"No, your highness."

The duke turned abstractedly to another, and gave orders right and left. In a few moments he again seemed, at the sight of the king, to be reminded of something.

"Was he a brave man?" asked he.

"He was one of Stålhandske's cavalry!" said the Finn, with emphasis, and with a pride which did not ill become him.

"When did he fall, and where?"

"In the last skirmish with the Pappenheimers."

"Search for him!"

The duke's command was executed without grumbling by these over-wearied soldiers, who, with good reason, wondered why it was that one of the youngest officers should be searched for that very night, when Nils Brahe, Winckel, and so many other gray-haired generals, were still lying in their blood on the battle-field. Not until early morning did those sent out return with the intelligence that Bertel's dead body was nowhere to be found.

"Hum!" said the duke, displeased; "great men have sometimes their little whims; what shall I now do with the king's ring?"

And the November sun rose blood-red over the field of Lützen. A new epoch dawned; the master was gone, and the pupils had now to see how they could carry out his work.

PART II. — THE SWORD AND THE PLOUGH.

INTERLUDE.

WHEN the Surgeon had ended his first story, his hearers sat for a time in silence, reflecting, perhaps, upon the death of the great king, or perhaps not realizing that the tale was ended. On the stuffed leather sofa sat the old grandmother, in her brown-plaid woolen shawl, and at her side the school-teacher, Master Svenonius, with his blue handkerchief and brass-rimmed eyeglasses; on the right, Captain Svanholm, the postmaster, who had lost his left forefinger in the last war; on the left, the pretty Anne Sophie, who was then eighteen years of age, and wore a high tortoise-shell comb in her thick brown hair; while around them on the floor, with and without seats, were six or seven frolicsome and mischievous little folks, all with wide open mouths, as though they had heard a ghost story.

The first one to break the silence was Anne Sophie, who, with a cry, sprang up from her chair, stumbled, and fell into Master Svenonius' arms. This little interruption had about the same effect on the company, who at that moment were in Lützen, as if all Isolani's Croats had suddenly charged into the peaceful chamber. The postmaster, yet warm from the heat of the conflict, jumped up and trod on the old grandmother's sore foot with his iron-shod heel; the schoolmaster looked quite dis-

concerted, not at all realizing the value of the
burden he held in his arms—undoubtedly the first
and the prettiest in his whole life; the children
scattered confusedly in all directions, upset their
benches, and crept behind the Surgeon's high-
backed chair; but young Andreas, who had just
been following Stålhandske's cavalry in the gallop
over the trenches, seized the Surgeon's silver-
headed Spanish cane, and placed himself in position to receive the Croats at the point of the bayo-
net. Old Bäck was the only one who maintained
his imperturbable composure; he took out his oval
tobacco-box, bit off a very little piece, and asked,
mildly: "What is the matter with you, Anne Sophie?" Anne Sophie loosed herself, blushing and
embarrassed, from the master's embrace, and looked
around after the culprit, declaring that somebody
had pricked her in the arm with a pin.

The old grandmother, who, when occasion required, was quick to scent out mischief, immediately instituted proceedings which resulted in the
discovery that Jonathan had inserted a pin in the
end of his rattan, and therewith disturbed his oldest sister, who had not yet recovered from the
effects of the battle of Lützen. The trial was
short and summary, like that of a court-martial;
and our good Jonathan received the hard sentence
of banishment to the nursery and learning an extra
lesson for the next day.

When, by action of the reigning powers, and
without undue bloodshed, order was again restored,
the company found opportunity for some conversation about the Surgeon's tale.

"It is altogether too tumultuous a story, my
dear cousin," began the old grandmother, regarding the narrator with one of those mild and ex-

pressive glances which yet in her old age captivated all hearts with their peculiar intelligence and kindness — " altogether too tumultuous, I must say. It seems to me that my ears are yet deafened by the tumult of the cannon. War is something horrible and detestable, when we consider all the blood that is shed on the battle-field and all the tears at home. When shall the day come when men, instead of tearing each other to pieces, will share the earth and our Lord's good gifts together in peace and harmony?"

Here the postmaster's martial sympathies rose in arms.

"Peace?—sharing?—and no war? Pshaw, cousin, pshaw! would you make an ant's nest of the world? Just think, what a state of things! Scribblers would ink over everything; cowards and petty despots would jump on honest men's noses; and when one nation domineered over another, people would bow humbly, thank their masters, and look like sheep. No, the devil take me! such men as Gustaf Adolf and Napoleon, they shake things up; they tap a little blood which has been spoiled by too much good living, and thereby the world gets healthier. I remember yet the 21st of August, at Karstula: Ficandt stood at the left, and I at the right . . ."

"If I might interrupt my honored brother in his speech," said the master, who had heard a hundred and seventy times before the Karstula story, in which Svanholm, then a sergeant, had lost the celebrated finger, " I would prove that the world would profit more by ink than blood. *Inter arma silent leges.* Should war prevail now, we would not be sitting here by our fire and our toddy in Bäck's chamber, but our place would be by a cannon on a

I

fortress-wall, linstock in hand, instead of a glass; powder in the pouch instead of snuff. But now, you see, it is the ink that has made you, brother, a postmaster; in the ink you live, and have your being; ink is your daily bread; and what would you be with blood alone and no ink, I ask?"

"What would I be? Devil take me! I . . ."

"Cousin Svanholm!" said the old grandmother, with an expressive glance around at the children.

The postmaster hushed instantly. The Surgeon realized the necessity of establishing peace between ink and blood.

"I mean," said he, "that nations go through this world very much like all the rest of us children of humanity. In their youth they are wild and lawless; they fight and rage and tear each other to pieces, man against man. Then they become older and wiser, invent gunpowder, place mass against mass, and let them in cold blood kill their brethren at long distances. Finally the world comes to reason, loads with powder only, as if for firing a salute, and seizes the pen, which is very sharp when required. And then begins the reign of universal common-sense, which is certainly the wisest, according to my understanding."

"Oh, a thousand dev——. . . . well, well, cousin, I am silent as a brick wall!" exclaimed the postmaster. "But I only ask, what kind of a man was Gustaf Adolf? What kind of a man was Napoleon? Were they birthday musicians, do you think? Were they wild and reckless?—yes, thanks for it . . . cousin, do you hear?—I don't swear. But you should have heard Ficandt—how like thunder and lightning he swore at Karstula!"

The Surgeon continued, without paying any heed to the postmaster:

"Therefore, the history of all nations begins with war; and soldier number one in the world's first company was called Cain. But as war is as old as the world, it is likely to exist as long as the world stands. I do not believe in the nice new ideas about an eternal peace. I think that so long as people share the earth between them, so long as human hearts retain selfish desires, they will be subject to the curse of war. Believe me, eternal peace consists in allowing people no longer to fight so blindly, slavishly, and frantically as before, but with glad courage, so that they may clearly comprehend the reason why, and be able to swear that their cause is a righteous one; for then they can strike with right good will."

"That is to say, to fight for an idea," observed the schoolmaster, thoughtfully.

"That is it, 'for an idea.' It is the honor of the Finnish soldier that he has always fought for the righteous object of defending his fatherland, without making an attack upon another man's house. Only once he went out to fight on foreign soil; and our Lord mercifully ordained that it was for the greatest and most righteous cause of all: namely, to defend the pure evangelical faith and freedom of conscience for the whole world. The Finn knew this in the Thirty Years' War; and therefore his efficiency. He felt within himself that his heart was of the same as Gustaf Adolf's — who, as far as I can see, was the greatest general who ever lived, while he fought and gained victories for the greatest cause worth bleeding for."

"Tell us a little more about Gustaf Adolf!" exclaimed Andreas, who understood, of all that the Surgeon had been saying, only this one name.

"Dear good uncle, a little more about Gustaf

Adolf!" chimed in the rest of the youngsters, who, with the greatest effort, had been kept within bounds by grandmother's stern looks and by sister Anne Sophie.

"No, thank you; the great king is now dead, and we will let him slumber in peace in the vault of Riddarholm church. And if the story thus loses much, it also gains something, namely: that the rest of the personages become more prominent. For hitherto we have scarcely had an eye for anything but the hero king, and grandmother was right in saying that our ears have been split by the cannon. Thus it has happened that both Lady Regina and the Jesuit, and especially Bertel, who is the hero, have passed by like shadows without life or substance. . . ."

"And Kätchen," interrupted the grandmother; "for my part, I would like, best of all, to know something more about this happy and well-mannered child. I will leave Regina alone; but this much I will say: that such a black-haired wild-cat, who can tear one's eyes out any minute, I would not give much for."

"And the fine Count of Lichtenstein, whom we have not seen since Würtzburg," added Anne Sophie; "I predict that he will in the end become Regina's betrothed."

"Aha! little cousin listens with delight to that part of it!" rejoined the postmaster, with a sly smile. "But I ask you, brother Bäck, not to busy yourself with love-nonsense; let us rather hear something more about Stålhandske, Lyydikäin, the little thick Larsson, and the Tavastlander Witikka. How the devil did the man get along without ears? I remember to this day, that on the 21st of August there was a corporal at Karstula . . ."

"Brother Bäck," interrupted the schoolmaster, who was always inexorable every time Karstula was mentioned, "brother Bäck, who has *justitia mundi*, the sword of justice, in his hand, cannot possibly fail to hoist the Jesuit Hieronymus up to the top of the highest pine on the Hartz Mountains."

"Take care, brother Svenonius," retorted the postmaster, dryly; "the Jesuit was a very learned man, who knew a great deal of Latin . . "

"I will tell you what I know about the Finns," said the Surgeon; "but I assure you in advance that it is altogether too little. Let us wait ten or twenty years longer, when some diligent man will take the pains to glean from the old chronicles our brave countrymen's exploits. Until then we must content ourselves with sketches, disjointed—and perhaps a little fanciful," added the Surgeon, in so low a tone as not to be heard by the little ones, whose belief in the veracity of the story he did not wish to disturb.

"And what became of the king's ring?"

"Why, that we will hear to-morrow evening."

CHAPTER I.

A MAN FROM THE CLUB WAR.

AWAY toward the north, beyond the fertile plains of Germany, is spread a stormy sea, whose level changes with ebb and flow, whose shores are covered every year with the ice of winter, and whose open straits have sometimes borne entire armies on their floating bridges of ice. For centuries, surrounding nations have battled for the possession of this sea, and colored its waves with their blood; but at the time of our story, a single power, the most puissant in the north, ruled over nine-tenths of its wide coasts. The Baltic had become almost an inland sea in the Swedish kingdom.

And the Baltic stretches its mighty blue arms east and north, and folds in its tumultuous embrace a daughter of the sea, a land of the waves which had sprung up from its bosom, and, still increasing, lifts her solid rocks high above her mother's heart. Finland is the best-beloved child of the Baltic. To this day she empties her treasures into her mother's lap; and the mighty sea is not uplifted by the offering, but draws lovingly and tenderly back, like an indulgent mother, that the daughter may grow, and every summer clothe with grass and flowers new shores laid open to the day. Happy the land which lulls in its bosom the waves of a thousand lakes, and stretches a shore of nine hundred miles toward the sea! The sea bears power, freedom, well-being and culture; the sea is the active civilizing element of earth; and a country which has communication with the sea can never stagnate in want and oppression, unless by its own fault.

And far away in the north of Finland extends a region which, more than any other, is the foster-child of the sea; for from time immemorial its gentle slopes have risen increasingly from the waves. Innumerable green islands rise along these coasts. "In my youth," says the gray-haired sailor, "great ships floated here where now a boat is rowed with difficulty;" and, a few years hence, herds will graze on the former bottom of the sea. The child at play loads its boat at the beach; look around you, little one, and mark well the spot where the waters trace their edges in the sand; when you become a man you will seek that strand in vain; far beyond the green plains you will hear its murmur in the distance; and when you one day stand there as an old man, a flourishing town will appear on the spot once occupied by your childhood's sea. Strange region, where the towns which had so wisely built their harbors by the deep bays and rivers, in two hundred years are miles away from the outer roadstead, while vessel keels and anchors are drawn up from the bogs fifty miles inland!

This region is East Bothnia. Its area is greater than that of many kingdoms; and it extends far up in the extreme north, to the borders of Lapland, where the sun never sets at midsummer, and never rises during the Christmas darkness. Three months of the year, nature is there awake in the unbroken splendor of day, and then you can read the finest print at midnight; three months the night continues, but a night of stars and boreal lights, a night of moonlight and glittering snow, frosty-clear, holy and solemn. The flower's beauty is more perishable there than human joy; seven months the plains are covered with blinding snow, and the lakes with ice solid as the ground; but never is spring more blithe than after such a winter of frost—though this is mingled with a melancholy which the heart well understands.

Along the coast of this northern land live two races, unmixed, and very unlike each other: a variegated picture of national and local peculiarities of language, habits, and temperament, sharply marked from parish to parish; yet all present certain common traits: activity, energy, and a frankness of demeanor which is peculiarly their own. It is not a geographical chance that the greatest and bloodiest battles in Finland's history have been fought on the soil of East Bothnia.

Twenty-five miles east of Wasa, on the low banks of Kyro River, lies Storkyro Parish, one of the richest parishes in East Bothnia, whose granary it is. Here grows, in fertile clay soil, the celebrated seed-rye which is shipped yearly in great quantities to Sweden. The whole parish is an almost unbroken plain of waving grain-fields, from which arose the well-known saying that "Storkyro fields and Limingo meadows have not their like in length and breadth." The inhabitants are Finns, of ancient Tavastlandish origin. Their old leaning church, built in the year 1304, is one of the oldest antiquities of the country.

It is there that we now invite the reader.

At the time of our story, this region was not nearly as well cultivated as in later times. The ravages of the Club War had retarded its prosperity, so that for a whole generation traces of them were seen; while other hard wars, with sweeping conscriptions, hindered time from healing these wounds. Therefore, in the summer of 1632, many a farm-house still stood desolate in the edge of the woods; the grain fields stretched but a little way from the banks of the river, and the unhealthy fogs of the morass covered the country when the nights were cool. The already-thinned forests still yielded fuel for the tar-pits; part of the peasantry fished among the Michael Islands; and the pastor, Georgius Thomæ Patur, did not then, like his present successor, have a safe yearly income of four thousand silver rubles.

It was therefore that the eye lingered with delight on Bertila's farm-house, in the vicinity of the church, more imposing and better built than any of the rest, and surrounded by the most fertile fields. The summer had advanced to the middle of August, and the harvesting had just begun. More than sixty persons, men, women, and children — for the East Bothnian peasant women work out-doors the whole summer—were diligently cutting the golden rye, which they gathered into sheaves, and placed with skillful hands in high, comely ricks. The day was warm, and the stooping posture which the work required was very tiresome; so it frequently happened that some idler among the workers straightened himself up and threw longing glances at the soft turf around the edge of the field, which seemed especially intended for a resting-place. But at the same time he did not forget to glance timidly at an old man in a wide gray homespun jacket, evidently a kind of overseer. Whenever anyone shirked a little, he heard his neighbor whisper, "Larsson is coming!" which instantly had a marvellous effect, not unlike a foretaste of the lash.

But Larsson—a little dumpy old man, between whose thick beard and bushy eyebrows gleamed an expression rather kind-hearted and good-humored than severe—was at this moment busy with one of the working women, who, on account of the heat and the heavy work, had sunk fainting on the ground.

To judge from her pale features, this woman was no longer young; she had perhaps seen six-and-thirty summers; but to judge from her slender form, or the mild, warm expression of her blue eyes, one could scarcely believe that she was past twenty. Her whole figure bore the stamp of rare but prematurely faded beauty, and of much suffering and much submission. She had worn a fine white flannel jacket, which was taken off on account of the heat, disclosing sleeves of the whitest linen, a red bodice, after the fashion of the peasantry, with a short striped woolen skirt, and a little checked handkerchief tied like a bandage around her head, to keep up her long flaxen hair. She had worked like all the others, but her strength was not as great as theirs. She had sunk down with the sickle in her hand; and those nearest her had, with evident respect and love, carried her to the soft grass, where they tried, with a drink of fresh water from the spring, to recall her to life.

"There now, Meri!" (Emerentia) said old Larsson, while with a fatherly sympathy he held the fainting woman's head on his knees, and bathed her temples with cold water; "there, my child, don't be foolish now, and die from your old friend; what joy would he then have on earth? . . She doesn't hear me, poor child! Where was there ever such a father as hers? To force that delicate creature to work in such a heat! Drink a little—that's right . . . it is real good of you; now open your beautiful eyes again. Do not be troubled, Meri; we will go up to the house. You shall rest there, and need not work any more to-day."

The pale and delicate woman tried to rise and take up the sickle. "Thank you, Larsson," said she, in a faint but melodious voice; "I feel better now. I will work; father wishes it."

"Father wishes it!" ejaculated the little old man, testily; "but you see I do not. I forbid you to work; I do, Meri: and even if your father were to turn me out of doors, and I had to go and beg my bread, you should not work more to-day. Well, well, dear child, don't take it so hard; your father is n't so stupid as all that; he cannot help understanding that you have n't arms like the rest of us. You are not to be blamed for that; you take after your dead mother, who was born a lady, and your education in Stockholm. . . . There, there! come, let us go home. Don't be stubborn, now, Meri!"

"Let go of me, Larsson; there he comes himself," exclaimed Meri, tearing herself loose and grasping the sickle, with which she again began to mow the golden straw. But as she bent down, it grew dark before her eyes; and, for the second time, she sank, pale and unconscious, between the waving stalks.

At that moment the efforts of all the laborers redoubled; for he approached in person, the stern and dreaded master of Bertila farm. Like a dark cloud, he came slowly along the path from the house, a tall old man of seventy, as yet little bent by age. His attire did not differ from that usually worn by the peasants in summer-time: wide shirt-sleeves, a long red-striped vest, short linen pantaloons, blue stockings, and skillfully-made bark shoes; but on his white head he wore a pointed cap, knit of red yarn, the height of which gave his tall figure a still loftier appearance. But in spite of the simplicity of his costume, his whole exterior was in the highest degree commanding. His tall straight form, decided bearing, sharp, penetrating look, and an habitual expression of resolution, love of authority, and severity, around the tightly-drawn upper lip, indicated at once the former political leader and the rich and powerful land-owner, accustomed to rule over many hundred subordinates. On seeing this old man, one understood why he was known in many adjacent parishes under the name of "the Peasant King."

Old Aaron Bertila, cold and calm, approached the spot where his only daughter lay in a fainting fit.

"Put her in the hay-wagon, and take her up to the house," ordered he; "she will be back to her work in a couple of hours."

"But, Bertila," began Larsson, excitedly.

Bertila turned around with a glance before which the other suddenly hushed;. then he walked on through the field as if nothing had happened, observing with a sure eye the diligence of the laborers, now blaming, now praising them; sometimes breaking off an ear, and examining closely the number and weight of the grains. From the barn one could overlook the whole great golden-yellow harvest field — a new piece of ground, more than a hundred acres in extent, lately reclaimed from the swamp. The old man gazed with proud satisfaction at this waving sea of grain; his bearing became more erect, his chest expanded, and he beckoned Larsson to him.

"Do you remember this tract as it was four-and-thirty years ago? Then Fleming's cavalry scoured the country like heathens; the village lay in ashes, and the fields were tramped down by horses' hoofs. Here, where we stand, close by the village, was the wilderness; naked, half-burned stumps stood between mud-puddles and quagmires; no road or path led hither; and even the very wolves of the forest thought this place too miserable to seek a den in it."

"I remember it well," replied Larsson, monotonously.

"Now look around, old friend, and say, who rebuilt this village from its ashes, more beautiful than ever before? Who tilled this wilderness; who made roads and paths; who measured the land; who drained the morass; who ploughed this gloriously fertile soil; who sowed this whole field which now waves in the wind, and will in a few days supply hundreds of human beings with its harvest? Say, Larsson, who is the man who did this great work?" and the old man's eyes shone with enthusiasm.

But the little dumpy person at his side seemed to be filled with a different feeling. He took off his old worn hat humbly, clasped his hands, and said, earnestly.

"Nothing is he who sows; nothing is he who waters; God alone gives the growth!"

Bertila, absorbed in thought, scarcely heard him; and continued, without suspecting his meaning:

"Yes, by Heaven! I have seen evil days, times of want, misery, and despair, which the sword brought upon the earth; and I have myself drawn the sword to destroy my enemy's home, and I have tried victory as well as defeat, both to my detriment. Therefore I have a right to rejoice in the work of peace. I know what the sword produces, and what the plough achieves. In the steel of the sword lurks an evil spirit, to revel in human blood and tears: the sword kills, the sword destroys; but the plough gives life and happiness. . . . You see, Larsson, the plough has made this field. Over there at Korsholm is the Finnish coat of arms, a lion with a naked sword. Were I king, I should say: 'Away with the sword, and here with the plough!' The plough is the true weapon of Finland. If we have bread, we have plenty of arms; if we have arms, we will drive our enemies from our homes; but, without bread, Larsson, what good is steel and powder to us?"

"Bertila," said Larsson, hesitatingly, "you are a strange man. You hate soldiers and war; but that I can easily understand: they burnt your farm, and drove your first wife and her little children into the woods to die. You yourself have fought at the head of the peasantry, and barely escaped the slaughter on Ilmola's ice. That such things are not easily forgotten, I well understand; but what I cannot comprehend is, that you, a friend of the peasantry, a soldier-hater, first took me, an old starving soldier, as overseer on your farm, then equipped my Lasse — God save the boy! — for the war, and finally sent your own grandson, Meri's child, our little Gösta, yet beardless, into the field among the king's cavalry."

Old Bertila's look darkened strangely. A sensitive chord had been touched, and he glanced shyly around, as if he feared a listener behind the walls of the barn.

"Who speaks to me of Meri's child?" said he, in a low voice. "I know none other than *my* son Gösta, born of my second wife during the journey to Stockholm; and God be merciful unto you if ever . . Let us forget that matter. Why I took you? why I sent the boy into the field? Well, . . . it does n't concern you."

"Well; then, keep it to yourself; I know already more than I wish."

"Tell me, if you can, Larsson, what elements are needed for an honest and Christian government?"

Larsson looked at him in silent astonishment.

"I will tell you. The sword is composed of two parts: the blade and the handle. So likewise for the plough two forces are necessary: one that draws and one that drives. And two forces conjoined form a Christian government: namely, the people and the king. But that which comes between brings dissension and ruin; it arrogates to itself the king's power and the people's property. It is a monster!"

"I know you hate the nobility."

"And therefore "—Bertila laid an emphasis on his words, and uttered them with an almost ironical smile, which seemed to turn his meaning into a jest —"therefore, you see, *my* son must either be *peasant* or *king*; nothing more, and nothing less!"

Larsson looked at him in dismay. He had not imagined the depth of ambition which had hitherto, deeply concealed, glowed in the old peasant's heart. He did not dare to believe what he, not without reason, considered the extreme of crazy presumption.

"You can certainly never hope," said he, timidly, "that Meri's son, with his birth—"

The tall old man's eyes flashed, but the words came almost inaudibly from his lips, as if he tried in vain to struggle against an inner impulse, to express for once, for the first and perhaps for the last time, the bold thought which had for many years been growing in his tempestuous soul.

"King Gustaf Adolf has only a daughter," said he, at last, with a peculiar expression.

"Lady Christina. . . . Yes."

"But the kingdom, in war with half the world, will need, after his death, a man on the throne."

"Bertila, what does this mean?"

"It means that in my childhood I heard the son of King Erik and the peasant girl Karin declared the successor to the crown."

"Are you out of your senses?"

Again an ironical smile flitted over the old man's lips.

"Do you not understand," said he, coldly, "how it is possible to hate soldiers and noblemen, and yet send one's son to war as the shortest road to distinction under a king's eyes?"

"I beg of you, Bertila, put aside such wild fancies; you are a sensible man, when the spirit of pride does not get possession of your restless mind. Your plan will fail; it must fail."

"It cannot fail."

"How? It cannot fail?"

"No! Have I not told you that Gösta must be either king or peasant?—which, I care not. If he wishes to remain a peasant, as I am, so be it."

"But if he neither will nor can remain a peasant? If he gets it into his head to become a nobleman, to fight for a coat of arms? . . . Remember that you have put him on the road to a noble title. He is already, as an officer, a nobleman's equal."

Bertila seemed lost in thought.

"No!" exclaimed he; "it is impossible. His blood . . . his education . . . my will."

"His blood! then you no longer remember that nobility flows in it from both sides? His education! —and you sent him to Stockholm at twelve years of age; you have allowed him to grow up among young patricians whom he has daily heard express scorn and contempt for the plebeian classes. Your will!—foolish father, to believe that you can, with the word of authority, bend a youth's inclination from the direction which such powerful influences have given it!"

The old man remained silent for a moment; then he said, with forced calmness:

"Lar-son, you are a credulous fool; you take in earnest what I joke about in a merry moment. I will answer for the boy. Let us speak no more about it. . . . But take care;—not a word of what has been said! Do you understand?"

"I am your old friend, Bertila. Since the moment when I, a horseman with Svidje Klas, helped you to escape from Ilmola, you have repaid me the service many times over; I can never desert you. But, you see, I love your children as my own—yes, even more; I cannot bear to have you make the boy unhappy. And Meri . . . Are you a father, Bertila? How do you treat your child, your only daughter, who complies with your smallest whim, who does everything, by submission and obedience, to atone for the fault of her youth? You treat her harder than the lowest of your servant girls; you let her, frail and weak, perform the heaviest tasks; you see her sink to the ground, and you do not lift up your own child. You are cruel, Bertila . . . more than cruel; you are an inhuman father!"

"That is something you do not understand," answered the old man, gloomily. "Such tender-hearted fellows as you do not comprehend what it means to follow one's way straight ahead, without looking either to the right or to the left. Meri takes after her mother. She has something of the fine lady in her, and that must be uprooted. She cannot become a queen, like Karin Månsdotter;

well, then, she shall be a peasant woman, from top
to toe. King or people. . . . I have said what I
think of the intermediate class, and now you understand why I act as I do. Come, let us return to the
laborers."

"And Meri . . . spare her to-day, at least."

"She shall work like the rest this afternoon."

CHAPTER II.

ASHAMED OF THE PEASANT NAME.

THE cabin of the East Bothnian peasant is in
our time more spacious, lighter, and more
respectable in its whole appearance, than is found
in any other part of Finland. Sometimes it consists of two stories, or has, at least, a garret; the
windows are often three panes in height. The
house is almost always painted, usually red, occasionally with white cross-beams and window-shut-
ters; but now and then yellow oil painting is used.
The whole bears evidence of skill and prosperity,
due to the fact that the East Bothnian neither
builds such large and compact villages as the
Tavastlander and the Åbo peasant, nor, except in
cases of necessity, such solitary farm-houses as the
rest of his countrymen.

At the time of our story, "smoke-huts" were
yet in general use among almost the whole Finnish
population; only peasants of Swedish origin used
fire-places with regular chimneys. But even then
were seen in the Finnish districts of East Bothnia,
nearest the coast, houses of more modern style,

copied from their Swedish neighbors. The newly-founded towns, which attracted the inland people to the coast, had already begun to accustom them to greater comfort; and the more wealthy the peasant became, the sooner did his house, like his person, assume a more improved aspect. It is true, the extravagance which the sumptuary laws of the sixteenth century so severely prohibited was found only on the estates of the nobility and the wealthy Åbo burghers; the home-brewed ale foamed not the less in the peasant's tankard, and Holland spices were kept in his closet for festive occasions.

Ever since the flames of the Club War destroyed the huts in Storkyro Village, the Swedish and Finnish styles of building were seen peacefully mingled together. Bertila's house, the largest and richest in the village, was built entirely after the new style: it had stairs, a front porch, and two little chambers adjoining the large room, one for the master and the other for his daughter. The rest of the people on the place lived mostly together in the large room; but now, in summer time, the younger portion slept outside. At that period, the large clock, with its blue and red case, which is now the chief ornament in every wealthy farm-house, did not exist. The large smoothly planed table, with its high seat for the master of the house, stood, surrounded by benches, by the innermost wall opposite the door. It was near the dinner time, and in the large fire-place sputtered a porridge-kettle. The room was as yet almost empty; a cat purred on the bench; a girl of fourteen stirred the porridge; and Meri sat, with a piece of knitting-work in her hand, not far from the fire-place.

Poor Meri had recovered from her fainting-fit, but was still very pale. Her long hair fell freely over her half-covered shoulders, and her look was now and then directed shyly toward the door, as if she feared every moment that her father would enter. Then again she looked at her knitting-work. She was making a scarf of the most beautiful colors, and singing at the same time an old Swedish folk-song:

"My scarf with roses now I weave,
That shall my dearest friend receive;
When from war's terrors to his home
To me returning he shall come."

We have stated that Meri was no longer young. The traces which suffering had left on her once blooming cheeks told of many a year of sorrow; but at this moment, when she looked at the scarf, her face had an almost child-like expression of inner satisfaction. It was evident that the work delighted her, and that the friend she sang of was very dear to her. Her life with her hard father had little joy for her; but when her eyes fell on the scarf, she seemed to read in its variegated figures a whole future of quiet bliss. For this scarf she lived; the thought was her only joy—an idolatrous joy—the thought of her son! And again she was heard to sing:

"Here weave I pearls so fine
For this dear friend of mine;
No king upon his throne
Shall this scarf's equal own."

At that moment Bertila, the father, entered, followed by Larsson and the whole gang of laborers. The old husbandman's look was dark; he could not conceal from himself that Larsson's predictions were too likely to be fulfilled. His son a nobleman! This possibility, which in his eyes was a disgrace, had up to this time never entered his mind.

The last words of Meri's song had just died away. At her father's entrance she hid her scarf quickly under her apron; but the old man's suspicious eye detected the secret.

"Do you sit there dreaming again, you idler, instead of serving the porridge!" exclaimed he, in a hard tone. "What have you in your apron? Out with it!"

Meri was obliged to show the half-finished scarf, her precious secret, before the eyes of all. The father looked at it a moment with contempt; then he tore it in two and threw it into the corner.

"I have told you many a time," said he, coldly, "that an honest peasant woman has nothing to do with such nonsense, suited only to the nobility. Let us say grace."

And the old man folded his hands, according to ancient custom, while all the others followed his example. But before the prayer passed any one's lips, Larsson stepped into the middle of the floor. His usually good-humored face flamed with indignation, and the honest and frank accent of his voice made every one forget to laugh at his little round figure.

"You ought to blush, Bertila," said he, "to scold your own daughter before all the folks! She works like a slave night and day, more than any of us; and you call her an idler! I tell you to your face, master of the house as you are, although I eat your bread, and without it have scarcely anything but a beggar's staff, that such an unjust father is not worthy of so good a daughter; and rather than see this misery day out and day in, I prefer to go and beg my bread. But you will have to answer, before our Lord, for your child. And now say your grace if you can; and may the food taste good to you. Farewell, Bertila; I will not endure this life any longer."

"Turn the boorish fellow, who defies his master, out of doors!" burst out Bertila, with unusual violence.

No one stirred from the spot. For the first time in his life the old peasant king saw his commands disobeyed.

"Dear master," began the oldest of the laborers, "we, and all the folks, think just so . ."

A powerful blow from the master stretched the speaker on the floor before he had time to finish. In vain did Larsson offer to go; in vain did Meri try to intercede; so strong was the sense of justice in this people, that they all, not from preconcerted action, but from their own conviction of the right, arrayed themselves, as one man, against the master's tyranny. Fourteen muscular men stood erect and resolute before the enraged Bertila, whose tall figure towered threateningly in the midst of the circle. One more stroke of his fist, and they would all have left his service, and perhaps shut him up in the little chamber until his anger should have subsided; for the higher to the north the Finnish peasant lives, the more sensitive is he to blows. Bertila knew his people, and wisely understood that his heat had led him too far. He sought some means of getting out of the difficulty without too great humiliation.

"What is it you want?" asked he, regaining self-possession.

Those spoken to looked at each other.

"You are wrong, master," said one of the boldest, at last; "you have scolded Meri undeservedly; you have wished to turn Larsson out of the house, and have struck Simon; you have done wrong!"

"Meri, come here!"

She went to him.

"You are no longer a child, Meri. If you can not endure to live with your father in his old age, then you are at liberty to stay on my farm at Ilmola. You are free; go, my child!"

Bertila knew his daughter. Those few words, "Go, my child!" uttered in a milder tone than she was accustomed to hear, were sufficient to soften her heart.

"Do not send me away, father," said she. "I never will forsake you."

This reply caused her defenders to waver, and the old man saw his advantage.

"Here with the catechism!" cried he, in a thundering voice.

The fourteen-years-old Greta stepped up with the book, as was the custom on sacred days, and read aloud:

"Ye servants, obey your temporal masters with fear and trembling, in the simplicity of your hearts. Ye servants, be submissive to your masters in all fear, not only the good and the mild, but also the unworthy."

These timely words did not fail of their effect. Bertila and his people lived at a period when the power of the master and father retained all its original and stern sanctity in essence, and not merely in title; a power "by the grace of God." The well-known words impressed upon them from childhood, the old man's commanding assurance, and Meri's example of complete submission to the paternal rule, all conspired to pacify the lately excited minds, and the revolt was quelled.

Grace was said. Each one took his seat without further murmurings; only the old Larsson stood, gloomy and hesitating, with his hand on the latch.

Then the door suddenly opened and a stranger entered. The new-comer was a bearded soldier, in a broad-brimmed hat decorated with a gracefully fastened eagle plume. He wore a yellow woollen jacket, with a girdle, and a long sword at his side; he had short top-boots, and held a cudgel in his hand.

"Well, by Saint Lucifer!" exclaimed he, merrily; "I come as if I were invited. God's peace, peasants! Make room at table; I am hungry as a monk during mass, and can't get to the parsonage in this cursed heat. Have you any beer?"

The old man in the high seat, whose mind was yet in a tumult under the calm surface, rose half-way, but seated himself again.

"Sit down, countryman," said the old man, mildly. "Aaron Bertila's table has also a place for self invited guests."

"Aha!" continued the new-comer, as he helped himself without any ceremony, apparently accustomed to look out for number one. "Aha, so you are Bertila! Glad to hear it, comrade! Honor for honor; I will then tell you that I am Bengt Kristerson, from Limingo, sergeant in His Majesty's brave East Bothnian regiment, and sent here to superintend the conscription. A little more ale in the mug, peasants. Well, well, be not afraid, girls, I won't bite. . . . Bertila," continued the soldier, with his mouth full; "what the devil!—is it you, peasant, who are Lieutenant Bertel's father?"

"I do not know that name," answered the old man, piqued by the soldier's patronizing manner.

"Are you crazy, old fellow? Do you not know

Gustaf Bertel, who only half a year ago called himself Bertila?"

"My son! my son!" exclaimed the old man, with a heart-rending voice. "Unhappy father that I am! He is ashamed of his peasant name!"

"Peasant name!" repeated the jolly sergeant, with such an immoderate laugh that the ale jug jumped about on the table. "Have you also names, peasants? Well, I declare if I don't feel like getting rid of mine! You are a bright chap, old fellow . . . tell me what the devil do you need a name for?" And with this he looked at his host with such good-natured impudence that the insulting words were considerably modified.

The old Bertila scarcely honored him with a glance.

"Fool that I was! I sent out a beardless boy, and thought I sent a man," added he, gloomily, to himself.

But the sergeant, who perhaps had taken a dram before, and had now peeped far down into the jug, did not seem inclined to drop a good subject.

"Don't look so fierce, old boy," continued he, in the same tone. "You peasants associate so much with oxen and sheep that you become just like them. If you were a bit civil, you would have sent a pretty girl to fill my jug. It is empty, you see—empty as your cranium. But you turnip-peelers don't appreciate the honor which is conferred upon you in having a royal sergeant for a guest. You see, old fellow, a soldier in these times is everything; he has a name that rings, because he has a sword that rings. But you, old ploughshare, have nothing but porridge in your head and a turnip in your breast. Fill your mug, old fellow; here's to the brave Lieutenant Bertel's success!

Do you refuse to drink the health of an honest soldier? . . . Out upon you, peasant!" And the sergeant, in the consciousness of his dignity, made bold to strike his fist upon the table with such force that the wooden platters danced about, and even the large wooden bowls seemed disposed to make for the floor with all their contents.

The first effect of this martial joke was that six or eight of the men rose from the benches, and seemed ready to teach the uninvited guest respect for the peasantry in a manner that would make itself felt. But the old Bertila prevented them. He had risen with apparent composure, approached the sergeant with a firm step, and without uttering a single word in reply, seized him by the neck with the left hand, placed the right on his back, lifted him from his seat, and carrying the good Bengt Kristerson to the door, threw him on a pile of shavings at the foot of the steps. So confounded was the jolly sergeant at this unexpected grasp, that he scarcely moved his sinewy arm to defend himself; in which event his seventy-year-old adversary could scarcely have come off victorious.

"Go!" cried Bertila, after him, "and keep your welcome in remembrance of the Storkyro peasants!"

Nothing makes so strong an impression on human nature as a resolute courage joined with a strong arm. When the old man again entered the room, he was surrounded by his people with admiration bordering on enthusiasm. Forgotten was all the animosity which had just before placed master and servants in a hostile attitude toward each other. The rivalry between the sword and the plough is as old as the world. The Club War, which had resulted from this rivalry, and considerably increased it, was still fresh in memory. These peasants, whose independent minds never bent, like many of their countrymen, beneath the oppression of their land-holders, saw with delight their human worth defended against a soldier's arrogance. They forgot, at this moment, that perhaps before long more than one of them would don the soldier's cloak to fight for his fatherland. Even the old peasant chief, elated over his successful exploit, had got over his bad humor. For the first time in a long period of years, they saw a smile on his lips; and when the meal was over he began to relate to them some of his former adventures.

"Never can I forget how we cudgeled the rascal Abraham Melchiorson, the man who, here in Kyro, seized our best peasants, and had them broken on the wheel, like malefactors. With fifty men he had gone up north. It was wintertime. He was a fine gentleman, who got the snuffles from the cold, and rode so grandly in a splendid wolf-skin cloak. But when he approached Karleby Church, we hid ourselves in the bushes, and came upon him like Jehu; beat twenty-two of his men to death, and pommeled him black-and-blue. But every time he expected a rap, he drew his wolf-skin cloak over his ears, and thus no club could reach the traitor. 'Wait,' said Hans Krank, from Limingo, who led us; 'that wolf we will yet whip out of his skin.' With this he drubbed Abraham so vigorously that he was obliged to let go his splendid fur. Krank had nothing on but a jacket, and it was cold enough, God knows; he thought the fur cloak a very nice thing, and drew it, unobserved, over his own shoulders. But, as all this occurred in the twilight, the others did not notice that Krank had crept into the wolf-skin but began again, with fresh courage, to belabor the same cloak, to which we had got used; and it is very certain that Krank had a warm drubbing that time. But Abraham Melchiorson became so light and agile, after he had got rid of his cloak, that he took to his heels, and ran in his jacket several miles to Husö Farm, where Såka Jakob, from Karleby, caught him, and the rascal was brought to Stockholm; but he did not have a chance to lament long for his wolf-skin cloak before the duke made him a head shorter."

"Yes," said Larsson, who usually took the part of Fleming and his people. "that time you had the upper hand. Eleven soldiers had remained alive, but feigned death; you stripped them to their bare bodies, and at midnight they crept, half-frozen, to the chorister's cottage, and were taken in. But the next morning you would bury them, living, under the ice, as you did at Lappfjärd River. You were wolves, and not human beings. The river was so shallow that you were obliged to push the men down in the ice-hole with poles when they tried to resist. Your women beat them on the head with their buckets."

"Hold your tongue, Larsson! you don't know all that Svidje-Klas has done," answered Bertila, irritated. "I say nothing about all those whom he and his people killed or broke on the wheel. But do you remember Severin Sigfridson, at Sorsankoski? When he had surrounded the peasants, he commanded his orderly to behead them one by one; but the man had not strength for more than twenty-four, and told the fine lord to behead the rest himself. Then the gentleman got angry, and made the peasants first cut the orderly into five pieces, and then do the same to each other, until only one was left."

"But how did you act, mad brutes, on Peter Gumse's farm? Your people sacked the house, broke all the windows, slaughtered the cattle, and set the cut-off heads, with their mouths wide open, as scarecrows in the window. Then the beams were sawed three-quarters through, so that when the inmates returned the whole house would tumble on their heads. And when you caught any horseman, you made him a target for your arrows."

"It isn't worth while for you to take Svidje-Klas' part. Do you remember the woman to whom one of Axel Kurk's men came, and killed her children before her own eyes? The poor mother could not stand it, but she and her half-grown daughter seized the drunken brute around the waist, beat him on the head with a pole, and then pushed him, half-fainting, under the ice. Then came Svidje-Klas, and cut the woman in two."

"Idle talk, which has never been proven," replied Larsson, gruffly.

"The dead keep silent, like good children. The five thousand slain at Ilmola tell no tales."

"Rather than molest the sergeant, you should have asked him for news from your son and mine," resumed Larsson, to get away from their usual subject of contention, the fatal Club War.

"Yes. . . . You are right. I must know something more about the boys and the war. I am going to Wasa to-morrow."

"Is he coming home soon?" asked Meri, shyly.

"Gösta—he will take his own time," replied the father, angrily. "He has now become a nobleman, who feels ashamed of his old father. . . He blushes for the peasant name."

CHAPTER III.

THE SOUTHERNER IN THE NORTH.

THE coast of Finland stretches due north until, a few miles south of Wasa, at about the sixty-third degree of latitude, it makes a decided curve toward the north-east. The great blue Bothnian Gulf follows the same direction, narrowing for a moment in the Qvark, then widening again, and leaning its high brow against Finland's breast. With greater freedom than elsewhere, the winds from the Arctic Ocean sweep against these coasts, driving between the islands, and beating the waves with terrible violence against the rocks. In the midst of this stormy sea lie Gadden's bare flat ledges, with their warning light-house and their far-projecting reefs. When the mountain winds shake their wings over these dangerous breakers, then woe unto the vessel which, without a sure rudder and tightly furled sails, ventures through the narrow passage at Understen: its destruction is certain. But in mid-summer it frequently happens that a light northern wind is the most welcome, promising clear skies with fine weather. Then fly the many hundred sails from the coasts out toward Qvark's islands and reefs; the nets are cast for shoals of herring; and the restless, murmuring sea frolics like a loving mother with her daughters, the verdant islands, nestling at her bosom.

THE SWORD AND THE PLOUGH.

With the exception of Åland, no part of Finland's wide coast is so rich with luxuriant islands as Qvark and its neighboring east shore. These innumerable islets and holms, of which the largest are Wallgrund and Björkö, are here sprinkled about, like drops of green in the blue expanse, and form a peculiar collection—Replot parish—inhabited only by fishermen. So numerous are these groups, so infinitely varied the sounds, so labyrinthine the channels, that in the Michel islands, a group consisting of several hundred, a strange vessel could not find its way out unless a native pilot was at the helm. Thirty cruisers would here be insufficient to prevent smuggling; there is only one means of putting a stop to this hereditary sin of the coast, and this means—a light tariff with few prohibitions—Finland, during late years, has tried with success and great advantage.

At the period described in the preceding chapter (the middle of August, 1632), the waters of the Baltic were plowed by the royal Swedish war-brig, "Maria Eleonora," bound from Stockholm to Wasa, to transport the recruits conscripted in East Bothnia for the German war. It was a clear and beautiful summer morning. Over the wide sea played that indescribable glitter which has something at once so grand and so enchantingly beautiful. A boundless field of snow, illumined by the spring sun, can rival it in splendor; but the snow is stillness and death, the shimmering wave motion and life. A sea at rest in its resplendence is grandeur clothed in the smile of delight; it is a slumbering giant who dreams of sunbeams and flowers. Gently heaves his breast; then the plank rocks under thy feet and thou tremblest not; he could swallow thee up in his abyss, but he mildly spreads his silver carpet under the keel, and he, the strong one, bears the frail bark like a child in his arms.

It was immediately after sunrise. On board the vessel there prevailed the monotonous silence of sea life during the morning watch, when no danger is apprehended. A part of the crew were still asleep below deck; only the mate, wrapped in a jacket of Dutch frieze, promenaded back and forth on the aft deck. The helmsman stood motionless at the rudder, the man at the round-top peered noiselessly ahead, and here and there on the forward deck were seen sailors, now fastening a loose rope end, now mending a pair of boots, now carrying wood to the galley, now polishing the cannon which were to salute Korsholm when they entered port.

The stern discipline of a modern man-of-war was at that time almost unknown. There were neither uniforms nor whistles, nor aught of that system of signals and commands which is now carried to such perfection. A man-of-war scarcely differed from a merchant vessel except in size, armament, and the number of the officers and crew. When one remembers that at that time there were neither whiskey nor coffee on board as a solace against the chill morning air—(they had, however, already learned from the Dutch to use an occasional quid of tobacco for this purpose)—then it is readily seen that sea life on the "Maria Eleonora" bore very little resemblance to that on one of our modern men-of-war.

By the green gunwale of the deck stood two female figures, wrapped in ample travelling hoods of black wool. One of these passengers was small in stature, and showed under the hood an old wrinkled face, with a pair of blinking gray eyes; she had bundled herself up in a thick wadded cloak of Nuremberg cloth. The other figure was tall and slender, and wore a tight-fitting capote of black velvet lined with ermine. Leaning against the gunwale, she regarded with gloomy thoughtfulness the receding waves and the vessel's glistening wake. Her features could not be seen from the deck; but if one could have caught her image in the mirroring wave, it would have revealed a classically beautiful face, irradiated by two black eyes which in lustre surpassed the shining wave-mirror itself.

"Holy Mary!" exclaimed the old woman volubly, in strongly accented Low-German. "When will all this misery, which the saints have imposed upon us on account of our sins, come to an end? Tell me, little lady, in what part of the world are we now? It seems to me as if it were a whole year since we sailed from Stralsund, for since we left the heretic Stockholm I have no longer kept an account of the days. Every morning when I arise I recite seven *aves* and seven *pater nosters*, which the reverend Father Hieronymus taught us as a protection against ghosts and evil witchcrafts. Who knows but that the world here comes to an end, when we have reached so far from the domain of the holy true believing church and Christian people! This sea has no limit—oh the horrible sea! I now appreciate the river Main which flowed so peacefully beneath our little turret window in Würtzburg. Say, little lady, what if over there at the horizon was the end of the earth and we should go with full sails right into purgatory?"

The tall, slender young girl in the velvet capote did not seem to listen to the loquacious duenna's effusive words. Her dark, brilliant eyes, under their long black lashes, rested pensively on the sea as if

L   7*

to read in its waves the interpretation of her heart's dreams. And when at times a long swell from former storms rolled under the little waves, and the ship gently careened, so that the guard neared the water and the mirrored image in the sea approached the girl on board, then a smile of mingled melancholy and pride passed over the beautiful pale features, and her lips moved almost inaudibly to confide her innermost thoughts to the wave:

"*It is only the great and majestic in life that deserve to be loved!*"

Then she added, transported by this thought:

"Why should not I love a great man?"

And she whispered these words with an unbounded enthusiasm. But instantly a shudder ran through her delicate frame, a dark flash shot through the glimmering enamel of her black eyes, and she uttered, almost trembling:

"*It is only the great and majestic in life that deserve to be hated!* . . . Why should I not hate . . ."

She did not finish the sentence; she bent her head against the guard; the flash in her eyes disappeared, leaving in its stead a moist tear. Two hostile spirits contended for this passionate soul. One said to her: "*Love!*" the other: "*Hate!*" And her heart bled under the terrible struggle between the angel and the demon.

It is unnecessary to mention, what the reader has probably already divined, that the slender young girl on board the "Maria Eleonora" was none other than Lady Regina von Emmeritz, the beautiful fanatic who in Frankfort-on-the-Main tried to convert Gustaf Adolf to the Catholic faith. The king, who knew the human heart, had not without reason considered this fanatical girl capable of anything if longer left a prey to the influence of the Jesuits. He had therefore, not from revenge, which was foreign to his great soul, but from noble compassion for a young and richly endowed nature, resolved to send her for a time to a distant land, where she could no longer be reached by the influence of gloomy monks.

The reader will remember that the king expressed this intention on the memorable night after the festival of the Frankfort burghers; and later in the summer Lady Regina was sent, by the way of Stralsund and Stockholm, to the stern old Lady Märtha Ulfsparre, at Korsholm. The noble king did not suspect that the demoniacal power from whose claws he wished to save his beautiful prisoner followed her even to Finland's remote shores; for Lady Regina had been allowed to choose for her companion the one of her waiting-women in whom she felt the most confidence, and she chose, not the light-hearted blonde Kätchen, her good genius, who was sent away to her home in Bavaria, but the old Dorthe, her nurse, who, secretly in the service of the Jesuits, had long nourished the fire of fanaticism in the young girl's soul. Thus the poor unprotected girl was given up to the dark power which, ever since her earliest childhood, had perverted her rich and sensitive heart with its dreadful teachings. And against this power she could only oppose a single but powerful feeling — her admiration, her fanatical love for Gustaf Adolf, whom she loved and hated at the same time, whom she would have been able to kill, and yet for whom she would herself have suffered death.

The shrewd Dorthe seemed to guess her mistress's thoughts; she leaned forward, winked with her small eyes, and said, in the familiar tone which a subordinate in her position so easily assumes:

"Oh ho! Is that the way it stands? Do they again come up, the sinful thoughts about the heretic king and all his followers? Yes, yes, the devil is cunning; he knows what he is about. When he wishes to catch a little frivolous girl of the common sort, he places before her eyes a young blooming dandy with long and well-curled locks and cavalier appearance. When he wishes to entangle a poor forsaken girl with great proud thoughts and noble aspirations, then he clothes himself in the form of a magnificent victor, who gains castles and battles; and little does the poor child care that the fine conqueror is a sworn enemy to her church and faith, and is working for the ruin of both."

Regina turned her tearful and glistening eyes away from the sea, and looked for a moment with distrust at the old counsellor.

"Say," said she, almost violently, "is it possible to be at once an angel of magnanimity and a monster of wickedness? Is it possible to be at once the greatest and the most despicable of human beings?"

Regina again looked toward the sea. The peaceful tranquillity of the morning rested on the glittering waters, and stilled the tempest within her. The young girl remained silent. Dorthe continued:

"'By their fruits shall ye know them.' Think, what evil has not the godless king done our church and us? He has slain many thousands of our warriors; he has plundered our cloisters and castles; he has driven out our nuns and holy fathers from their godly habitations, and the devout father Hieronymus has been frightfully abused by his people, the heretic Finns. Us he has driven away in exile to the ends of the earth. . . .."

Again Regina looked over at the islands and the inlets, bathed in their mild morning glory. When the dark demon whispered hatred in her ears, radiant nature seemed to preach only love. On her lips hovered the transporting thought: "What matters it if he has slain thousands, if he has driven out monks and nuns, if he has driven us, ourselves, into exile; what matters all this, if he is great as a man, and acts according to the dictates of his faith?" But she kept silent from fear; she dared not break with all her preceding life. She caught up, instead, one of Dorthe's words, as if to dispel the cloud of hatred and malediction which, with its dark mist, enveloped her heart in the midst of this peaceful and lovely picture of a sea in the fresh splendor of a summer morning.

"Do you know, Dorthe," said she, "that the Finns whom you hate live on the coast of this sea? Do you see the strip of land over there in the east? It is Finland. I have not yet seen its shores, and yet I cannot detest a country which is bathed by so glorious a sea. I cannot think that evil people can grow up in the heart of such a nature."

"All saints protect us!" exclaimed the old woman, while her lean hand hastily made the sign of the cross. "Is that Finland? Saint Patrick preserve us from ever setting foot on its cursed soil! Dear lady, you have, then, never heard what is said of this land and its heathen people? There an eternal night prevails; there the snow never melts; there the wild beasts and the still wilder human beings lie together, like brothers and sisters, in dens and caves. The woods are so filled with hobgoblins and imps that when one of them is called by name a hundred monsters immediately creep forth from the leaves and branches. And people bewitch each other with all kinds of evils, changing their enemy into a wolf; and every word they speak becomes real, so that when they wish to make a boat or an axe, they say the word and directly they have what they utter."

"That is a pretty picture which you draw," said Regina, smiling for the first time in many weeks, for the freshness of the sea had a good influence on her dreamy soul. "Happy is the land where people can create whatever they wish for with a single word. If I am hungry and desire beautiful fruit, I have but to say, *peach!* and right away I have it. If I feel thirsty, I say, *spring!* and instantly a spring gurgles at my feet. If I have sorrow in my heart, I say, *hope!* and hope returns; and if I long for a beloved friend, I mention his name, and he stands at my side. A glorious land is Finland, were it such as you represent it to me. Even if we lived with wild beasts in a cave, under the eternal snow, we would look at each other and say, *Fatherland!* and at the same moment we would sit hand-in-hand on the banks of the Main, beneath the shadow of the lindens, where we often sat when I was a child, and the nightingales of our native land would sing blithely for us as before."

Dorthe turned angrily away. The vessel now steered its course between the rocks and islands, moved with gentle speed past the outermost reefs, of which many that now stand high above the surface of the water were at that time washed by the briny wave.

"What is the name of the long richly-wooded stretch of land to the left?" asked Regina of the helmsman, standing near.

"Wolf's Island," answered the man.

"There you hear it yourself, dear lady," exclaimed Dorthe. "Wolf's Island! That is the first name we hear on Finland's coast, and that shows us what we have to expect."

The vessel now turned to the north, sailed between Långskär and Sundomland, again veered off toward the east, passed Brändö, went smoothly over the shoals which now exclude large vessels from these waters, into Wasa's then superb harbor, and saluted with sixteen cannon-shots the ramparts of Korsholm.

CHAPTER IV.

PEASANT, BURGHER, AND SOLDIER.

IT was decided, as a mark of re-established friendship between father and daughter, that when Aaron Bertila should seat himself in his handsome cart, for a day's travel to Wasa, Meri should take a seat by his side, in order that she might purchase, in town, herrings, hops, and a few spices, such as ginger and cinnamon, which were already making their appearance in the houses of the wealthier peasants. Both father and daughter had their own plans concerning that journey; but neither wished to acknowledge to the other that it was news from Germany that each especially sought. Larsson had in the meantime been charged with the general supervision over the work at home.

It was just at the time when Gustaf Adolf and Wallenstein stood opposite each other at Nuremberg. Soldiers were needed more than ever, and Oxenstjerna wrote letter after letter from Saxony, to hasten the arrival of additional reinforcements. Notwithstanding the height of the harvest season, the war, which was also in the height of its harvesting, caused a great number of the conscripts from the neighboring villages to stream down to Wasa, from thence to be transported to Stockholm, and so on to meet Wallenstein's threatening hosts in Germany.

At that time the military drill was not nearly so complicated and difficult as now: to stand passably well in the ranks, to rush straight upon the enemy at the first command, to aim surely (as the East Bothnians had learned to do in the seal-hunts), and to hew down manfully,— these were the chief things. And thus one can understand that many of these peasant boys, just taken from the plough, had sufficient time to fall with honor at the side of their king on the battle-field of Lützen.

The town of Wasa was then only twenty years old, and much smaller in extent than now, not merely on account of its youth, but also because Korsholm fields, which belonged to the crown, hindered all extension on the south side. Around the old Mustasaari church, on the northern extremity of Köpman and Stora streets, were a few compact rows of newly-built one-story houses, painted red, with six or eight insignificant shops. Along the quays stood store-houses, and the neighborhood around was filled with fishermen's and sailors' huts in scattered groups— for regular plans and straight streets were considered by the architects of the sixteenth century rather superfluous, and the closer people built their houses together the safer they considered themselves in unquiet times.

A borough, as Wasa then was, regarded itself as one common family; and as a compensation for the insignificance of their own dwellings, the inhabitants looked with a sort of pride on the high green ramparts of Korsholm, near them on the south.

The long-credited story, confirmed by Messenius, that Korsholm had been built by Earl Birger and received its name from a large wooden cross which was there raised both as a religious symbol, a sign of victory, and a refuge, was founded on the equally old tradition that the celebrated earl, on his expedition to Finland, landed upon this very coast. Later researches have thrown doubt upon this story and Korsholm's origin at the same time; but certain it is, that the fortress is very old, nay, so old that it is scarcely remembered, save as the remains of something more ancient. It is a fact that it has never, so far as is known, offered resistance to an enemy; its situation made it unimportant to Finland's defence; and since Uleå and Kajana castles were erected, shortly before the time of our story, it had ceased to be regarded as a military post. Its principal use was now partly to afford a residence for the governor of the northern districts, partly to lodge other crown officials, to serve as a prison, and, together with its appanage of land, to yield a nice income for the support of the governor. The governor of the northern part of Finland, Johan Månsson Ulfsparre of Tusenhult, who was soon after succeeded by Colonel Ernst Creutz of Sarvelax, lived only by intervals at Korsholm; yet it is said that his seventy-year old mother, Lady Märtha, ruled with a stern hand over both castle and estate during his absence.

Between the peasants and the burghers of the new towns there prevailed at that time an unnatural and injurious rivalry, originating in the efforts of the government to suppress the country trade for the advantage of the towns, and, in a singularly narrow-minded way, regulate the exchange of produce. Therefore, when the old and powerful peasant chief, with his daughter, drove in through the country toll-gate from the Lillkyro side, a few of the citizens nodded a greeting to the well-known old man for the sake of his wealth; but the more haughty among the merchants, who feared Bertila's personal influence with the king, looked at him with unfriendly eyes, and gave vent to their ill-feeling in mocking words, uttered loudly enough to reach the old man's ears.

"There comes the Storkyro peasant-king!" said they; "and Wasa hasn't prepared any triumphal arch! He thinks himself too good to thresh in the barn; he means to enter the army and become generalissimo at once. Take care! Do you not see how ungracious he looks, his cabin majesty! If he could have his way, he would plough up all Wasa into a grain-field!"

With the hot-blooded Bertila, anger was seldom far off; but he concealed his resentment, and urged forward the horse, that he might soon arrive at the house of the sailor's widow where he generally stayed when in town. He had not gone far, however, on Köpman street—which in our time is not one of the broadest, but was then extremely narrow—before it was blocked up by a crowd of drunken recruits, who, in an ale-house near by, had inaugurated their new comradeship and strengthened themselves for the long journey in prospect. Two under-officers had joined the crowd as its self constituted leaders, and rushed, with a bold, "Out of the way, peasant!" toward the new-comer.

Bertila, already irritated and unable to restrain his anger, answered the shout with a rather ungentle cut of the whip, which knocked off the speaker's broad-brimmed hat with its eagle feather. Then the fray begun. The man rushed upon the peasant's cart, and the whole crowd followed him.

"Aha, old fellow!" exclaimed the merry sergeant, Bengt Kristerson, whom Bertila had so ignominiously thrust out of doors in Storkyro; "now, we have you here at our mercy, and I shall thank you for your gracious treatment yesterday. Make room, boys; the old fellow is mine; that codfish I mean to scale myself."

Bertila was too old to depend further on the strength of his fist, and looked around for a place of retreat. Armed with the whip, he jumped from the cart, which had stopped close by the steps of the shop, and gave the horse a cut, so that the latter, with the cart and the daughter, cleared its way through the yielding throng and galloped up the street. But if Bertila had intended to seek a refuge in the shop, he was disappointed, for the door was shut in his face by the inhospitable owner. The old champion, seeing escape cut off, placed himself with his back against the shop-door and threatened the assailants with his long whip.

"Let us thrash the proud Storkyro peasant!" screamed a young Laihela boy, who, during the one week that he had carried a musket, had been able to forget his peasant name, but not his peasant language.

"Your father was a better man, Matts Hindrikson," said Bertila, with contempt. "Instead of ranting against his own people, he helped us, like an honest peasant, to pommel Peter Gumse's cavalry in former days."

"Do you hear, boys?" cried one of the subalterns, "the dog brags of having given brave soldiers a thrashing!"

"We will not allow any one to tyrannize over us!"

"The peasant shall dance after our whip!"

"And not we after his!"

And five or six of the most excited of the soldiers, who had lately worn the peasant jacket themselves, rushed to pull Bertila down from the steps. The old man would have been lost, had not his adversary of the day before, the jolly sergeant, thrown himself between him and the aggressors.

"Hold on, boys!" cried Bengt Kristerson, in thundering tones. "What the devil are you thinking of? Are you honest soldiers? Do you not see that the old man is seventy years of age—and yet you go six against one? *Blitz-donner-Kreutz-Pappenheim* [the sergeant had learned this potent oath, which never failed of its effect, in the proper school], is that war-like? What do you suppose the king would say about it? Out of the way, boys; the old man is mine; I alone have the right to wash him clean. You should have seen how he lifted me yesterday like an old glove and threw me down the steps. It was a manly stroke, and now it has to be repaid."

Courage and magnanimity seldom fail of their impression. Those standing nearest willingly gave way. The sergeant advanced to the steps. Bertila could have reached him with the whip, but he did not strike. He knew his people.

"Do you know what it means, peasant?" cried the sergeant, with an air of authority which would have become General Stålhandske himself, "do you know what it means to throw his royal majesty's soldier down the steps? Do you know what it means to knock off the hat of the defender of the evangelical faith and the conqueror of the powerful Roman emperor, who with his own hand has gained fourteen battles and run his sword through sixteen or seventeen living generals? Do you know, peasant, if I were in your place . . ."

"If I were in the place of his royal majesty's soldier," answered Bertila, coolly, "I would respect an honest man in his own house and a grandsire in his old age. And if I were Bengt Kristerson, if I had conquered the Roman emperor and run my sword through seventeen living generals, I would still not forget that Bengt Kristerson's father, Krister Nilson, was a peasant in Limingo, and fell on Ilmola ice like an honest fighter against Fleming's tyranny."

The sergeant for a moment seemed dumbfounded. Then he stepped close up to his adversary, and said, with a grim aspect:

"Do you know, peasant, that I could impale you on this?" and so saying he drew his frightful long sword half-way out of the scabbard.

Bertila looked at him coldly, with crossed arms.

"Are you not afraid, old fellow?" resumed the conqueror of the Roman empire, evidently discomposed by the peasant's firm attitude.

Bertila felt his advantage.

"When did you ever see an honest Finn afraid?" said the old man, almost smiling.

The sergeant was not a vicious man. He felt suddenly inclined to magnanimity; his fierce mien changed into the blustering and jovial air which became him so well.

"Do you know, boys," said he, with a glance at his comrades, "that the old ox has both horns and hoofs? He might have become something in the world if he had been among cavaliers. Yesterday, when they were fourteen against one — for you must know, boys, that all fourteen of the laborers helped to lift me on the clodhopper's back, and then every one had marks from it — yes, as I say, yesterday I would have beaten the old fellow black and blue, had it not been for the presence of women who sat with us at table. But to-day *we* are fifteen against one; and so I propose that we let the old man go."

"He is as rich as Beelzebub," cried some of the crowd; "he shall treat us to a keg of ale."

Bertila drew out a little leather purse, took some of Carl IX.'s silver coins, and threw them contemptuously among the rabble. This irritated the soldiers anew; several arms were raised, and the storm threatened to burst forth again, when suddenly the whole crowd turned and rushed down to the harbor. Cannon-shots were heard; it was the brig "Maria Eleonora," which saluted Korsholm.

CHAPTER V.

THE ARRIVAL AT KORSHOLM.

EVERYBODY in Wasa who had life and feet had gone down to the harbor to enjoy the uncommon spectacle of a man-of-war. Five or six hundred people lined the shore, rowed out in boats, or climbed the masts of the yachts or the roofs of the store-houses to get a better view. Two hundred recruits regarded with mingled curiosity, fear, and pride, the vessel which was to take them from their fatherland, perhaps forever; and behind them stood a large group of mothers, sisters, and sweethearts, shedding bitter tears at the thought of the approaching separation.

The governor, Ulfsparre, was away in Sweden. His lieutenant, Steward Peder Thun, with his garrison, received the new-comers; the recruits formed a row on both sides, and the captain of the " Maria Eleonora " offered his arm politely to Lady Regina, to escort her to Korsholm. But at this moment the proud young girl remembered that she was a prisoner; she refused the officer's arm, and walked alone, with a princely bearing, followed by her old servant, through the ranks of the recruits and the staring crowd.

Such an unusual sight put all Wasa in a terrible state of curiosity. In an instant there arose and spread the strangest reports about her.

"She is a princess of Austria," said some; "the emperor's daughter, taken prisoner during the war, and sent here for safety." Others pretended to recognize in her the Queen Maria Eleonora; but why did she come to Korsholm?

"I will tell you," whispered a tinker, with an important air. "She is in league with her German countrymen against the king and the country, and therefore she is to be imprisoned in this remote and secure fortress of Korsholm."

"That is not true," rejoined another, who had received from returning soldiers a vague idea of the conspiracies against the king's life. "It is," added he, with a shy voice, as if fearing to be heard by the object of his story, " it is a nun from Wälskland, hired by the Jesuits to make away with the king. Six times has she given him deadly poison, and six times has he been warned in dreams not to drink. When for the seventh time she offered him the draught, the king drew his sword and forced her to swallow her own poison."

"But how can she then be here alive?" remarked an elderly lady, innocently.

"Alive?" repeated the story-teller, without being disconcerted. "Oh, that is a question. Those creatures can dissemble wonderfully. . . . Yes, indeed, do you remember the Dutchman last year who swallowed melted lead? I do not wish to say too much—but just look! The black-haired nun is as pale as a corpse!"

"Has she given the king poison?" exclaimed a trembling female voice close by. It was Meri, who, with bated breath, drank every word.

"What nonsense!" replied a sea-captain, with the air of knowing more than all the rest. "When I was in Stralsund last spring, I saw those same eyes, which one cannot easily forget. The girl was then brought to Stockholm, and one of the guards told me the whole story. She is a Spanish witch, who has sold herself to the evil one, to be for seven years the most beautiful woman on earth. Only look at her: do you not see that the devil has kept his word? But see, in those eyes is something dark that burns and bewitches. When she became so handsome, she went to the Swedish camp and gave the king a love-potion, so that he neither heard nor saw anybody but her for seven whole weeks. This seemed to his generals a sin and a shame, as the enemy pressed them hard; and so they took her secretly one night and sent her here, to spend the seven years of beauty at Korsholm."

"Did the king love her?" asked Meri, in agitation.

"I think he did," answered the sea-captain, gruffly.

"Did she also love the king?"

"There surely are in the whole world no more curious people than women. How the deuce can you expect me to know all about it? the evil one is smarter than other folks, that is certain. She gave the king a copper ring . . ."

"With seven circles inside each other, and three letters, engraved on the plate?"

"What the deuce!—do you know that already? I have heard of the seven circles, but not of the plate . . ."

Meri took a deep breath: "He wears it still!" said she to herself, with a secret joy. Meri was superstitious, like all the people of her time. It never entered her mind to doubt the possibility of witches, enchantments, and love potions; but this strange dark girl, who loved the king and was loved by him in return . . . could she not be innocent of the horrible things they said about her? The poor forgotten one was seized with a violent desire to approach this mysterious being who had stood so near the great king. The moments were precious; in a few hours she must return to Storkyro. She took courage, and followed the stranger to Korsholm.

The old residence within the ramparts of the castle was, in spite of its fine prospect, more gloomy than magnificent. Frequent changes of governors, who only lived there a little while at a time, had given to the two-story granite building, with its side wings for prisoners, a dreary and deserted appearance. It resembled a jail more than a mighty chieftain's castle. The gloominess was increased by its present inmates—the stern Lady Märtha, with her old maid servants, some invalid soldiers, and the bearded jailors. Had Gustav Adolf recollected the condition of the place, he would probably not have sent his young prisoner to such a dispiriting abode.

Lady Märtha was prepared for her young guest, whom they had described to her as a dangerous and depraved person, for whose cunning no bar was strong enough, no wall thick enough. She had therefore had a little dark chamber within her own bedroom prepared for Lady Regina and her duenna, and made up her mind to watch the wild girl's slightest motions like an Argus. Lady Märtha was in reality a good honest soul but a sharp and stiff-necked lady of the old school, who had brought up all her children with the rod, and never considered them too old to receive a merited chastisement. It never entered her mind that a lonely, defenceless and forsaken young girl, far away in a strange land, needed a comforting hand, a motherly kindness; Lady Märtha held that a spoiled child should be tamed by discipline, and then, as she believed, it would be time enough to think of a milder mode of treatment.

When Lady Regina, accustomed to the freedom of the sea, entered this gloomy dwelling, an involuntary shudder passed through her slender frame. Her spirits were not lightened when she was received on the steps by the old lady herself, in a close linen cap and a long dark woolen cloak.

It is possible that Regina's bow was somewhat stiff, and her whole bearing somewhat proud, when she greeted the old Lady Märtha on the castle steps. But Lady Märtha did not allow herself to be intimidated by it. She took the young girl by both her hands, shook them vigorously, and nodded a greeting, about midway between a welcome and a threat. Then she surveyed her guest from top to toe, and the result of this survey fell in low-spoken words from her lips:

"Stature like a princess . . . no harm; eyes black as a gypsy's . . . no harm; skin white as milk . . . no harm; haughty . . . ah, ah, that is bad; we will see about that, my sweet friend."

Regina, impatient, made a motion to proceed. But Lady Märtha was not one to let go her hold.

"Wait a bit, my dear," said the stern dame, as she tried to collect the little stock of German words which still remained in her memory's scrap-bag; "with patience, one may go a long way. One who crosses my threshold must not be a head higher than the door-post. Better to bend in youth than creep in old age. There . . . that's the way for a young person to greet one who is older and wiser . . ." And before Regina was aware, the strong old lady had put her right hand on her neck, her left against her waist, and, with a hasty pressure, forced her proud guest to bow as profoundly as one could reasonably ask.

Lady Regina's pale cheeks were covered with a flush as red as the evening sky that precedes a storm. Higher and prouder than ever rose the girl's slender form, and her dark eyes shot forth a flash, which did not, however, frighten Lady Märtha. Regina said nothing, but old Dorthe undoubtedly felt disposed to give Lady Märtha a lesson in civility in her mistress's behalf, for she, with her lively southern gesticulations, ascended two steps higher on the stairs, and screamed, beside herself with anger:

"Miserable Finnish witch! how dare you treat a high-born lady so shamefully? Do you really know, base jailor, whom you have the honor of receiving in your house? You do not? Then I will tell you. This is the high-born gracious Lady Regina von Emmeritz, born Princess of Emmeritz, Hohenlohe, and Saalfeld, Countess of Wertheim and Bischoffshöhe, heiress of Dettelsbach and Kissingen, and more. Her father was His Highness the Prince of Emmeritz, who owned more castles than you, ragged witch, have huts in your town. Her mother was Princess of Würtemberg, related to the Electoral House of Bavaria; and her still living uncle, His Highness, worthy of honor and glory, the Prince Bishop of Würtzburg, is lord of Marienburg, and the town of Würtzburg, with all the lands belonging to it. You take advantage because your heretic king has seized our land and city and made us prisoners, but the day will come when Saint George and the Holy Virgin will descend and destroy you, ye heathen; and if you dare to harm a hair of our heads, we will raze this castle to the ground, and exterminate you, miserable witch, and your whole town . . ."

It is probable that old Dorthe's eloquence would not have come to an end for some time yet, had not Lady Märtha made a sign to her servants, at which they, without any ceremony, took the old woman, and carried her off, in spite of her resistance, to one of the small rooms on the lower floor, where she was left to herself, to reflect further upon her lady's aristocratic lineage. But Lady Märtha took the amazed Regina, half by force, half willingly, by the arm, and led her to the room allotted for her, adjoining her own, and commanding a view of the town. Here the stern lady left her for the present, yet not without adding the following admonition at the door:

"I will tell you, my friend: to obey is better than to weep; the bird that sings too early in the morning is before evening in the claws of the hawk. Follow the habits of the country you are in. It is now seven o'clock. At eight, supper is brought in; at nine, you go to bed; at four in the morning you get up; and if you don't know how to card and spin, I will provide you some sewing, so that time shall not hang heavy on your hands. Then we will talk together again; and when your waiting-woman learns to hold her tongue you may have her back. Good-night; don't forget to say your prayers; a psalm-book lies on the dressing-table."

With these words Lady Märtha closed the door and Regina found herself alone. Solitary, imprisoned, far away in a foreign land, unprotected, left to the mercy of a hard keeper,—her thoughts were not the most cheerful. She fell on her knees, and prayed to the saints, not the prayers of the heretic psalm-book, but according to the rosary of rubies which her uncle, the bishop, had given her at her christening. What were her prayers? Only heaven and the dark walls of Korsholm know that, but a sympathizing heart can imagine. She prayed for the saints' assistance, for the victory of her faith, and the downfall of the heretics; she prayed also that the saints might convert King Gustaf Adolf to the only saving church; that he, another Saul, might become another Paul. Finally she prayed for freedom and protection. . . . And the hours went by; her supper was brought in, and she perceived it not.

Lady Regina looked out of the little window, where lay a landscape in the sunset glow—a quiet bay, with its golden water-mirror; it was not the luxuriantly-blooming Franconia, with its ripening vineyards; it was not the rushing Main; and the town over there was not the rich Würtzburg, with its rows of cloisters and its lofty spires. It was the poor, bleak Finland, and an arm of its sea; it was the newly built Wasa, with its church, Mustasaari, the oldest in East Bothnia; one could plainly see the reflection of the sun on the small Gothic windows with stained glass from Catholic times, and it seemed to Regina that she saw the transfigured saints looking out from this, their former temple. And was not the eye of the setting sun itself, at this moment, the look of such a saint, who, with beatific serenity, gazed down on the world's strife? All was so still, so atoningly placid; the evening radiance, the landscape's pretty verdure, the freshly mowed fields with their rows of sheaves, the small red houses with their shining windows, all invoked devotion and peace.

Then Lady Regina heard in the distance a mild, melancholy song, simple and unaffected, but sung as though from nature's own heart, on a lonely evening, with a setting sun, by the shore of a resting sea, when all sweet memories waken in a yearning breast. At first, she did not listen to it; but the song came nearer; . . . now it was obstructed by a cottage wall, now by a group of hanging birches; now it was heard again, free, loud, and clear, and finally one could distinguish the words.

CHAPTER VI.

LOVES OF THE SOUTH AND NORTH.

AS the lonely voice came nearer, the words of the song could gradually be distinguished. It was a gentle heart which sang, in uneven but impassioned strains, its sorrows and its yearnings, by the shore of the sea, in the glory of a beauteous August evening, in the far off regions of the North.

> The sunshine over the round world lies—
> Over land and ocean's surge ;
> And the moon sails up through the evening skies,
> Above the horizon's verge ;—
> But never on maiden forgotten and lone
> Shall fall the sun's clear light,
> And never the blithe moon shall look down
> On the faith of a faithless knight.
>
> For the friend—the only one I held dear—
> Dwells far in his castle of stone ;
> He walks in glory, but leaves me here
> With all my griefs alone ;
> He has friends an hundred, and I but one ;
> He has palace and towns and land :
> I scatter my pearls in the setting sun,
> I sing to the sea and strand.
>
> At his castle the bird rests in her flight,
> Under the southern sky,
> And sits in a tree-top and sings all night
> Of solitude's woe—as I.
> He listens : for strangely the little bird's tone
> Thrills the proud heart of the knight ;
> And ere he guesses, the night has flown,
> As vanishes love's delight.

The longer Lady Regina listened to these simple tones, which were to her at once so strange and yet in their deep melancholy so familiar, the more was she moved by the echo of a regret that so nearly resembled her own. She was seized with a longing to breathe the fresh evening air; the little window long resisted her efforts to open it, but all Lady Märtha's prudence had not been able to prevent the hinges from becoming so old and rusty that they finally yielded to the young girl's repeated attempts. Only two or three hours had she been an inmate of this prison, and yet she inhaled the evening fragrance as a life-prisoner breathes the air of freedom. Her heart expanded, her eyes regained their fire, her thoughts were filled with dreamy ecstacy, and she sang, softly, so as not to be heard by her jailor, but clearly and melodiously, a song which can be but imperfectly reproduced in the following words:

  So deep my smart,
  Thus I impart
To thee, O Virgin, all my heart;
  For honor dear,
  My soul's wish e'er
Is but to die, without a fear.

  Amidst earth's kings
  My loved one flings
His javelins, like the Lord's lightnings;
  Great when in wrath
  All in his path
He crushes—yet he mercy hath.

  But all denied:
  If thou decide,
My dagger in his heart I hide;
  Holy One—thou
  God's Mother!—Oh,
Protect him from the deadly blow!

> Let him but see
> Thy majesty,
> And I will ask no more of thee ;
> Oh, guard his throne,
> His life, his crown,
> And let my soul his sins atone.

The solitary person who had sung the first song slowly approached the castle walls. It was a peasant woman, whose pale yet once beautiful features wore an expression of winning gentleness. She was apparently trying to catch the song of the stranger; but she did not succeed, on account of the suppressed tones and the unknown language. She seated herself on a stone, at a little distance from the wall, and bent her mild gaze steadily toward the prisoner in the castle window, who in turn regarded her with dark penetrating eyes. These two seemed to understand each other perfectly ; for the language of song needs no other lexicon than the heart. Or did a presentiment tell them, the girl of seventeen and the woman of thirty-six, that they both loved the same man, that both sang their shipwrecked love on a far distant strand, but in so infinitely different a manner?

Up in the north the summer nights are clear until the beginning of August, when a light transparent veil spreads itself over land and sea as soon as the sun goes down. By the middle of August (the time of which we are speaking) this veil has grown thicker, and casts a mild, soft shade over the leaves and groves of summer. Then the moon rises upon this world of vanishing green ; and there is nothing more sadly beautiful to be found in all nature than such an August evening, when the eye, accustomed to three months' unbroken day, shrinks from the darkness, though seeing this darkness in

8*

its loveliest aspects, like a mild sorrow irradiated by a heavenly glory. This impression returns every year, even though one lives to be a hundred; it is light and darkness which struggle at the same time for the world and the human heart.

The two singers felt the power of this impression; they both sat mute and motionless, quietly regarding each other in the deepening twilight; neither said a word, yet each understood the other's innermost thoughts.

Suddenly the pale woman outside rose, turned toward the town, and seemed to be listening to some sounds which disturbed the holy peace of evening.

Lady Regina followed the motions of the unknown attentively, leaning out of the window that she might see better. All nature was silent and calm; only in the distance was heard the stroke of oars on the sea, or the melancholy, prolonged tone of a shepherd's horn. This stillness, increased by the first darkness of the autumn, had in it something at once holy and solemn. Jarring strangely upon the peace and quiet came the indistinct noise from the distant town. It was not the surge of the sea, or the roar of the rapids, or the crackling of wood fires; although it resembled all these sounds. It was rather the murmur of an enraged mob, actuated at once by fury and want. . . In a short time the reflection of a fire was seen afar off in the northern part of the town.

With the speed of the wind the lonely figure outside the wall hurried away in the direction of the threatening danger. . . . We will, for a moment, precede her.

The arrival of the man-of-war for the transportation of the recruits had placed these in a state of excitement which had been heightened by sorrow, pride, and ale. With their under-officers at the head, they had thronged around the dram-shops; and at this time, when the soldier was all-important, it was often necessary to overlook his license, in order to keep him in good humor. The superior officers consequently pretended not to notice that two hundred young men, with the combative disposition of the East Bothnians, intoxicated themselves to excess; and it is possible that this policy would have been the right one, had not a peculiar circumstance, dangerous to peace, brought their unrestrained passions to a full blaze.

The brave sergeant, Bengt Kristerson, had not neglected this opportunity to do himself all possible credit. Inflated with the thought of his own dignity, he had jumped up on a table and thoroughly demonstrated to his new comrades:— first, that it was really he who had conquered Germany; secondly, that he would long ago have driven Emperor Ferdinand, alive, into the river Danube, had the latter not been in league with Satan, and bewitched the whole Swedish army, the king first of all; thirdly, that on the night of the Frankfort ball, he, Bengt, had stood on guard outside the king's bedchamber, and plainly seen Beelzebub, in the form of a young girl, occasion a terrible commotion there; and fourthly (and to this conclusion the sergeant came quite naturally, in the inspiration of the moment), that the weal or woe of the whole kingdom and of the world depended upon the witch who was now imprisoned within Korsholm's walls.

"You will see that the black-haired witch brings the plague to the town," observed, thoughtfully, a Malax peasant, with a shaggy appearance and very light hair.

"The wolf-cub!"

"The king's murderess!"

"Shall we endure it to have her sit in peace and quiet, and destroy both king and country with her witcheries?" cried a drunken recorder who had joined the company.

"Let us duck her in the sea!" shrieked a Nerpes peasant.

"Let us club her on the spot!" exclaimed a Lappo peasant, with an eagle nose and dark bushy eyebrows.

"And if they don't give her into our hands we will set fire to Korsholm, and burn the owl and the nest at the same time," said a ferocious Laihela peasant.

"Better that than to have the kingdom ruined," remarked a grave-looking seal-hunter from Replot.

"Torches!" shrieked a Wörå peasant.

"To Korsholm!" howled the whole crowd. And excited, as is usually the case, by their own words, the horde rushed to the large open fire-place of the dram-shop, and snatched up all the burning brands that were to be found. But as ill-luck would have it, there was a great quantity of flax hanging in bundles on the walls of the room. One of the recruits, in his drunkenness, swung his brand too high, the flax took fire, the strong draft from the open door fanned the flame, and in a few moments the ale-house was in full blaze. All rushed out. Nobody had time to realize how it happened.

"It is witchcraft!" shrieked some.

"The witch at Korsholm will have to pay for this!" cried others; and the whole raging mob hastened at full speed to the old castle.

CHAPTER VII.

THE SIEGE OF KORSHOLM.

MERI (for the solitary singer was none other than she) had scarcely realized the purpose of the mad crowd, before she hurried with the speed of the wind, and by the shortest way, back to Korsholm. In the moonlight, which shed its silver rays over the landscape, she could plainly distinguish Regina's dark locks, which, blacker than the night, stood in relief from the room in the background, like a shadow in the midst of shade. And under these locks shone two eyes, dreamy, deep, like the glimmer of the stars in the dusky mirror of a lake. The words died on Meri's lips; all the strange reports rose like spectres before her imagination. She who sat so lonely up there at the window, was she not, after all, a southern witch, a transformed sorceress, weeping over her fate in being compelled to spend the seven years of her beauty within these walls, and then again become what she had been before—a frightful monster, half woman and half serpent?

Meri stood as if petrified at the foot of the wall.

But nearer and nearer was heard the murmur of the wild crowd, and the lights of the brands began to be reflected on the castle. Then the superstitious peasant-woman took courage, and raised her voice so that it could be heard at the window.

"Fly, your grace!" said she, rapidly, in Swedish.

"Fly! A great danger threatens you; the soldiers are wild and frantic; they say that you have tried to murder the king, and they demand your life."

Regina saw the pale shape in the moonlight, and before her imagination rose all the stories she had heard about this land of witchcraft. During her ten months' stay among the Swedes she had in some measure learned to understand their language; she did not immediately comprehend the other's meaning, but a single word was sufficient to fasten her attention.

"The king?" repeated she, in broken Swedish. "Who are you, and what have you to tell me about the great Gustaf Adolf?"

"Waste not a moment, your grace!" continued Meri, without listening to Regina's question. "They are already at the gates, and Lady Märtha, with her six soldiers, will not be able to protect you against two hundred. Quick! If you cannot come out through the door, tie together sheets and shawls and let yourself down from the window; I will receive you."

Regina began to understand that some danger threatened her; but far from being terrified by it, she heard it with a secret pleasure. Was she not a martyr to her faith, transported to this wild land for her zeal in trying to convert the mightiest enemy of her church? Perhaps the moment was at hand when the saints would grant her a martyr-crown, dearly bought by life itself. Why should she shun an honor which she had so recently craved? Was it not the tempter himself, who, in the pale woman's form, tried to lure her from an imperishable glory? And Regina answered: "*Et dixit diabolus : da te præcipitem ex hoc loco, nam scriptum est : angelis suis mandavit de te, ut te* *tueantur ne ullo modo lædaris.*"* At these words the moon appeared round the corner of the wall and threw its melancholy light on the beautiful girl's face. Her cheeks glowed, her eyes burned with an ecstatic brilliance. Meri looked at her full of wonder and dread . . and again it flashed through her mind that something must be wrong with a being of such a singular appearance, and who spoke so strangely. An indescribable fear seized her, and she fled, without knowing why, away through the moonlight, back to the town.

In the meantime Regina in her chamber had heard the murmur from the castle yard. The drunken horde had been checked by a well-barred gate, and stood clamorous on the outside, threatening not to leave a stone of the castle standing, unless the witch was immediately given up to them. But Lady Märtha, although just awakened from her sound sleep, was not one to be easily scared. She had been in more than one siege in her younger days, and understood, like a wise commander, that a fortress does not fall at big words. "One who gains time, gains all," thought Lady Märtha, and she therefore began to negotiate for capitulation, with the request to know what the besiegers especially wanted, and why they wanted it. In the meantime, half a dozen rusty muskets were hunted up, with which the castle's invalids were armed; the six keepers were provided with clubs and pikes; the servant girls themselves were ordered to seize the flails with which more than one of Fleming's cavalry received their death-blow during the Club War. Thus prepared, Lady Märtha thought she could with

* "And Satan saith unto him: 'Cast thyself down; for it is written, He shall give His angels charge concerning thee, that they may preserve thee, so that no harm may befall thee.'" Compare Matthew iv, 6, where the Lutheran text differs from the Catholic.

safety break off negotiations; she therefore advanced in person to the inside of the gate, and began a scolding lesson which had in it strong words and but little music.

"You crazy scamps!" shrieked the brave dame, with more force than elegance, "may the devil take you, as many as you are, drunken ale-bibbers! Pack yourselves off this instant, or, as sure as my name is Märtha Ulfsparre, you shall have a taste of 'Master Hans' on your backs! you villains, sots, shameless knaves, night loafers!"

"Master Hans" was a good-sized stick of braided rattan which seldom left Lady Märtha's hand, and for whose impressive maxims all the inmates of the castle entertained a deep respect. But whether the noisy crowd did not understand "Master Hans'" excellent qualities, or whether, in the uproar, Lady Märtha's words were only heard by those standing nearest, the mob continued to press on with loud cries, and the strong gate shook upon its hinges.

"Out with the witch!" shrieked the wildest, and some of them began to throw brands against the gate, in the hope of setting it on fire.

Lady Märtha had on the ramparts two clumsy cannon from the time of Gustaf I, called "the hawk" and "the dove." Their innocent employment had long been to respond to the salute of vessels arriving in the harbor, and on solemn occasions, such as christening days and royal nuptials, to interpret in loud tones the official sentiments of pleasure. It is true, these guns were mounted on some old disused ramparts outside of the present fortifications of the castle—the high fence with its iron spikes—and the cannons were consequently more easily accessible to the enemy than to the besieged. But Lady Märtha calculated very correctly that a cannonade from the ramparts would overawe the enemy, and serve as a signal of distress to summon assistance from the man-of-war and the town. She therefore ordered two of her soldiers to steal out under cover of the night, load "the hawk" and "the dove," and directly after the shot was fired—with powder only—return quickly to the castle.

The effect of this was instantaneous. The hue and cry ceased directly; and Lady Märtha did not let the opportunity slip from her hands.

"Do you hear, you pack of thieves?" screamed she, mounted on a ladder so that her white night-cap was seen in the moonlight a few feet above the gate; "if you don't this minute take yourselves off from His Royal Majesty's castle, I will let my cannon shoot you into fragments, like so many cabbage stalks; you noisy, drunken swine! I suppose you know that angry dogs get torn skins, and the chicken who sticks his neck in the jaws of the fox will have to look around to see where his head is. I shall have you cut to pieces, you ruffians!" continued Lady Märtha, more and more excited; "I will make mince-meat of you and throw you to the . ."

Unfortunately, the brave commander was not allowed to finish her heroic harangue. One of the crowd had found a rotten turnip on the ground, and flung it so skilfully at the white night-cap shining in the moonlight, that Lady Märtha, struck right in the brow, was obliged to retire, and for the first time in her life had to leave a sentence unfinished. An irrepressible laugh now rose among the crowd, and with it Lady Märtha's supremacy was hopelessly impaired. The enemy stormed more and more arrogantly against the gate, the hinges bent, the boards gave away, finally half the gate fell in with a terrible crash, and the whole crowd of the besiegers rushed into the court-yard.

Now one could have wagered three against one that Lady Märtha would be obliged to capitulate. But no; she withdrew quickly, with all her force, to the interior of the castle, barring the entrance, and placed her musketeers at the windows, threatening to shoot down the first person who attempted to enter. Such resolute courage, on any other occasion, would not have failed of its effect; but the infuriated rabble neither heard nor saw. One of the men in front, who had found a crowbar, began to batter the door.

Then arose confusion and outcries at the rear of the crowd. Those in the middle turned round and discerned through the open gateway, as far as one could see in the uncertain moonlight, the whole space outside filled with head upon head and musket upon musket. It was as if an army had sprung up from the earth to annihilate the disturbers of the peace. Could it be all the bloodless shades of the long deceased champions of Korsholm had risen from their graves to avenge the violence that had been committed against their old fortress?

In order to explain the unexpected sight which was now presented to the view of the belligerents, we must remember that a great part of the country people from the adjacent regions had flocked to the town to witness the departure of the recruits. It ought also to be mentioned that the Storkyro peasant king had remained over night in Wasa, probably in the secret expectation of hearing some news about Bertel from the crew of the "Maria Eleonora." The burning of the ale-house and the march of the noisy crowd toward Korsholm had set all Wasa in commotion, and when Meri arrived in breathless haste, imploring her father to save the imprisoned lady, she found open ears everywhere. The East Bothnian is soon ready for battle; and when the peasants learned the wrong which had been done Bert la, their foremost man, the old animosity against the soldiers awakened within them. They forgot that many of their own sons and brothers had just donned the recruit's jacket; they could not possibly neglect so welcome an opportunity to give the soldiers a thrashing, both in the name of humanity and in defense of the king's castle. They therefore marched, with Bertila at the head, about a hundred strong, to the rescue of the castle; and what in the moonlight might have been taken for pikes and muskets, was scarcely anything but hastily-snatched poles and rails—the usual weapons in the fights of that region.

As soon as the soldiers saw that they were attacked from the outside, they tried to hide their consternation by loud shouts and threats. Uncertain of the enemy's strength, some of them began to think of a possible retreat over the spiked fence; others believed that they had to deal with a whole army of spectres, called up through the strange witch's incantations, which seemed, even to the most courageous, uncomfortable and unpleasant. They were soon roused from their delusion, however, by the well-known sounds of Malax Swedish and Lillkyro Finnish, which could with very good reason be thought to come from human lips, and not from ghosts. At the moment when the forces of the outer enemy clogged up the gateway, a silence arose, as if by agreement on each side, during which could be distinguished a voice from the castle window and another from the rampart, both speaking at once:

"Didn't I tell you so?" shrieked Lady Märtha bravely, from the window: "didn't I tell you, tipplers, vagabonds, that you ought to think seven times before you stuck your noses between the wedge and the tree, and if the tail has once got into the fox trap, there is no other resource left than to bite it off. A big mouth needs a broad back, and now hold yourselves in readiness to pay the fiddler!"

And with this, Lady Märtha drew back; very likely from fear of a new volley of rotten turnips.

The other voice from the rampart was that of an old man, who in powerful tones cried to the soldiers:

"If you will lay down your arms and give up your leaders, then the rest may go in peace. If not, there shall be a dance, the like of which Korsholm has never seen, and we will see to it that the bows are well-rosined."

"May all the devils take you, peasant lubber!" replied a voice from the court-yard, by which could be plainly recognized the jolly sergeant, Bengt Kristerson. "If I had you between my fingers, I would—*blitz-donner-kreutz-Pappenheim!*—teach you to propose to brave soldiers a cowardly surrender! Go ahead, boys; let us clear the gateway and drive the gang back to their porridge kettle!"

Fortunately, none of the soldiers were provided with fire-arms, and very few with swords, as the recruits had not yet obtained weapons. Most of them had, besides their extinguished brands and some fragments of broken wagons, only sticks snatched from a wood-pile in the yard. Thus equipped, the crowd bore down upon the entrance.

At the first assault, the soldiers were received with such energetic blows of the rails, that many drew back with bloody heads. But soon the crowd at the gate became so dense that no arm could be lifted, no blow dealt, and a frantic struggle took place between those in front, while those from both sides closed around them and finally pressed them so tightly that no one could move hand or foot, and they expected every minute to be squeezed to death. Here were seen vigorous arms trying in vain to overthrow an enemy; there, broad shoulders exerting themselves to make their way through the crushing mass. Finally the pressure from within became so strong that the foremost ranks of the peasants were thrust aside or thrown down, and about half of the soldiers cleared a way toward the open plain outside the ramparts, while the other half, again penned up, were obliged to remain in the court-yard.

Then began a regular battle. They fought with poles and sticks, with whips and fists. Here rained down many a blow which might better have been bestowed on Isolani's Croats; here was performed many a daring exploit which would have been better suited to the battle-fields of Germany. The soldiers, although superior in numbers, were divided by the gate into two detached corps, and soon had the worst of it. Part of them, numbering the youngest of the recruits, took to flight, and scattered themselves toward the town; others were overpowered and badly beaten; others again—the old experienced soldiers—retired to the ramparts, where, secure from attack in the rear, they defended themselves with desperate courage.

Victory now seemed to incline decidedly toward the side of the peasants, when the strife received a new impetus. The forces at the gate, who, on account of the struggle outside the ramparts, had forgotten the enemy within, were surprised by the enclosed soldiers, who rushed out to help their comrades. These now found breathing space, and in their turn attacked the peasants with increased fury; the affray became more and more involved, the victory more and more uncertain; both parties had defeats to revenge, and the rage of both increased as the strength on both sides became more equal.

And over this scene of tumult and confusion, of lamentation, cries of victory, threats, and wild conflict, the clear and silvery August moon beamed like a heavenly eye upon the self-inflicted anguish and misery of earth. All the inlets of the bay shone in the moonlight; in the tree tops and on the moist grass there glittered millions of dewdrops, like pearls on midsummer's green robe. All nature breathed an indescribable calm; a gentle breeze from the great shining sea in the west passed softly over the coast; in the distance was heard the monotonous roll of the surf upon the beach, and the stars looked down, silent and twinkling, into the dark waters.

When the yard was found empty, Lady Märtha and her soldiers ventured out to behold from a nearer standpoint the strife on the ramparts. The stout-hearted old lady undoubtedly felt inclined to take part in the contest in her way, for she was heard to cry to the peasants in a loud voice:

"That's right, boys! drum ahead! let the stick fly! many have danced after worse fiddles!" And to the soldiers she screamed: "Good luck to you, my children; help yourselves to a little supper; Korsholm offers the best the house has. Be at ease; your witch is in good keeping; Korsholm has bolts and bars for you too, miscreants!"

But as if a capricious fate wished to convict the old lady of untruth and put all her prudence to shame, a tall, dark female form appeared at that moment on the top of the rampart, and outlined itself against the moonlit sky.

Lady Märtha felt the words die on her lips when, in dismay, she recognized her well-guarded prisoner. How Regina had got out through locked doors and closed windows was to the good dame such an inexplicable enigma that she was for an instant infected by the superstitious belief in the strange girl's alliance with the powers of darkness. She gave up all idea of catching the fugitive, and expected nothing less than to see large black wings grow out of her shoulders, and to see her, like an immense raven, soar aloft toward the starry firmament.

The reader, on the other hand, can easily find a natural explanation. The din of the conflict and the sound of the two cannon shots had reached Regina's lonely chamber. Every moment she expected to be seized by executioners and dragged to a certain death; and so glorious did the lot of dying for her faith seem to her, that her impatience was increased to the highest degree when the noise down below continued, but still, after an hour's interval, no human feet were heard to approach her door. Finally the thought ran through her fanatical soul, that the prince of darkness envied her so grand a fate, and that the strife going on below was instigated by him in order to prepare for her, instead of a glorious death, a languishing life in captivity, without profit or joy. She remembered the singer's advice, to lower herself down through the open window by means of sheets and shawls; quickly she formed her resolution, and before many minutes stood in view of all the combatants on the rampart.

As they became aware of the tall form up there in the moonlight, they were seized with the same superstitious dread which had just paralyzed Lady Märtha's quick tongue. The contest gradually subsided, and continued only at the most remote points; friend and foe were affected by a common horror, and near the rampart there was a silence so deep that one could hear in the distance the sea's low murmur against the pebbly beach.

And Lady Regina spoke with a voice so loud and clear that if her Swedish had not been so imperfect she could have been very well understood by all within hearing.

"Ye children of Belial!" said she, in tones which, though slightly trembling at first, soon became firm and calm, "ye people of the heretic faith, why do ye delay to take my life? Here I stand without weapons, without any human protection, with the high heaven above me and the earth and sea at my feet, and say to you: Your Luther was a false prophet; there is no salvation except in the true universal Catholic Church. Therefore, be converted to the Holy Virgin and all the saints; acknowledge the Pope to be Christ's vicegerent, as he truly is, that you may avert from your heads the sword of St. George, which is already raised to destroy you. But me you can kill in order to seal the veracity of my faith; here I stand; why do you hesitate? I am ready to fall for my faith!"

It was Lady Regina's good fortune that her

speech was not understood by those to whom it was addressed, for so strong was the power of Lutheranism, in this fervid time when nations and individuals sacrificed life and welfare for their religion, that even the humblest and most ignorant were filled with burning zeal and a blind hate to the Pope and his followers, of which all our crabbed but pithy old psalm-books yet to-day bear plain witness. Had this mass of people, both peasants and soldiers, heard Regina extol the Pope and declare Luther a false prophet, they would inevitably have torn her to pieces in their rage. As it was, the young girl's words were an unmeaning sound in their ears; they saw her firm bearing, and the respect which courage and misfortune united always inspire did not fail to have its effect upon the enraged throng, a few moments before so furious, now irresolute, and at a loss what to think or do.

Lady Regina again expected, in vain, to be dragged to death. She descended from the rampart and mingled in the shyly yielding crowd; all could see that she was utterly unprotected, and yet not a hand moved to seize her.

"It is not a being of flesh and blood, it is a shadow," said an old Wörå peasant, hesitatingly. "It seems to me that I see the moon shine right through her."

"We may test that," exclaimed a shaggy fellow from Ilmola, laying his coarse hand rather roughly on Regina's shoulder.

It was a critical moment; the young girl turned around and looked her assailant in the face with such dark, deep, shining eyes, that the latter, seized with a strange emotion, immediately drew his hand back, and stole away abashed. A large number of those standing nearest followed him. None could explain the power of those dark eyes in the moonlight, but all felt their mysterious influence. In a few moments the space around Regina was vacant, the strife had ceased, and a patrolling force, which at last arrived, put an end to the disturbance by arresting the most refractory of the combatants.

. . . .

But not long did the rivalry engendered by the Club War continue between the peasants and the soldiers—between the industrious *plough*, Finland's pride, and the conquering *sword*, which at this time was drawn to subdue the Roman emperor himself.

Of Regina we will only say that she allowed herself, with a sigh over the martyr-crown she had missed, to be taken back to the dark and solitary prison-chamber under Lady Märtha's charge. But Bertila returned with his daughter to Storkyro: the older person with thoughts of a coming greatness, the younger with the memory of a past joy. And it should be observed that all this occurred during two days of the summer of 1632—before King Gustaf Adolf's death, which was described at the end of the first story.

. . . .

Days and months go by, and human destinies change form, and the swift word is obliged to check its flight and remain awhile mute in expectation of the evenings which are to come. For the Surgeon's tales, like a child's joy or sorrow, lasted but a single evening—short enough for those who sympathetically listened to them, and perhaps sufficiently long for the others. But never was the thread of the story clipped in the middle of its course, without young and old thinking to themselves: there is still more coming. And the Surgeon had to promise this. He had much yet to relate about the half-spun skein of two family histories; and next time it will probably be spun longer—if not to the end, at least to the knot, which means that the skein has reached its right length.

PART III.—FIRE AND WATER.

INTERLUDE.

SIX weeks elapsed before the Surgeon again saw gathered around him his story-loving listeners, large and small. It had happened that in this interval an accident had befallen the old man. Nearly everybody in this world, and especially old bachelors, have some hobby. Bäck had now got it thoroughly into his head that he ought to have a certain comfort in his old days. He had in the garret a pretty large sack of feathers, and he was accustomed to increase it every spring and autumn by bird shooting. To what use these feathers were to be put, he informed no one; when asked about it, he usually answered:

"I will do like Possen at the Wiborg explosion: if Finland should need, I will go up in a tower and shake my feathers in the air; then there will be as many soldiers as the sack has feathers."

"You talk like a goose, brother Andreas," replied Captain Svanholm, the postmaster. "In our day, soldiers must be made of sterner stuff. The devil take me, but I think you consider us warriors only chickens."

"Yes," added the Surgeon, when the captain was about to continue, "I know what you mean to say: precisely like Ficandt at Karstula."

However, the fact was, that one fine April day the Surgeon had gone to the bay on a shooting expedition, with decoy-ducks. He was accompanied by an old one-eyed corporal named Ritsi, a name meaning Fritz. He had in his youth been a journeyman, and wandered around Germany with a pack on his back; but he brought nothing home in it except his name.

There was still ice in portions of the bay, with frequent openings of clear water. The old men strolled along the edge of the ice, discharging their guns every little while, but without much result, as both of them had rather poor eyesight. It happened early in the morning that Bäck thought he saw a pair of fine ducks at the farther edge of the ice, which could only be reached by making a long circuit. He set off, and sure enough the ducks were there. He stole as near as he dared; he aimed; he fired; the ducks shook themselves a little, but did not stir from the spot. "Those creatures are pretty tough," thought Bäck; and he bent down, reloaded, and fired again at thirty paces, with the same result. Feeling a little flat, Bäck went nearer, and discovered for the first time that he had been shooting his own decoy-ducks, which the wind had driven, unobserved, from the inner edge of ice to the outer.

The old gentleman now resolved to return with his game; but this was easier said than done. The wind had separated the ice where he stood from the ice which held Ritsi, and the loose block was drifting toward the sea. The two old friends looked sadly at each other; it was scarcely a dozen yards between them, and yet the corporal could not assist his friend and master, for there was no boat to be had. Bäck was driven slowly but surely out to sea.

"Good-by now, comrade!" cried the Surgeon,

while he could yet be heard by the corporal.
"Tell Svenonius and Svanholm that my will is
locked up in the lower bureau-drawer to the right.
Tell him to have the bells rung for me next Sunday. As for the funeral, you need not give yourself any trouble; I will attend to that myself."

"God have mercy!" cried the corporal; and
he wiped his single eye with the inside of his
jacket-skirt, and returned to the town slowly and
tranquilly, as if nothing had happened.

Now it must be said, to the honor of the good
town, that the rest of the Surgeon's friends were
far from taking the matter as coolly as the corporal.
The postmaster cursed and swore; the schoolmaster marched out at the head of his boys, and
the old grandmother quietly sent off a couple of
able-bodied pilots in their safe boats to cruise
between the blocks of ice and hunt for the Surgeon. Half the town was in motion; there was
a great bustle and running about, those who made
the most fuss accomplishing the least.

Two days passed with no trace of the Surgeon;
on the third day, the pilots came back without having found their game. The Surgeon was now given
up for lost, and they ceased to search for him. There
was sincere mourning in the town; for an heirloom
like the old man Bäck—the uncle of all and confidant of all—was one of the little town's household
guardian spirits, without whom it was impossible
to conceive how the general welfare could be
maintained. But what was to be done? When,
on the third Sunday after the unfortunate birdhunting, nothing had been heard from the Surgeon,
not even a cry or chirrup, the bells were rung, according to custom, for his poor soul, a fine eulogy,
composed by Svenonius, and interlarded with both

Latin and Hebrew flowers of rhetoric, was read in the church, and the most wise town council appointed a day in the coming week for taking an inventory of the property of the old comrade so unexpectedly cut off.

I hope, however, that the reader, who has noticed the title of this veracious story, will not be alarmed. It would really be very hard if the Surgeon should be taken away just now, when Regina sits confined at Korsholm under Lady Märtha's stern hand, and Bertel yet bleeds on the battlefield of Lützen. And what would become of the tender-hearted Meri, of the Storkyro peasant-king, and so many of the other remarkable persons of this story? Patience; the Surgeon had certainly gone through worse experiences in his day; it wasn't for nothing that he was born on the same day as Napoleon.

Everything was arranged for the inventory. A surprising neatness prevailed in Bäck's garret-chamber; something very unusual had occurred there: the place had been swept and scrubbed. All his effects were set in order—the medicine-chest was dusted, the stuffed birds were placed in a row, the sacred collection of eggs exposed to profane eyes. The silver-headed Spanish cane stood gravely in the corner; the old peruke hung with a meditative air on its hook; the innermost mysteries of Bäck's bureau—the locks of hair from former times—were drawn forth to be valued in rubles and kopeks, probably not at a high figure. All was in order, as we said; an alderman with an official mien had taken his seat at the old oak table, where a blank document, stamped with the big seal of the government, now occupied the place usually reserved for the Surgeon's carpenter tools;

a clerk sharpened his pencil opposite the alderman, and the old grandmother, as landlady of the house, had presented herself, with moist eyes, to deliver up Bäck's property, as the old man had neither kith nor kin.

One thing, however, was still unopened and unexamined: it was the worn sealskin trunk under the Surgeon's bed. The alderman's eyes occasionally turned there with a pious thought of the percentage he would derive from the inheritance; but what the trunk contained, and who would be the rightful heir, no one knew.

It was time to commence. Svanholm and Svenonius were called up as appraisers. The alderman coughed once or twice, assumed his most magisterial air, opened his mouth, and spoke:

"Whereas, it has come to the knowledge of the most wise town council that the former Surgeon of the High Crown, the before-mentioned Andreas Bäck, while engaged in the pursuit of ice-bird shooting of birds on the ice, on the aforesaid ice accidentally lost his life in a deadly way; and whereas, he therefore, although not found in body, must certainly be considered dead in soul, correctly and according to law . . . . ."

"I would most humbly beg to be excused from that!" said at this instant a voice from the door; and the effect thereof was marvellous.

The wise alderman lost both his wits and his official bearing; he turned his eyes upward, and his eloquent tongue for the first time refused its office. The clerk, with the name and dignity of secretary, jumped up like a rocket, knocking his head against the wall behind him, and tumbling over the learned Svenonius, who was somewhat deaf, and had neither heard the awful voice nor understood the slightest thing about the commotion. The most excited one, however, was the brave Svanholm; one could have sworn that he had not, even at Karstula, experienced such an ordeal. He suddenly became as white as a sheet, and vainly commanded his refractory left foot to wheel about. The only one who maintained any degree of self-possession was the old grandmother; she put her spectacles on her nose, went straight up to the new-comer, and shook her respected head dubiously, as if to say (what she did not say, however), that it was very unbecoming in corpses to peep about.

But old Bäck—for who else could it be?—was not at all daunted. His feelings were of an entirely different kind. When he saw his dear old chamber so shamefully fixed up, his precious effects so glaringly paraded, and the officious alderman actively engaged in what Bäck considered none of his business, he was seized, excusably enough, with righteous indignation, took the representatives of the law by the neck, one after the other, and threw them without ceremony from the room. Then came the turn of brother Svenonius, who was also not spared; and finally of brother Svanholm, who, likewise, before he could utter a word, found himself rolling his whole length down the stairs. All this was done in the twinkling of an eye. The place was now cleared of all except the grandmother. When Bäck met the old lady's mildly reproachful glance, he came to his senses, and felt ashamed.

"Well, well," said he, "you must not take it ill, cousin; I shall teach sweepers and dusters to disorder my room. . . . Be so kind as to take a seat, dear cousin. But it is enough to provoke a stone, to see such nonsense. Just look how these rogues have scrubbed my room and dusted all my birds! It is scandalous!"

"Dear cousin," interrupted the grandmother, at once vexed and pleased; "I am the one to be blamed for all that; we couldn't possibly think but that you had been drowned."

"Drowned indeed!" muttered the Surgeon. "I will tell you, cousin, a bad penny is not got rid of so easily. It is perfectly true that I floated around on that miserable block of ice three whole days and nights. It wasn't exactly a warm bed and well-spread table, but it answered. I had my old gun with me, and managed to shoot a venturesome seal. It was pretty oily, I can assure you, but I thought: 'better lack bread than wit.' I had a tinder-box, and salt too; so I made a fire of my game-bag, and fried myself a beef-steak. On the fourth day I drifted to firm ice at West Bothnia, and marched ashore. 'Now it is time to start for home,' thought I; so I sold my gun, and started, although the sledging was bad enough. And I tell you what it is, cousin, they would been spared from upsetting my room, and sticking their noses into my things, had not the Swedes raised the charges more than four times what they were when I was young. Before I got to Haparanda, my purse was empty. Then I thought: 'let the *collegium medicum* go to the devil;' and so I began my old practice with the lancet and '*essentia dulcis*,' as I went along; and all the old grannies . . . God bless you, I thought you were going to sneeze! . . . and all the old grannies were amazed to see old times come again. In this manner I managed to reach home . . . a little too late, but still in time to throw my uninvited guests down-stairs."

It is easy to see that the Surgeon found it difficult to forgive his friends for invading his peaceful domains. Had they robbed him of his treasures, or disgraced his name, he could have pardoned them; but to put his room in order was more than human magnanimity could excuse! Little by little the storm was allayed through the old grandmother's wise mediation; and so the day came when the reconciliation was celebrated with a third story. It is true that some simple-minded people still looked upon the Surgeon as a ghost; the council doubted his right to live when he had been legally declared dead; the postmaster swore by a thousand devils over his sore back, which still bore marks of the encounter with brother Bäck; Svenonius sighed over a hole in his twenty-years-old black coat, which, in honor of the solemn occasion, he had worn at this neck-breaking reunion. But the old grandmother smiled just as mildly; Anne Sophie was as gentle as ever; the little folks were as uproarious; and thus it happened that the sunshine scattered the mists, and the horizon cleared for the fortunes of the imprisoned Regina.

"My dear friends," began the Surgeon, "it may seem strange to you that I should call this story 'Fire and Water.' All that concerns 'The King's Ring' and how 'The Sword and the Plough' fell into strife, you can understand without puzzling your brains. But now some of you probably think that I intend to divert you with natural science, since I let the elements figure as a title. That would certainly be well enough; I have a great respect for nature, but I hold the opinion that in a story human beings are the main thing. If we are looking at pictures, we can with hearty pleasure regard a fruit-piece or a game-piece; but so far as I understand, figure-painting, with fine human forms, is superior. I will tell you at once that I do not by any means intend to describe conflagrations and deluges, but I have chosen my title from the fact that human dispositions sometimes have a remarkable resemblance to the elements—some to fire, some to water, some even to light air. I intend to tell you about four persons, of whom two belong to the first sort and two to the second. This title by no means says all that might be said, for most titles have the fault of expressing but one of many sides. I also thought of calling this part 'The Coat of Arms,' when I realized that it could with just as much reason be called 'The Axe'. I might have frightened you with the terrible title of 'The Curse'; but when I came to think of it, I found that it could just as well be called 'The Blessing'. Consequently you will have to be contented with the elements.

"I have now said all that I desired in explanation, and will leave you to guess the rest."

CHAPTER I.

SPOILS FROM THE BATTLE-FIELD.

IT is necessary the reader should remember, what has already been explained, that all the events described in the narrative of "The Sword and the Plough" occurred before the battle of Lützen, which ended Part I, "The King's Ring."

Returning now to Lützen and the 6th of November, 1632, we must forget for awhile that "The Sword and the Plough" ever existed, and imagine that we still stand by the bloody bier of the great hero-king, where, the day after the battle, he lay embalmed in the village of Meuchen.

It was a glorious but terrible sight when the Pappenheimers made their charge upon the Finns on the east side of the river Rippach. Mail-clad, irresistible, the cuirassiers descended upon Stålhandske, whose Finnish troopers reeled under this crushing attack: their horses, weary from the long conflict, recoiled, fell backwards, and for a time gave way. But Stålhandske rallied them again, man against man, horse against horse ; they fought with their last strength, indifferent to death ; and friends and enemies were mixed together in bloody confusion. Here fell Pappenheim ; here fell his bravest men ; half of Stålhandske's cavalry were trampled under the horses' hoofs, and yet the strife raged without interruption until twilight.

At Stålhandske's side rode Bertel ; and so it happened that he met Pappenheim. The youth of twenty was not able to cope with this arm of steel; a blow of the brave general's long sword struck Bertel across the helmet with such crushing force that his eyes were blinded and he became insensible. But in falling he unconsciously grasped his faithful horse, Lappen, by the mane, and Lappen, confused by the tumult, galloped away; while his master, with one foot in the stirrup and his hands convulsively twisted in the mane, was dragged with him.

When Bertel opened his eyes, he was in dense darkness. He remembered vaguely the adventures of the hot struggle; the last thing he there saw was Pappenheim's lifted sword. The thought entered his mind that he was now dead and lying in his grave. He put his hand to his heart, it beat;

he bit his finger, it pained him. He realized that he was still living, but how and where it was impossible to guess. He stretched out his hand and picked up some straw. Under him he felt the damp ground, above him the empty air. He tried to raise himself up, but his head was as heavy as lead. It still felt the weight of Pappenheim's sword.

Then he heard not far from him a voice, which, half complaining, half mocking, uttered the following words in Swedish:

"Ghosts and grenades! Not a drop of wine! Those scoundrelly Wallachians have stolen my flask; the miserable hen-thieves! Holloa, Turk or Jew—it is all the same—bring here a drop of wine!"

"Is that you, Larsson?" said Bertel, in a faint voice; for his tongue was half paralyzed by a burning thirst.

"What sort of a marmot is it that whispers my name?" responded his neighbor, in the darkness. "Hurrah, boys! loose reins and a brisk gallop! When you have emptied your pistols, fling them to the devil, and slash away with swords! Cleave their skulls, the brutes; peel them like turnips. Beat them, grind them to powder! The king has fallen.... Devils and heroes, what a king!.... To-day we shall bleed; to-day we shall die; but first we must be revenged. That's the way, boys! Hurrah!.... Pitch in, East Bothnians!"

"Larsson," repeated Bertel; but his comrade did not hear him. He continued in his delirium to lead his Finnish boys in the conflict.

After awhile a streak of the late autumn morning dawned in through the window of the miserable hut where Bertel lay. He could now distinguish the straw which was strewn over the bare ground; and on the straw he saw two men asleep.

The door opened; a couple of wild bearded men entered, and pushed the slumberers rudely with the butts of their guns.

"*Raus!*" cried they, in Low Dutch; "reveille has sounded!"

And outside the hut was heard the well-known trumpet-blast, which at that time was the usual signal to break camp.

"They may spear me like a frog," muttered one of the men, sulkily, "if I know what our reverend father intends to do with these unbelieving dogs. He might as well give them a passport to the archfiend, their lord and master."

"Blockhead!" retorted the other; "do you not know that the heretic king's death is to be celebrated with great pomp and state at Ingolstadt? The reverend father intends to hold a grand *auto-da-fé* in honor of the solemn occasion."

The two sleepers rose, half awake; and Bertel recognized, by the faint morning light, the little thick-set Larsson, of the East Bothnians, and his own faithful Pekka. But there was no time for explanations. All three were led out, bound, and packed into a cart; after which the train, consisting of a long line of wounded men and baggage-wagons, under guard of the Croats, set itself slowly in motion.

Bertel now realized that he and his countrymen were prisoners of the Imperialists. His memory soon cleared, and he learned from his companions in misfortune how it had all happened. When the faithful Lappen felt the reins loose, he galloped with his unconscious rider back to the camp. But a swarm of the rapacious Croats were here, com-

mitting their depredations, and when they saw a
Swedish officer dragged half-dead after the horse,
they took him with them in the hope of a good
ransom. Pekka, who would not desert his master,
was taken prisoner at the same time. Larsson, for
his part, had, at the Pappenheimers' attack, ventured too far among the enemy, received a pike
thrust in the shoulder and a wound in the arm,
and being unable to cut his way through, had been
borne along by the stream. Who had conquered,
Larsson did not know with certainty.

It was now the third day after the battle; they
had marched in a southerly direction a day and
night without stopping, and then rested a few hours
in a deserted and plundered village.

"Cursed pack!" exclaimed the little captain,
whose jovial disposition did not abandon him
even in the jolting peasant cart; "if only they hadn't
stolen my flask, so that we might have drank Finland's health together! But these Croats are a
thieving set, compared to which our gypsies at
home are innocent angels. I wish I had a couple
of hundred of them to hang on the ramparts of
Korsholm, as they hang petticoats on the walls of
a Finnish garret."

In the meantime the march continued, with brief
halts, for three or four days, not without great suffering and discomfort for the wounded, who, badly
bandaged, were hindered by their fetters from as-
sisting each other. In the beginning they trav-
eled through a plundered region, where with difficulty they obtained the slightest refreshment, and
where the population everywhere took to flight before the dreaded Croats. But they soon came to
richer sections, where the Catholic inhabitants
showed themselves only to curse the heretics and

exult over their king's fall. The whole Catholic world shared this rejoicing. It is stated that in Madrid brilliant spectacles were performed, in which Gustav Adolf, another dragon, was conquered by Wallenstein, another St. George.

After seven days' tiresome journey, the cart with the captive Finns drove, late one evening, over a clattering draw-bridge, and stopped in a narrow castle yard. The prisoners, still disabled from their wounds, were led out and taken up two crumbling flights of stairs into a turret room in the form of a half-circle. It seemed to Bertel as if he had seen this place before; but darkness and fatigue did not allow him to clearly distinguish objects. The stars shone in through the grated windows. The prisoners were refreshed with a cup of wine, and Larsson exclaimed, joyously:

"I wager that the thieves have stolen their wine from our cellars, while we lay in Würtzburg; for better stuff I never drank!"

"Würtzburg!" exclaimed Bertel, thoughtfully. "Regina!" added he, almost unconsciously.

"And the wine-cellar!" sighed Larsson, mimicking him. "I will tell you something, my dear boy:

'The biggest fool in the world
Is he who believes a girl;
When love, the heart-thief, comes to harry,
Espouse the girl, but the wine-cup marry.'

"As far as Regina is concerned, the black-eyed maiden sits and knits stockings at Korsholm. Yes, yes, Lady Märtha is not one of those who sigh in the moonlight. Since we last met I have had news from Wasa through the jolly sergeant, Bengt Kristerson. He had fought with your father, he said.

10

There is no 'nonsense about the old man; he carried Bengt out at arm's-length, and threw him down the steps there at your home in Storkyro. Bengt swore he would stuff the old man and twelve of his men into the windmill, and grind them to groats; but Meri begged them off. Brave fellow, Bengt Kristerson!—fights like a dragon and lies like a skipper. Your health!"

"What else did you hear from East Bothnia?" asked Bertel, who, with a youth's bashfulness, colored at the thought of revealing to the prosaic friend his life's secret, his love for the dark-eyed, beautiful and unhappy Regina von Emmeritz.

"Not much news, except scant harvests, heavy war-taxes, and conscriptions. The old men on the farm, your father and mine, squabble as usual, and make up again. Meri pines for you, and sings sorrowful songs. Do you remember Katri?—splendid girl; round as a turnip, red as mountain-ash berries, and soft about the chin as a lump of butter. Your health, my boy!—she has run away with a soldier!"

"Nothing else?" said Bertel, abstractedly.

"Nothing else! What the d——l do you want to know, when you don't care for the most buxom girl in all Storkyro? '*Ja, noch etwas,*' says the German. There has been a great fray at Korsholm. The recruits got it into their heads that Lady Regina had tried to kill the king with witchcraft, so they stormed Korsholm, and burned the girl alive. Cursedly jolly!—here's to the heretics! We also know how to get up *autos-da-fé.*"

Bertel started up, forgetting his wounds; but pain overpowered him. Without a sound, he sank fainting in Larsson's arms.

The honest captain became both angry and

troubled. While he bathed Bertel's temples with the wine left in the tankard, and finally brought him to life again, he gave vent to his feelings in the following words — crescendo from piano to forte, from minor to major:

"There, there, Bertel . . . what ails you? Does the devil ride you, boy? Are you in love with the girl? Well, well, calm yourself. Faint like a lady's maid? Courage!—did I say they had burned her? No, my boy, she was only roasted a little, according to what Bengt Kristerson says, and afterward she scratched both eyes out of Lady Märtha and climbed like a squirrel up on top of the castle. Such things happen every day in war. . . Well, you have got your eyes open at last. So you are still alive, you milk-baked wheat-cake! Are you not ashamed, boy, to be like a piece of china? You a soldier? A pretty soldier you are! *Blitzdonnerwetterkreutspappenheim!* you are a pomade-pot, and no soldier! Curse it! now the tankard is empty!"

The little round warrior would undoubtedly have continued to give free reins to his bad humor, especially as he had no longer any consolation in the tankard, had not the door opened and a female form stepped in among the prisoners. At this sight, the captain's puffy although now somewhat pale face brightened perceptibly. Bertel was pushed aside, and Larsson leaned forward, so as to see better; for the light of the single lamp was quite dim. But the result of his survey did not seem especially satisfactory.

"A nun! Ah, by Heaven . . . . to convert us!"

"Peace be with you," sounded a youthful voice, of fresh and agreeable tone, from under the veil. "I am sent here by the reverend prioress of the convent of Our Lady, to bind your wounds, and, if it is the will of the saints, to heal them."

"Upon my honor, beautiful friend, I am very much obliged; let us then become a little better acquainted," replied the captain, somewhat more mildly disposed, and stretched out his hand with the intention of raising the nun's veil. Instantly the latter drew back a few steps; and just then two soldiers, of forbidding aspect, appeared at the door.

"Ah, I understand!" exclaimed Larsson, startled. "The devil! what proud nuns they have here! When I was in Franconia, at Würtzburg, I used to get at least half a dozen kisses a day from the young sisters in the convent; for such sins are never refused absolution. Well," continued the brave captain, when the nun still lingered, hesitating, at the door, "your reverence must not take offence at a soldier's freedom of speech. *Nunquam nemo nasitur caballerus,* says the Spaniard; an honest soldier is born a gallant. Your reverence sees that I, although an unbelieving heretic, can talk Latin like a true monk. When we were at Munich I lived in intimate friendship with a genuine Bavarian nun, twenty-seven years old, brown eyes, Roman nose . . ."

"Hold your tongue!" whispered Bertel, impatiently. "You will drive the nun away."

"I haven't said a word. Walk in, your reverence; don't be frightened. I wager it is a good while since your reverence was twenty-seven. *Posito,* as the Frenchman says, that your reverence is an old granny."

The nun returned in silence, accompanied by

two sisters-in-waiting, and began to examine the wound on Bertel's head, which had been badly dressed. A delicate white hand drew out a pair of scissors and cut off the youth's hair at each side of the broad mark left by Pappenheim's sword. Within twenty minutes Bertel's wounds were dressed by a skilful hand. The youth, touched by this compassion, raised the nun's hand to his lips and kissed it.

"Upon my honor, beautiful matron," cried the voluble captain, "I feel half inclined to be jealous of my friend, who is fifteen years younger than I. Now deign to stretch out your gentle hand and plaster this brave arm, which has conquered the piety of so many pious sisters."

The nun, still without speaking, began to undo the ragged scarf which covered Larsson's wounds. Her hand, in doing this, happened to touch his.

"*Potz donnerwetter!*" burst out the captain, with a connoisseur's surprise. "What a fine, soft little hand! I beg your pardon, amiable lady doctor; *ex ungua leonem*, says Saint Homer, one of the fathers of the church . . . for I also have studied the fathers of the church . . . that is to say, in good Swedish, by the paw one knows the lion. I wager ten bottles of old Rhine wine against a cast-off stirrup, that this little white hand is much better fitted to caress a cavalier's cheek than to finger rosaries night and day."

The nun drew her hand away for an instant, and seemed to hesitate. The gallant captain began to fear the consequences of his gallantry. "I will say nothing more; I am as silent as a Carthusian monk. But I do say, that one who dares to presume that such a soft hand belongs to an old granny . . . well, well, your lovely reverence hears that I am silent."

"*Tempus est consummatum, itur in missam,*" said a sepulchral voice at the door, and the nun hastened to finish dressing the wound. In a few moments the two prisoners were again alone.

"I have heard that voice before," remarked Bertel, thoughtfully. "Are we then surrounded by nothing but mysteries?"

"Bah!" replied the captain, "it was a bald-headed, jealous monk. Bless me, what a sweet little hand!"

CHAPTER II.

TWO OLD ACQUAINTANCES.

THE following morning, as the late autumn sun sent its first rays into the turret-room, Bertel arose and went to take a look out of the narrow grated window. It was a glorious prospect. Below him wound a magnificent stream, on whose further shore lay a town with thirty spires, and beyond were seen a number of still verdant vineyards.

At the first glance, Bertel recognized Würtzburg. Castle Marienburg, where the prisoners were confined, had, at the Swedes' retreat, fallen again into the bishop's hands; but on account of the insecurity of the times, his princely grace had not returned there himself, but remained most of the time in Vienna. The castle had suffered much from the last conquest and the attendant plundering; one tower had been destroyed, and the moat was filled up in several places. At present there were only fifty men in the garrison, but there were sick and wounded, nursed by the sisters of charity from the convent in the town. When Bertel inspected his prison more closely, he thought he recognized Regina's chamber, the same one where the beautiful lady with her maid contemplated the strife, and where the Swedish cannon-ball shattered the image of the saint in the window.* This discovery seemed beyond value to the romantic youth. Here had she stood, the wondrously beautiful unhappy daughter of the prince; here had she slumbered the last night before the assault. It was in Bertel's eyes a sacred place; when he pressed his lips to the cold walls, he fancied that he kissed the traces of Regina's tears.

Like a flash, a strange thought ran through his mind. If the nun who visited them yesterday could have been a disguised princess! . . . if the delicate white hand belonged to—Regina! That would be a miracle, but . . . love believes in miracles. Bertel's heart beat violently. The gentle nurse's care had already greatly improved his neglected wounds. He felt twice as strong already.

His companions in misfortune, tired from the journey, were still asleep. Then the door opened softly, and with noiseless step the nun entered, to bring the wounded men a healing draught. Bertel felt his head swim. Overcome by his violent emotion, he fell on his knees before her.

"Your name, you angel of mercy, who remember the imprisoned!" exclaimed he. "Tell me your name, reveal your face! . . . Ah, I should

* Here the Surgeon seems to have forgotten that Regina's room was in the tower shot down at the seige.—*The Author.*

recognize you among a thousand. . . . You are Regina herself!"

"You are mistaken," said the same fresh voice which Bertel had heard yesterday. It was not Regina's voice, and yet it was a very familiar one; but whose?

Bertel sprang up, and snatched the veil from the nun's head. Before him stood the pretty and gentle Kätchen, with a smiling face. Bertel stepped back, bewildered.

"Impudent one!" said Kätchen, and hastily covered her face. "I had desired to have you under my charge, and you force me to leave my place to another."

Kätchen disappeared. That same day, in the afternoon, a nun again entered the room. Larsson delivered an eloquent harangue, raised her hand to his lips, and pressed upon it a resounding kiss. Then he swore by a million devils, he had kissed an old withered hand, whose surface was like hundred-year-old parchment.

"Verily, my dear Bertel," said the deceived captain, with philosophic resignation, "there are things in nature which must eternally remain an enigma to human sagacity. This hand, for example . . . *manus, mana, manum,* hand, as the old Roman so truly expressed himself . . . this hand, my friend, would undoubtedly occupy a conspicuous place in the Greek poet Ovid's Metamorphoses, which we formerly studied in the cathedral school at Åbo, the time my father wanted to make me a priest. Yesterday I could have pledged my soul that it was a delicate lady's hand; and to-day I will let them shave me into a monk if this hand does not belong to a seventy-year-old washerwoman. *Sic unde ubi apud unquam post,* as they expressed themselves in olden times. That is to say: so can a pretty girl become a witch before any one knows it."

The prisoners' wounds healed rapidly under the careful nursing of the nuns. The dark autumn storm roared around the castle turrets, and the heavy rains beat against the small windows. The vineyards withered; a thick and chilling mist arose from the Main, and obscured the view of the town.

"I can't stand it any longer," grumbled Larsson. "These wretches give us neither wine nor dice. And may Saint Brita forgive me, but the devil may kiss their nuns; I will neither kiss hand nor mouth, for *habeo multum respectum pro matronibus*,—I have much respect for old women. No, I can't stand it, I will jump out of the window..."

"Do it," said Bertel, provoked.

"No, I will not jump out of the window," rejoined the captain. "No my friend, *micus ameus*, as we used to express ourselves.... I shall instead honor this fellow-prisoner of ours with a game of pitch and toss."

And the captain, fertile in resources, was pleased to honor Pekka for the thirtieth time with the monotonous game which constituted his diversion, and which was played with a six öre piece of Charles X.

"Tell me, rather," resumed Bertel, "what they are building there on the square in Würtzburg opposite us?"

"A tavern," answered Larsson. "Heads!"

"It seems to me to look more like a pyre."

"Tails!" repeated Larsson, mechanically. "Plague on it, what ill-luck I have! That cursed

P

Limingo peasant wins from me horse, saddle, and stirrups."

"The first morning of our imprisonment," continued Bertel, "I heard them say something about an *auto-da fé*, in celebration of the battle of Lützen. What do you think of it?"

"I? What should I have against burning a dozen witches, much to our amusement?"

"But if it now concern us? If they were only waiting for the bishop's arrival?"

Larsson opened his small gray eyes, and stroked his goatee. "*Blitzdonnerkreutz!* . . . the miserable Jesuits! They would roast us like turkeys—us, the conquerors of the holy Roman empire! . . It seems to me, friend Bertel, that in such desperate circumstances, *in rebus desperatus*, an honest soldier could not be blamed if he should quietly steal away—for example, through the window . . ."

"It is seventy feet above the Main, and the flood is straight beneath."

"The door?" . . . continued the captain, inquiringly.

"It is guarded night and day by two armed men."

The honest captain sank into melancholy reflections. Time passed; it became afternoon; it became night. The nun with the evening repast was not heard from.

"Festivities begin with fasting," muttered the captain, gruffly. "May I turn into a fish if I don't wring the neck of our neglectful nun the first time she shows herself."

At that instant the door opened and the nun entered, but this time without attendants. Larsson exchanged an expressive glance with his comrades, approached the nun hastily, seized her by the neck, and held her fast against the wall.

"Keep still, like a good child, most reverend abbess," mocked the captain. "If you make a sound, it is all over with you. I ought really to throw you out of the window to swim in the Main, so as to teach you *punctum preciosum*, that is to say, a precise punctuality in your attendance upon us. But I will let grace prevail instead of justice. Tell me only, you most miserable of all meal-bringers, *miserabile pecorale*, what is the meaning of that fire they are preparing on the square, and who is going to be roasted there?"

"For the sake of all the saints, speak low!" whispered the nun, in a scarcely audible voice. "I am Kätchen, and have come to save you. A great danger threatens you. The prince bishop is expected to-morrow, and Father Hieronymus, the implacable enemy of you and all other Finns, has sworn to burn you alive in honor of the saints."

"The little, delicate, soft hand!" exclaimed Larsson, in delight. "Upon my honor, if I was not a booby not to recognize it immediately. Well, then, my charming friend, to Saint Brita's honor I will take a kiss on the spot . . ."

And the captain kept his word. But Kätchen tore herself from him, and said rapidly:

"If you do not behave yourself, young man, you will furnish fuel to the flame, that is certain. Quick, bind me fast to the bed-post and tie a handkerchief over my mouth."

"Bind you fast . . ." replied the captain roguishly.

"Quick! The guards have had wine and are asleep, but in twenty minutes they will be visited by the father himself. Take their cloaks and hasten out. The watchword is 'Peter and Paul.'"

"And you, yourself?" demurred the captain.

"They will find me bound; I have been overpowered and gagged."

"Noble girl! Crown among all Franconia's sisters of charity! Had I not sworn never to marry . . Well, hurry up, Bertel! Hurry, Pekka, you lazy dog! Farewell, little rogue! One more kiss . . . good-by!"

And the three prisoners hastened out.

But scarcely were they outside the door, on the dark spiral staircase, before they felt themselves seized by iron hands, thrown down and bound.

"Take the dogs down to the treasure-room!" said a well-known voice.

It was the voice of the Jesuit Hieronymus.

CHAPTER III.

THE TREASURE-ROOM.

OVERPOWERED and bound hand and foot, the prisoners soon found themselves in the dark, damp dungeon, hewn deep in the rock, where the bishop of Würtzburg had kept his treasure before the Swedes saved him the trouble. No ray of light penetrated into this musty vault, and the moisture from the rocks trickled through the crevices and dripped monotonously on the ground.

"Lightning and Croats! may all demons take you, cursed earless monk!" yelled the captain, when he again felt the firm ground under his feet.

"To shut us up, the officers of his royal majesty and the crown, in such a rat-trap! *Diabolus infernalis multum plus plurimum!* . . Are you alive, Bertel?"

"Yes. In order to be burned alive to-morrow."

"Do you think so, Bertel?" asked the captain, almost sadly. "I know this treasure-room. On three sides is the rock, on the fourth a door of iron, and the man who guards us is harder than rock and iron. Never shall we see Finland again. Never shall I see *her* more . . ."

"Listen to me, Bertel; you are a sensible fellow, but that does not hinder you from sometimes ta king like a milksop. You are in love with the black-haired Regina; well, well, I will say nothing about that: *Amor est valde lurifaxius,*—love is a bandit,—as Ovid so truly expresses himself. But I cannot stand whimpering. If we live, there are enough other girls to kiss; if we die, then we will say good-riddance to them. So you really think that they intend to roast us like plucked woodcocks?"

"That depends upon yourselves!" answered a voice from the darkness. All three prisoners started with affright.

"The evil one is amongst us!" exclaimed Larsson.

Pekka began to say his prayers. Then the clear rays of a dark-lantern pierced the gloom, and all perceived the Jesuit Hieronymus standing alone near the captives.

"It depends upon you," repeated he. "To fly is impossible. Your king is dead, your army is beaten, the whole world acknowledges the power of the church and the emperor. The pile is ready for your bodies to be burned in honor of the saints. But the holy church, in its clemency, has thought of a way of still sparing you, and has sent me here to offer you mercy."

"Indeed!" exclaimed Larsson, mockingly. "Come, reverend father, loose my bonds and let me embrace you. I offer you my friendship, and of course you believe me. How says Seneca?— *homo homini lupus, wir Wölfe sind alle Brüder.*"*

"I offer you mercy," continued the Jesuit, coldly, "on three conditions, which you certainly will not refuse. The first is, that you abjure your heretic faith and publicly join the only saving church."

"Never!" exclaimed Bertel, fiercely.

"Be still!" said the captain. "Well, *posito* that we abjure the Lutheran faith?"

"Then," continued the Jesuit, "you shall, as prisoners of war, be exchanged for the high-born lady and princess Regina von Emmeritz, whom your king tyrannically sent in captivity to the North."

"It shall be done!" answered Bertel, eagerly.

"Be still!" cried Larsson. "Well, go on; *posito* that we accomplish the high-born lady's deliverance?"

"Then there remains but a trifle. I demand of Lieutenant Bertel King Gustaf Adolf's ring."

"Your purse or your life, in highwayman fashion!" said Larsson, derisively.

"You ask what I do not possess," answered Bertel.

The Jesuit looked at him distrustfully.

"The king commanded Duke Bernhard to give you the ring, and you must have received it."

* We wolves are all brothers.

"All this is entirely unknown to me," said Bertel, with perfect truth, but feeling surprised and overjoyed at the unexpected intelligence.

The Jesuit resumed his smiling composure.

"If that is the way the case stands, my dear sons," said he, "let us talk no more about the ring. As far as your conversion to the true church is concerned . . ."

Bertel was about to answer, but was interrupted by the captain, who for some moments had been engaged in a certain rubbing motion with that part of his body not reached by the light of the lantern.

"Yes, so far as that matter is concerned," Larsson hastened to interpose, "you know, reverend father, that there are two sides to it: *questio an* and *questio quomodo*. Now to speak first of *questio an*, my late rector Vincentius Flachsenius used to say, in his time, always place *negare* as *prima regula juris*. Your reverence will undoubtedly find it unexpected and pleasant to hear a royal captain talk Latin like a cardinal. Your reverence ought, therefore, to know that we, in Åbo Cathedral school, studied both Cicero, Seneca, and Ovid, also called Naso. For my part, I have always considered Cicero a great talker, and Seneca a blockhead; but as for Ovid . . ."

The Jesuit moved toward the door, and said, dryly:

"Thus you choose the stake?"

"Rather that than the disgrace of an apostasy!" exclaimed Bertel, who had not noticed Larsson's hints and signs.

"My friend," the captain hastened to add, "my friend thinks, quite sensibly and naturally, that the ugly part of the matter would be the public scandal. Thus, reverend father, let us confer about *questio quomodo.* *Posito* that we become good Catholics, and enter into the emperor's service . . . But deign to come a little nearer; my friend Bertel is rather hard of hearing ever since he had the pleasure of making the acquaintance of the great Pappenheim."

The Jesuit cautiously advanced a few steps closer, yet not without convincing himself by a glance that retreat stood open.

"It is I who decide the manner," said he, haughtily. "Yes or no?"

"Yes, yes, of course," replied Larsson, quickly, as he continued to rub himself. "Consequently we are in clear waters both with *questio an* and *questio quomodo.* Your reverence has a most persuasive eloquence. We now come to *questio ubi* and *questio quando,* for according to *logicam* and *metaphysicam* . . Pardon me, worthy father, I don't have a word of objection; I consent to it all. But," continued the captain, as he lowered his voice, "deign to cast a glance at my friend Bertel's right forefinger. I will tell your reverence, my friend is a great rogue; I am very much mistaken if he does not have the king's ring on at this very moment."

The Jesuit, carried away by his curiosity, came a few steps nearer. Swift as an eel, Larsson, unable to rise on account of his bonds, rolled himself between the Jesuit and the door, and when the monk wished to retreat, he found that the captain had scraped against a sharp stone the ligatures which held his right arm, with which he suddenly embraced the Jesuit's legs, and drew him down over him. Father Hieronymus made desperate efforts to free himself; the lantern was broken into fragments, the light extinguished, and a thick darkness enveloped the wrestlers. Bertel and Pekka, both unable to get up and help, rolled themselves toward the spot, but without reaching it. Then the brave captain felt a sharp pain in his shoulder, and directly afterwards a warm stream of blood. With a *Blitzdonnerkreutz!* he wrenched the dagger from his enemy's hand and returned the stab. The Jesuit now sued for mercy in his turn.

"With the greatest pleasure, my son!" answered the captain, mockingly. "But only on three conditions: the first is, that you abjure Loyola, your lord and master, and declare him a great milksop. Do you agree to it?"

"I agree to everything," sighed the father.

"The second is, that you start off and hang yourself to the first hook you find in the ceiling."

"Yes, yes, only let go of me."

"The third is, that you travel to Beelzebub, your patron saint," . . . and with these words, Larsson flung his enemy violently against the rocky wall, after which the place became quite silent. The dagger was now used hastily to cut the prisoners' bonds, and then it only remained to find the door.

When the three fugitives, after having bolted the door of the treasure-room from without, reached the dark narrow staircase which led to the upper regions of the castle, they stopped a moment to consult together. Their situation was anything but enviable, for they knew of old that the stairs led to the bishop's former bedchamber, from whence two or three parlors had to be crossed before they came to the large armory, and through that to the castle-yard, after which they still had to pass the closed drawbridge and the guard. All the rooms except the bedchamber, which the

Jesuit himself seemed to have taken possession of, had only two hours before, when the prisoners were brought down, been filled partly with soldiers, partly with the sick and their nurses.

"One thing grieves me," whispered Larsson, "and that is that I did not draw the fur off the fox when I held him by the ears. In the garments of piety I could have gone scot-free through purgatory, like another *Saulus inter prophetas*. But as it is, my friend Bertel, I ask, in my simplicity: how shall we get away from here?"

"We will fight our way through. The garrison are asleep; the darkness of night favors us."

"I confess, my friend, that if anybody, even were it I, Larsson himself, should call you a coward, I would call that fellow a liar. It is true that you once, as good as *solo*, alone, *alienus*, all by yourself, took this castle; but you had then at least a sword in your hand and a few thousand brave boys in the rear. . . . Hush! I hear a tread on the stairs;—no, it was nothing. Let us push on cautiously. Here it stands one in need to tread like a maiden: that stupid Limingo peasant tramps as if we had a squadron of cavalry at our heels."

The fugitives had ascended about thirty or forty steps, and the way still led upward, when a faint ray of light glimmered at the top of the passage. They came to a door, which stood ajar. They stopped and held their breath; not a sound was heard. The brave captain now ventured to push in his head, then his foot, and finally his whole stout person.

"We are on the right track," whispered he; "boots off! the whole company must march in stockings—*posito* that the company has stockings. March!"

The bishop's bedchamber, which the three now entered on tip-toe, was a large and once magnificent room. A flickering lamp dimly illumined the precious Gobelin tapestry, the gilded images of the saints, and the ebony bedstead, inlaid with pearl, where the rich prelate used to fall asleep with his goblet of Rhine wine beside him. No living creature was to be seen; but from one of the windows which overlooked the court-yard they could see the castle chapel opposite brilliantly lighted, and filled with people. Even the castle-yard, which was lighted by the reflection from the windows, was thronged with people, many of whom carried candles in their hands.

"I will let them salt and pickle me like cucumbers in a jar, if I understand what all those people are doing here in the middle of the night," muttered the captain testily. Perhaps they have come to see three honest Finnish soldiers roasted by a slow fire like Åland herrings!"

"We must look for weapons, and die like men," said Bertel, as he searched through the room. "Hurrah!" exclaimed he, "here are three swords, just what we need."

"And three daggers," added Larsson, who, in a large niche behind the image of a saint, had found a small arsenal of all sorts of weapons. "The reverend fathers have a weakness for daggers, as the East Bothnians have for their sheath-knives."

"I think," joined in the close-mouthed Pekka, as he caught sight of a good-sized flask in a corner, "I think that as it is Christmas night . . . ."

"Brave boy!" interrupted the captain, inspired by this prospect; "you have a remarkable scent when it is a question of something to drink. Pious Jesuit! you have accomplished some good in the world! Christmas night, did you say? Blockhead! why didn't you tell us at once? It is as clear as day, that half Würtzburg is streaming to the castle to hear Father Hieronymus say mass. By my honor, I am afraid he will make them wait some time, the good pater. Here goes, my friend; I drink to you; an officer ought always to set his troops a good example. Your health my boys... Damnation!... the miserable monk has cheated us; I have swallowed poison; I am a dead man!" And the honest captain became pale as a corpse.

But both Bertel and Pekka had hard work to restrain their laughter, notwithstanding their dangerous situation, when they saw Larsson at once white from fright and black from the fluid he had drank and spilled over himself.

"Be more moderate another time," said Bertel, "and you will avoid drinking ink."

"Ink! I might have known that the carless scrawler would be up to some deviltry. Two things trouble me to-night more than all *autos-da-fé*: that the sweet Kätchen, with the soft hand, deceived us, and that I have swallowed the most useless stuff in the world—ink. Bah!"

"If we had nothing else to do, I could show you something that ink has done," rejoined Bertel, as he hastily turned over a pile of papers on the writing-table. "Here is a letter from the princely bishop... he is coming to-morrow... we are to be solemnly burned... they will tempt us to abjure our faith, and promise us grace... but burn us, nevertheless! Infamous!"

"Roman fashion!" observed the captain, phlegmatically.

In the meantime Larsson had drawn out three

monks' cloaks; they put them on, and now ventured to proceed farther in the dangerous regions. The next two rooms were empty. Two rude beds gave evidence that some serving brothers had their abode here, and were now gone to mass.

"Bravo!" whispered Larsson, "they will take us for sheep in wolves' clothing, and believe that we also are going to attend mass.... Hark! didn't you hear something?—a woman's voice? Be quiet!"

They stopped, and heard in the darkness a young female voice, praying:

"Holy Virgin, forgive me this time, and save me from death; I will to-morrow take the veil, and serve you all my life!"

"It is Kätchen's voice!" said the captain. "Can it be that she is innocent, poor child? Upon my honor, it would be base of a cavalier not to rescue a sweet girl with such a soft hand!"

"Let us be off!" whispered Bertel, in vexation. But the captain had already found a little door, bolted on the outside; beyond the door was a cell, and in that cell was a trembling girl. Her eyes, accustomed to the darkness, distinguished the monk's garb; she threw herself at the captain's feet, and exclaimed:

"Grace, my father, grace! I will confess all; I have favored the prisoners' flight, I have given wine to the guard. But spare my life, have mercy upon me for the saints' sake! I am so young. I do not wish to die yet!"

"Who the devil has said that you shall die, my brave girl?" interrupted the captain. "No, you shall live, with your soft hand and your warm lips, as true as I am not a Jesuit, but Lars Larsson, captain in the service of his royal majesty and the crown and herewith take you . . . as my wedded wife, for better or for worse," continued the captain, undoubtedly because he considered that the well-known formula must be said to an end when he once began it.

"Away, away! with or without the girl, but away!—they are coming, and we still have to pass the large armory!"

"Allow me to tell you, my friend, Bertel, that you are the greatest fiddle-faddle I know; *maximus fiescus*, as the ancients so truly expressed themselves. How is it, my girl, you are not a nun, but only a novice? Well, it is all the same to me. You shall be my wedded wife, in case I ever marry. Here is a cloak; there now, put that on and look bold."

"It is no cloak, it is a mass-robe," whispered Kätchen, who had scarcely time to recover from her amazement.

"The deuce! a mass-robe! Wait; you take my cloak and I will take the robe. I will chant *dies iræ*, in their ears so that they all will be astonished."

The sound of several voices in the armory outside interrupted the captain in his priestly meditations.

"They have missed the Jesuit; they are looking for him, and we are lost through your silly nonsense," whispered Bertel, in exasperation. "We must now be careful not to betray ourselves. Come along, all of you."

"And the Latinist first!" exclaimed the captain.

All four went out. In the armory were some thirty sick-beds, but only two sisters in attendance. This sight was reassuring, but all the more dangerous was the meeting with the two monks, who stood in excited altercation close by the door. When they saw Larsson in the mass-robe, and behind him three figures in cloaks, the pious fathers were greatly startled. The captain raised his arms to bless them, uttered a solemn *pax vobiscum*, and was about to steal by with a grave step when he was checked by the foremost monk.

"Reverend father," said the latter, as he closely eyed the unknown prelate from head to foot, "what procures our castle this honor at so unusual a time?"

"*Pax vobiscum!*" repeated the captain devoutly. "The pious Father Hieronymus commands you to say mass the best you know how. . . . His reverence is sick . . . he has toothache."

"Let us seek his reverence," said one of the monks, entering the smaller room. But the other seized Larsson by the robe, and looked at him in a way which did not at all please the brave captain.

"*Quis vus e, quid eltis!*" repeated the captain, nonplussed. "*Qui quoe quod, meus tuus suus* . . . go to the devil, you bald-headed baboons!" roared Larsson, unable to restrain himself longer, and pushed the resisting monks into the chamber and bolted the door. Then all four hastened down to the court-yard. Behind them arose a great outcry; the monks shouted with all their might, the nuns joined in, and soon the attention of the crowd of people who thronged the court-yard began to be attracted.

"We are lost," whispered Kätchen, "unless we can reach the drawbridge by the back way."

They hastened there. The tumult increased. They passed the guard at the large sally-port.

"Halt! Who goes there?"

"*Peter and Paul*," answered Bertel, promptly. They passed out. Fortunately the drawbridge was down. But the whole castle was now in alarm.

"Let us jump into the river; the night is dark; they will not find us!" cried Bertel.

"No," said Larsson, "I will not leave my girl, if it should cost me my neck."

"Here stand three saddled horses! Be quick!"

"Up, you sweetest of all the nuns in Franconia! up in the saddle!" and the agile captain swung the trembling Kätchen before him on the horse's back. They all galloped away in the darkness. But behind them was tumult and uproar; the alarm-bells sounded in all the turrets, and the whole of Würtzburg wondered what could have happened on this Christmas night.

CHAPTER IV.

THE DUKE AND THE LIEUTENANT.

ONE spring day in March, 1633,—three months after the events narrated in the last chapter —we find Lieutenant Bertel in an ante-chamber of the little military court which the Duke Bernhard of Weimar held sometimes at Cassel, sometimes at Nassau, or at other places where the cares of war brought him. Adjutants came and went, orders flew in all directions, for the duke had a large portion of southern and western Germany as his department, and the times were very troublous.

After waiting a long time, the young officer

was conducted to the duke. The latter looked up distractedly from his charts and papers, and seemed to expect to be addressed. But Bertel kept silent.

"Who are you?" said Duke Bernhard, abruptly and harshly.

"Gustaf Bertel, lieutenant in his royal majesty's Finnish cavalry."

"What do you want?"

The youth colored, and made no reply. The duke perceived this, and regarded him with displeased looks.

"I understand," said the latter at length; "you have, as usual, been duelling with the German officers on account of the girls. I will not tolerate such things. A soldier should reserve his weapon for his fatherland."

"I have not been fighting, your highness."

"So much the worse. Then you come to ask a furlough to Finland. You remain, lieutenant. Good-morning."

"I do not come to ask a furlough."

"Indeed; then what the deuce do you come for? Can you not speak out, sir, quick and short! Leave it to priests to make prayers, and to girls to blush."

"Your highness has received a ring from his majesty the late king . . ."

"I do not remember it."

". . . which his majesty requested your highness to deliver to an officer of his life-guard."

The duke passed his hand over his high brow.

"The officer is dead," said he.

"That officer am I, your highness. Wounded at Lützen, I was directly afterwards taken prisoner by the Imperialists."

Duke Bernhard beckoned Bertel nearer, looked

at him searchingly, and seemed satisfied with his examination.

"Close the door," said he, "and seat yourself here at my side."

Bertel obeyed. His cheeks glowed with anxiety.

"Young man," said the duke, "on your brow you bear witness of your origin, and I ask no further proof. Your mother is a peasant's daughter, of Storkyro, in Finland, called Emerentia Aronsdotter Bertila."

"No, your highness. The person you mention is my elder sister, born of my father's first marriage. I have never seen my mother."

The duke looked at him with surprise.

"Very well," said he, doubtfully, as he hastily glanced through some papers in his portfolio; "we will, however, speak of this *sister* of yours, Emerentia Aronsdotter. Her father had rendered great service to King Charles IX., and was urged to request some sign of favor. He asked to be allowed to send his daughter, then his only child, to Stockholm, in order to be educated with young ladies of rank at the court."

"I know little about that."

"At thirteen years of age, the young peasant girl was sent to Stockholm, where her father's vanity and wealth procured her a residence, dress, and education, far above her rank. He burned with ambition; and as he himself could not gain a noble crest, he depended upon his daughter's high birth on her mother's side, for Bertila's first wife was an orphan girl of the family Stjernkors, deprived of her inheritance through the war, and then disowned by her haughty family on account of her marriage with the rich peasant Bertila."

"All this is unknown to me."

"The young Emerentia suffered very much in Stockholm from the envy and derision of her aristocratic companions, for many of them were poorer than she and could not endure to see a plebeian placed at their side as an equal. But her beauty was as extraordinary as her goodness and intelligence. Within two years she had acquired the refined habits of the best circles, while she preserved the rustic simplicity of her heart. This rare union of mental and physical graces reminded old persons of a lovely image from their youth . . . Karin Månsdotter."

At these words the duke gave the young man a sharp glance. But Bertel's expression did not change. All this was to him new and incomprehensible.

"Well," continued the duke, after a pause, "this beauty was not long unobserved. A very young man of high birth speedily fell in love with the beautiful maiden, who was then only fifteen, and she returned his attachment with all the devotion of first love. This attachment did not long remain unobserved by those around the patrician youth; policy trembled, and the pride of the nobility felt itself offended by this distinction bestowed upon a girl of low birth. They resolved to marry the young girl to an officer, like herself of humble origin, but distinguished for his valor in the Danish war. This intelligence came to the ears of the young couple. Poor children! they were so young, he seventeen, she fifteen, both inexperienced, and in love. Shortly afterward the young man went to the war in Poland; the young girl's marriage came to naught, and she was sent back by the offended nobility to her cabins in Finland, in disgrace. Do you wish to know anything more, Lieutenant Bertel?"

"I do not understand, your highness, what the account of my sister's life has to do with . . ."

". . . the ring you ask for? Patience. When the young man left for the war, and for the last time had a secret meeting with his beloved, she gave him a ring, whose earlier history I do not know, but which was supposed to have been forged by a Finnish sorcerer, and to have all the qualities of an amulet. She conjured her lover to constantly wear this ring on his finger in danger and in war, as he would thus become invulnerable. Twice was this warning forgotten; once at Dirschau . . ."

"Great God!"

". . . and the second time at Lützen."

Bertel's emotion was so violent that the blood all left his cheeks, and he stood pale as a marble statue.

"Young man, you now know a part of what you ought to know, but you do not yet know all. We have hitherto spoken of your sister; we will now speak of you. It was his majesty's intention to offer you a nobleman's coat of arms, which your brave sword had so well earned. But the old Aaron Bertila, actuated by his hatred of the nobility, solicited as a favor that the king would give you opportunity of gaining any other distinction, but not allow you to accept a noble name. The king could not refuse this entreaty from a father . . . and therefore you are still a commoner by name. But I, who am not bound by any promise to your father, I offer you, young man, what has heretofore been refused you—the spur and escutcheon of a knight."

"Your highness . . . this favor makes me dumb; how have I deserved it?"

Duke Bernhard smiled with a strange expression.

"How? My friend, you have only half understood me."

Bertel said nothing.

"Very well; with or without your knowledge or will, I regard you already as a nobleman. We will talk together about it another time. Your ring . . ah . . I have forgotten it. Do you remember how it looked?" And the duke looked zealously in his portfolio.

"They say that the king wore a copper ring, on the inside of which were engraved magic signs, and the letters R. R. R."

"It is possible that I have mislaid it, for I cannot find it. But who the deuce has time to think about such childish things? The ring must have been stolen from my private casket. If I find it again, you shall have it. If not, you know that which is worth more. Go, young man; be worthy my confidence and the great king's memory! No one ought to know what I have told you. Farewell; we shall see each other again."

CHAPTER V.

RECONCILIATION.

ONCE more we hasten from spring in Germany back to winter in the North. Before we proceed farther in the bloody path of the Thirty Years' War, we will make a visit to two of the

chief persons in this narrative, high up in East
Bothnia.

It was at Advent time, 1632. A violent storm,
mingled with flurries of snow, beat against the old
ramparts of Korsholm, and drove the autumnal
waves of the Baltic against the ice-bound shore.
Navigation for the year was over; no one crossed
that stormy sea. The newly conscripted recruits
had, at the end of July, left for Stralsund, by way
of Stockholm. News from the seat of war was impatiently awaited. Suddenly, in the middle of
November, a rumor spread through the country
that the king was dead. Such rumors fly through
the air, no one knows how or from whence: great
misfortunes, like presentiments, are known at a
long distance; as a remote earthquake, far beyond
its circle, causes a qualm in the mind. But this
report had more than once before been both circulated and refuted; people relied on King Gustaf
Adolf's good fortune; and as corroboration failed
to come, they forgot the story in the belief that it
was false.

It is a common experience in life, that, as we
hate those to whom we have done a wrong, we feel
kindly disposed toward persons to whom we have
had an opportunity of doing good. Lady Märtha
was not a little proud of her brave defence of
Korsholm against the drunken soldiers, and did
not neglect to attribute the preservation of the
castle to the heroism she had then displayed. That
she had saved Regina's life, gave the latter a great
importance in her eyes; but neither could she refuse her admiration to the courage and self-sacrifice which the young girl had shown on that occasion. The high-born prisoner was her pride; she
did not omit to watch all her steps like an Argus,

but she gave Regina a finer room, let her have old Dorthe again as a waiting woman, and provided her with an abundance of good food. Regina had grown somewhat less proud and cold; she could sometimes answer Lady Märtha with a word or a nod; but of all the nice things that were offered her—the choice meats and beer, and many other delicacies—she took little or nothing. She had sunk into an apparent indifference; she told her beads devoutly, but in other respects let one day pass like another.

Lady Märtha held the deep conviction that her prisoner, if not exactly the Roman emperor's own daughter, was yet a princess of the highest birth. She therefore hit upon the unlucky idea of trying to convert so distinguished a person from her papist heresy, in the supposition that she would thereby accomplish something very remarkable when the war ended and Regina was exchanged. Thus Regina became exposed to the same proselyting attempts which she herself had undertaken with the great Gustaf Adolf, but Lady Märtha's zeal was of a grosser and more awkward sort. She overwhelmed the poor girl with Lutheran sermons, psalm-books, and tracts, occasionally made her long speeches interspersed with proverbs, and when she found this was without avail she sent the castle chaplain to preach to the prisoner. Of course all this fell upon deaf ears. Regina was sufficiently firm in her faith to listen with patience, but she suffered from it; her stay at Korsholm became each day more unendurable; and who can blame her if she sighed with secret longing for the day when she should regain her freedom?

Dorthe, on the contrary, flamed up every time the heretic preacher or the plucky old lady began with their sermons, and rattled through a whole string of prayers and maledictions both in Latin and Low Dutch, the result of which was usually that she was shut up for two or three days in the dungeon of the castle, until the longing for her mistress made her manageable. And so passed a half year of Regina's captivity.

A better result of Lady Märtha's good-will was that Regina was allowed to embroider, and that fine materials were ordered for her in the autumn from Stockholm. Thus it became possible for her to embroider a large piece of silk with the Virgin Mary and the Infant Christ in silver and gold. Märtha, in her innocence, considered the work an altar-cloth, which Regina possibly might present to Wasa church, as a proof of her change of sentiments. A warrior's eyes, on the other hand, would have discerned in it an intended flag, a banner of the Catholic faith, which the imprisoned girl quietly prepared, in expectation of the day when it should wave at the head of the Catholic hosts.

Still, Lady Märtha was not quite satisfied with the Holy Virgin Mary's image, which seemed to her surrounded by too large a halo to be truly Lutheran. She was therefore considering how she could find for her prisoner a more suitable occupation. It happened now and then that Meri, the daughter of the Storkyro peasant king, when she was in town, made an errand to Korsholm, and, in order to gain the favor of the lady of the castle, presented her with several skeins of the silkiest linen floss, which none in the whole region could spin so well as Meri. Lady Märtha consequently took the notion one fine day to permit her prisoner to learn to spin, and gave her Meri as a teacher in this art. Meri in her heart desired nothing better.

The near connection in which the imprisoned lady had stood to the king, gave her an unsurpassable interest in Meri's eyes. She wished to hear something about him—the hero, the king, the great, never-to-be-forgotten man, who stood before her memory in more than earthly splendor. She wished to know what he had said, what he had done, what he had loved and what hated on earth; she wished for once to feel herself transported by his glory, and then die herself, forgotten. Poor Meri!

So Meri made her second acquaintance with Lady Regina in the castle. She was at first received with coldness and indifference, and her spinning scarcely pleased the proud young lady. But gradually her mild and submissive demeanor won Regina's good-will, and a captive's natural desire to communicate with beings outside the prison walls finally caused her heart to open. They spun very little, it is true, but they talked together like mistress and servant, especially during the days when Dorthe was shut up for her vicious tongue; and it was quite opportune that Meri recalled from former and brighter days some knowledge of the German tongue. Meri well knew how to lead the conversation toward one subject—the king; and Meri was quick-sighted; she soon divined Regina's enthusiastic love. But Regina was far from having any suspicion of Meri's earlier life; she attributed her questions to the natural curiosity which such lofty objects always excite in the uncultivated. Sometimes she seemed astonished at the delicacy and nobility of the simple peasant woman's expressions and views. There were moments when Meri's personality appeared to her an enigma full of contradictions; and then she asked herself whether she ought not to consider this woman a spy. But the next instant she repented this thought; when the spinner looked at her with her clear, mild, penetrating gaze, something convinced Regina's heart of her sincerity.

They were both sitting thus one day in the beginning of December, while Dorthe was again locked up for unseasonable remarks to the chaplain. There was a bright contrast between these two beings, whom fate had brought together from such different spheres, but who on one point shared the same interest. The first, young, beautiful, proud, dark, flashing, a princess even in her captivity; the other, of middle age, blond, pale, delicate, mild, humble, free, yet submissive. Regina, now seventeen years of age, might have been thought twenty; Meri, thirty-six, had in her whole appearance something so childlike and innocent that at certain moments she might have been thought seventeen. She might have been Regina's mother; and yet, although she had suffered so much, she seemed almost like a child in comparison with the early matured Southerner at her side.

Lady Regina had spun for some time, and had broken many threads. Vexed and impatient, she pushed the distaff away and resumed her embroidery. This had happened so often that her teacher had become accustomed to it.

"What a pretty picture!" said Meri, looking at the piece of silk. "What does it represent?"

"God's Holy Mother, *Sancta Maria,*" answered Regina, making the sign of the cross, as she was always in the habit of doing when she mentioned the Holy Virgin.

"And what is it for?" asked Meri, with a *naïve* familiarity.

Regina looked at her. Again a suspicion arose in her mind, but it immediately passed away.

"I am embroidering the banner of the holy faith for Germany," replied Regina, frankly and boldly. "When it shall wave, the heretics will flee before the wrath of the Mother of God."

"When I think of the Mother of God," said Meri, "I always imagine her as mild, and good, and peaceful; I imagine her as a mother, transcending in her love." Meri said these words with a peculiar tremor in her voice.

"The Mother of God is heaven's queen; she will contend against the godless and destroy them."

"But when the Mother of God takes to strife, King Gustaf Adolf will meet her with uncovered head and lowered sword, bend his knee to her, and say: 'Holy Virgin, I am not fighting for thy glory, but for that of thy Son, our Saviour.' And then the Holy Mary will smile and answer: 'One who fights for my Son also fights for me; for I am a mother.'"

"Your king is a heretic," answered Lady Regina, excitedly; for nothing irritated her so much as opposition to the Catholic faith, of which the doctrine of the Virgin Mary as heaven's ruler is a characteristic part. "Your king is a tyrant and an unbeliever, who draws all the anger of the saints upon his head. Do you know, Merchen, that I hate your king?"

"And I love him," said Meri, in a scarcely audible voice.

"Yes," continued Regina, "I hate him like death, sin, and perdition. If I were a man and had an arm and a sword, it would be the aim of my life to destroy his army and his work. You are fortunate, Merchen; you know nothing about war; you do not know what Gustaf Adolf has done to us poor Catholics. But I have seen it, and my country and my faith cry for revenge. There are moments when I feel that I could kill him."

"And when Lady Regina raises her white hand with the gleaming dagger over the king's head, then the king will expose his breast, where the great heart beats, look at her with a glance of sublimity and calmness, and say: 'Thou delicate white hand, which worketh the picture of the Mother of God, strike, if thou canst; my heart is here, and it beats for the freedom and enlightenment of the world.' And then the white hand will sink slowly down, the dagger will drop from it unperceived, and the Holy Virgin's picture on the banner will smile again, for she knew full well that it would be so; it would have been just the same with herself. For none can kill and none hate King Gustaf Adolf, because God's angel walks at his side and turns human hatred into love."

Regina forgot her work, and looked at Meri with her large, dark, moist eyes. There was much that surprised and moved her in these words. But she kept silent. Presently she said:

"The king wears an amulet."

"Yes," said Meri, "he wears an amulet; but it is not the copper ring, of which people speak; it is his exalted human heart, which renounces everything for truth and nobleness. When he was quite young, and had neither name nor renown, only his blond hair, his high brow, and his mild blue eyes, he wore no amulets; and yet blessing and love and happiness went by his side. All the angels in heaven and all beings on earth loved him."

Regina's black eyes glistened with tears.

"Did you see him when he was young?" said she.

"Did I see him? Yes."

"And did you love him, as did all the others?"

"More than all the others, my lady."

"And you love him still?"

"Yes, I love him . . . much. Like you. But you would kill him, and I would die for him."

Regina sprang up, weeping, clasped Meri in her arms and kissed her.

"Do not think that I wish to kill him. . . . I— O Holy Virgin!—I, who a thousand times would have given my life to save his! But, Merchen, you cannot understand the torture, the heartrending anguish, of loving a man, a hero, the personification of what is highest and grandest in life, and yet being commanded by a holy faith to hate this man, to kill him, to persecute him to the grave! You do not know, happy one, who only need to love and bless, what it means to be tossed between love and hate, like a ship on high waves; to be forced to curse one whom you must bless even in death, and then to sit within the walls of a prison, a prey to the conflicting feelings which incessantly strive for supremacy in your innermost soul. Ah, there was a night when I tried to reconcile my love with my faith, and to lead him, the mighty one, in the way of blessedness. If the saints had allowed my weak voice to overcome his unbelief, then the poor Regina would have followed him with joy as his humblest slave, his whole life through, and received in her breast all the lances and balls which sought his heart. But the saints did not grant me, unworthy one, so great an honor; and therefore I now sit here, a prisoner on account of my faith and my love; and even if an angel broke down the

prison walls and said to me: 'Fly! your country
awaits you!' then I would answer: 'It is his will,
the beloved for whose sake I suffered and for whose
sake I remain.' . . . And you still believe that I
wish to kill him!"

Regina wept long and bitterly, with all the violence of a passion which, long repressed, suddenly
bursts into flame. Meri stroked the black locks
from her brow, looked mildly and tenderly into
the tearful eyes, and said, with prophetic inspiration: "Do not weep; the day will come when you
will be able to love him without cursing him."

"That day will never come, Merchen!"

"Yes, the day will come, when King Gustaf
Adolf is dead."

"Oh, then may it never come! Rather would
I suffer all my life; since it is for his sake."

"Yes, lady, the day will come. Not because
you are young and he is older. But have you
never heard it said of a child who was gentler and
better than other children: 'It will not live long,
it is too good for this world!' So it seems to me
about King Gustaf Adolf. He is too great, too
noble, too good, to live long. God's angels wish
to have him before his body withers and his soul
grows weary. Believe me, they will take him
from us."

Regina looked at her, almost terrified.

"Who are you, who speak such words? . . .
How your eyes glitter! You are not the one you
seem. Who are you, then? . . . Oh, Holy Virgin,
protect me!"

And Regina started up, with all the superstition which belonged to her time. Doubtless she
could not have accounted for her fear; but Meri's
conversation had from the first seemed strange to

her, coming from the mouth of an uncultivated peasant woman in this barbarous land.

"Who am I?" repeated Meri, with unchanged mildness. "I am a woman who loves; that is all."

"And you say the king will die?"

"God alone prevails over human destiny, and the greatest among mortals is still but mortal."

At this moment some one turned the key of the door, and Lady Märtha entered, more solemn than usual, and also somewhat paler. She wore, instead of her bright striped woolen jacket, a deep mourning attire, and her whole appearance indicated something unusual. Regina and Meri both started at the sight.

Meri became pale as death, went straight to Lady Märtha, looked her sharply in the face, and said, monotonously, with great effort:

"*The king is dead!*"

"You know it already?" answered Lady Märtha, surprised. "God preserve us! the bad news came an hour ago by a courier from Torneå."

Regina sank down in a swoon.

Meri, although her heart was breaking, retained her self-possession, and tried to restore Regina.

"The king has then fallen on the battle-field, in the midst of victory?" asked she.

"On the battlefield at Lützen, the sixth of November, and in the midst of a glorious victory," replied Lady Märtha, more and more surprised at Meri's knowledge of the events.

"Awake, gracious lady," said Meri to Regina; "he has lived and died like a hero, worthy the admiration of the whole world. He has fallen in the hour of triumph, in the highest lustre of his glory; his name will live in all times, and this name we will both bless."

Regina opened her dreamy eyes, and clasped her hands in prayer. "Oh, Holy Virgin," said she, "I thank thee that thou hast let him go in his greatness from the world, and thus taken away the curse which rested upon my love!"

And Meri kneeled at her side in prayer.

But below, in the castle-yard, stood a tall white-haired old man, his hard features distorted by grief and despair.

"Curse upon my work!" said he. "My plan is frustrated beforehand, and the object for which I have lived slips from my grasp. Oh, fool that I was to count upon a human being's life-thread—to hope that the king would acknowledge his own, and live until the son of Aaron Bertila's daughter had time to win a brilliant fame in war, and ascend to the Swedish throne! The king is dead, and my descendant is only a boy, who will soon be lost among the crowd. Now it is only wanting for him to obtain a nobleman's coat of arms and place himself with the rest of the vampires between the only true powers of the state, the king and the people. Fool, fool that I was! The king is dead! Go, old Bertila, into the grave—to the fratricide King John, and the destroyer of aristocracy, King Charles, and bury thy proud plans among the same worms which have already consumed Prince Gustaf and Karin Månsdotter!"

And the old man seized Meri, who just then came out, violently by the hand, and said:

"Come, now we have neither of us anything more to do in the world!"

"Yes," said Meri, with suppressed grief, "we both have still a son!"

CHAPTER VI.

THE BATTLE OF NÖRDLINGEN.

THE Swedish lion had hitherto, through the agency of Gustaf Adolf and his men, advanced from victory to victory, overthrowing all adversaries by his tremendous blows. But the day of misfortune came at last, in a great and murderous battle, wherein the Swedish arms suffered a bloody defeat.

Wallenstein, the insatiable yet indispensable, had died a traitor's death in Eger. Gallas, the destroyer of armies, overran middle Germany, took Regensburg, and advanced against the free city of Nördlingen, in Swabia. Duke Bernhard and Gustaf Horn hurried with the Swedish army to its defence. They had only seventeen thousand men, while Gallas had thirty-three thousand.

"Let us attack," said the duke.
"Let us wait," said Horn.

They expected five thousand men as a reinforcement; and fourteen days elapsed. Then Nördlingen needed supplies, and began to signal with beacon fires on the towers at night. Again the duke wished to attack; again Horn preferred to fortify himself and relieve the city without battle. They called him, the brave man, a coward; and, indignant, but with dark forebodings, he resolved to fight. But the Swedes went to the conflict confident of victory; for repeated successes had made them over-bold.

The battle was fought on the 24th of August, 1634. Outside Nördlingen are forest-crowned heights called Arensberg, and between these and the city is a smaller height. Upon the latter the Imperialists had constructed three earthworks.

The Swedish army occupied Arensberg; Horn on the right and the duke on the left wing. The watchword was the same as at Breitenfeld and Lützen: *God with us!*

Early in the morning a heavy rain fell. Once more the prudent Horn wished to wait, but the duke was in command, and ordered an advance. Horn obeyed, and the right wing marched down into the valley between the heights. The impatience of the cavalry hastened the attack. From the very beginning, it was unfavorable. The Imperialists' cannon in the earthworks made breaches in the ranks of the cavalry, and the enemy's superior force compelled them to retire. Horn sent two brigades to storm the middle earthwork. They took it, and pursued the enemy. Piccolomini checked their course, and drove them back to the earthworks. There the powder happened to take fire. With a deafening explosion the earthworks flew into the air, and several hundred Swedes and Finns with it. This was the first calamity.

Upon this position, however, depended the victory. For a moment the spot was vacant; Piccolomini's soldiers, frightened by the report and the destruction, could not be persuaded to go there. Finally they did so. Horn asked for help, in order to expel them. The duke sent the young Bohemian, Thurn, with his yellow regiment. He made a mistake, attacked the wrong earthwork, and engaged with a largely superior force. Seventeen times he attacked the enemy, and as often was he repulsed. In vain did Horn storm the height. Thurn's error was the second calamity.

On the left wing the duke had begun the battle against the artillery and cavalry. At the first encounter the Imperialists were repulsed, and the duke's German cavalry pursued them with loose rein and disordered ranks. But Tilly's spirit seemed that day to give the Imperialists new courage. They opposed their well-ordered and superior ranks to the assailants, checked them, and drove them back with loss. The duke tried to get reinforcements into Nördlingen, but failed. In vain did he drive Gallas before him. New masses of the enemy constantly blocked his way, and in his rear the Croats plundered his baggage-wagons.

It was about noon. Horn's troops had endured the fire of the enemy for eight consecutive hours, and were worn out with wounds and fatigue. With every hour their hopes of victory sank, but their courage remained the same, unflinching and persistent. They had observed the disorder in their left wing. Down in the valley things were in a desperate condition. Piccolomini's bullets every instant fell in the underbrush, and sprinkled the sundered branches with blood. Then Horn proposed to withdraw to Arensberg, and the duke, who was in distress, was obliged at last to consent. He considered the matter nearly two hours; and these two hours he would afterwards have been willing to buy back with his own blood.

It was three o'clock in the afternoon. Horn ordered the Finnish cavalry to make a feigned attack, so as to cover the retreat, and began, like a prudent general, to withdraw in good order. The Imperialists perceived his intention, and pressed on with double force. They began to hope, what they had never dared to hope before, that even the Swedes might be conquered; and Piccolomini's dumpy figure flew through the ranks, urging his men to bear down with their collected forces upon the unprotected sides of the Swedish columns, open them, and crush them.

In the valley behind the Swedes, and between the heights, flowed a stream with steep banks, and swollen from abundant rains. At the little village of Hirnheim the stream was spanned by a single bridge, and this point Horn had guarded in good season, in order to secure the retreat. The artillery passed first over the bridge, and reached Arensberg heights in safety. The first columns of Horn's division had also reached Hirnheim and the rest were only a short distance from it, when a new calamity occurred—the third and most disastrous of this day of calamities. Duke Bernhard had undertaken to check the enemy with his division, until Horn and his men had crossed the stream. But too soon he discovered that in this he had consulted his bravery rather than his prudence. The enemy's forces became more and more concentrated, and their attack increased in violence. Three times De Werth charged the duke's cavalry; three times was he repulsed. The fourth time he broke through the duke's lines. The latter sent a squadron to take him in the flank. In vain. Beside himself with rage, the duke snatched his gold-embroidered banner from an ensign's hand, and, followed by his bravest men, rushed into the thickest ranks of the enemy. All in vain. His brave men fell, his horse was shot from under him, the banner was torn from his hand; wounded and overpowered, he came near being taken prisoner, when a young officer at his side gave him his horse, and he escaped with difficulty. His foot-soldiers had already fled, unable to contend against the cavalry on the plain; and when the duke galloped away, bleeding, and with loose reins, the whole division followed him in the wildest flight, believing that all was lost.

Just at this moment, Horn's infantry crossed the narrow bridge. Then arose from the rear confused cries that the battle was lost and the enemy close at their heels. First, single horsemen, then whole squads of the duke's cavalry, rushed along the road to the bridge, rode in among the foot soldiers, trampled some under their horses' feet, and threw the rest into terrible confusion. Horn tried to make his voice heard, his nearest officers tried to stay the horsemen's frantic course; but without avail. On the narrow bridge everything was crowded pell-mell: men, horses, wagons, the dead and living together; and finally the duke's whole division rushed to this fatal spot. Like lightning Piccolomini's division was in the wake of the fugitives; he sent some light cannons up on the heights, discharging them among the thickest masses of human beings, where every ball made a broad sweep of dead and wounded. Instantly the Croats were there also; and now the cannons had to cease, so as not to kill both friend and foe. The long pikes and broad swords of the Imperial cavalry made dreadful havoc. All that bore the name of Swede or Finn were doomed to destruction.

Gustaf Horn, of Kankas, the valiant and judicious Finnish general, whom Gustaf Adolf called his "right hand," and who from the beginning had dissuaded from this unfortunate battle, was the last to retain courage and self-possession at this fearful moment, the last to give up. With the remnants of three regiments, he had taken his post at the bridge, and the fleeing throng surged by him, without being able to draw him into the current. They conjured him to save his life; but to these appeals he opposed his stubborn Finnish will, and held his post. The enemy could scarcely believe their eyes when they saw him not only stand his ground, but boldly attack. For a moment the pursuit was checked—the only thing which Horn hoped to gain by his intrepid onset. Gallas sent one of the best Spanish brigades against him. Horn drove them back with bloody heads. Intoxicated with triumph, De Werth fell upon him with his dragoons. Equally bloody was their reception. From all directions the enemy's circle closed in, and Horn was attacked from three sides at once. They offered him life if he would surrender. He answered with a sword-thrust, and his men gave the same response. Not one of them asked quarter. At last, when nearly all around him had fallen, he was overpowered by numbers and taken prisoner, after which the few surviving champions surrendered.

When the Swedish army, in full flight, rushed over Arensberg, Duke Bernhard of Saxen-Weimar tore his long hair, and exclaimed, in his despair, that he was a fool, but Horn was a wise man. At a later period, the duke comforted himself with Alsace; but that day he had reason to repent his precipitancy. Six thousand Swedes and Finns, and with them their German allies, covered the blood-stained heights of Nördlingen; six thousand were taken prisoners, among them the two Finns, Horn and Wittenberg, who were treated very honorably by the enemy. Of the other ten thousand, one-half were wounded, and most of the remaining mercenaries deserted. The army had lost four thousand baggage-wagons, three hundred flags, and all the artillery. A miserable remnant made its way to Mentz, plundering as it went, and suffering from extreme want.

More than the loss of these twelve thousand men was the loss of Sweden's martial honor, and the restoration to the enemy of their confidence in victory. The battle at Nördlingen became the turning-point in the Thirty-Years' War, and excited mingled joy and consternation throughout Europe, until Banér's genius and success restored to the Swedish arms their lost lustre.

Among those who fought to the last by Horn's side, at the bridge, were the East Bothnians and our old friend Captain Larsson. The little thick-set captain had on that occasion no time to open his voluble mouth, a fate which had seldom happened to him. His whole round figure dripped with sweat in the summer heat; he had been fighting since the dawn, yet had not received the smallest scratch on his fleshy frame. It must be said, to his honor, that at Nördlingen he thought little of either Rhine wine or Bavarian nuns, but faithfully cut and thrust as best he could. We will not, however, affirm that he impaled thirty Imperialists on the point of his trusty sword, as he afterward asserted in good faith. He was one of those who were taken prisoner with Horn; and what most provoked the good captain was not his capture, but the vexation of seeing the Croats afterwards empty at their ease the Swedish stock of wine, which they had taken with the baggage-wagons.

Another of our friends, Lieutenant Bertel,

fought the whole day at the duke's side. He it was who offered his horse when the duke's horse was shot. That the duke did not forget this service, we will by and by see. Bertel was, like Larsson, engaged in the hottest conflict; but, less fortunate than the latter, he received several wounds, and was finally borne along with the stream of fugitives to Arensberg. Almost without knowing how, he found himself the next day far from the battle-field, and proceeded with the fragments of the duke's army to Mentz.

CHAPTER VII.

THE PRODIGAL SON.

WE are now at Epiphany, in the mid-winter of 1635. In the large sitting-room of Aaron Bertila, in Storkyro, a fire of pine logs crackles on the spacious hearth; for at that time heavy forests still surrounded the fertile fields. Outside, a snow-storm is raging, with sweeping blasts; the wolves howl on the ice of the stream; away in the clefts of the hill the hungry lynx prowls stealthily around.

It is Epiphany evening, an hour or two after sunset. The Storkyro peasant-king sits in his high-backed chair, at a little distance from the hearth, listening with distracted thoughts to his daughter Meri, who, by the light of the fire, reads aloud a chapter of Agricola's Finnish New Testament: for at that period the whole Bible was not yet translated into the Finnish language.

Bertila has grown very old since we last saw him, in his full vigor. The great thoughts that are constantly revolving under his bald forehead give him no peace; and yet his bold plans are now, after the king's death, completely shattered, like shipwrecked fragments floating around on the tumultuous billows of a dark sea. Great and strong souls like his generally end by destroying themselves. All the changes and misfortunes of his turbulent life had not been able to break his iron will; but the grief over a frustrated hope, the vain attempt to build anew the fallen castles in the air, the sorrow of seeing his own children tear down his work—all this preyed like an eager vulture upon his inner life. A single thought had in two years made him twenty years older; and this thought was presumptuous even to madness. It ran thus:

"Why is not one of my line at this moment King of Sweden?"

At times Meri raises her mild blue eyes from the holy book, and regards her old father with searching disquietude. She, too, has become older in appearance. The quiet sorrow is like autumn in green groves: it breaks not, it kills not; but it makes the fresh leaves wither on the tree of life. Meri's glance is full of peace and submission. The thought which always shines within her soul, like a setting sun, is this:

"Beyond the grave I shall meet again the pride of my heart; and he will no longer wear an earthly crown!"

Near her, on the left, sits old Larsson, short and thick in form, like his hearty son. His good-natured jovial face has for the time assumed a more solemn expression, befitting the holy reading to which he listens. His hands are folded as in prayer, save when, with his usual thoughtfulness, he heaps together the burning brands, so that Meri can see better.

Behind him are devoutly seated a part of the numerous laborers; and these groups, illumined by the reflection of the fire, are completed by a purring gray cat, and a large shaggy house-dog, which has curled himself up in a ring under Meri's feet, seemingly proud to serve her as a footstool.

When Meri, in her reading, came to the place in Luke, xvth chapter, where it speaks of the Prodigal Son, the old Bertila's eyes began to glisten with a sinister light.

"The reprobate!" muttered he to himself. "To waste one's inheritance, what is that! But to forget one's old father . . . by God, that is shameful!"

Meri read farther, until she came to the Prodigal Son's repentance: "And he arose and came to his father. But when he was yet a great way off, his father saw him, and had compassion, and ran, and fell on his neck, and kissed him."

"What a simpleton of a father!" said Aaron Bertila again to himself. "He ought to have bound him with ropes, and beaten him with rods, and driven him away from his house back to his riotous living and his empty wine-cups!"

"Father!" whispered Meri, with mild reproach. "Be merciful, as our Heavenly Father is merciful, and takes the lost children in His arms."

"And if your son ever returns . . ." began Larsson, in the same tone. But the old man interrupted him.

"Hold your tongues, and don't trouble yourselves about me," he answered, gruffly. "I have no longer any son . . . who falls in repentance at my feet," added he, directly, when he saw two large clear pearls glisten in Meri's eyelashes.

She continued: "And the son said unto him, Father, I have sinned against Heaven, and in thy sight, and am no more worthy to be called thy son."

"Stop reading that!" burst out the old man, in a rage. "See that my bed is in order, and let the folks go to rest; it is late."

At this moment horses' hoofs were heard outside in the creaking snow. This occurrence, unusual on the evening of a sacred day, made Larsson go to the low window and breathe on the frost-covered pane, so as to look out into the storm. A sleigh, drawn by two horses, worked its way with difficulty through the snowdrifts into the yard. Two men in sheepskin cloaks jumped out.

Seized with a sudden intuition, Larsson hurried out to meet the travellers, and quick as lightning Meri was at his side. The door closed creakingly behind them, and there was some minutes' delay before it opened again. And now a young man in a soldier's garb entered, with bowed head, threw aside his plumed hat, white with the snow, and going straight to old Bertila, knelt down, and bent his beautiful curly head still lower, as he said:

"Father, I am here, and ask your blessing!"

And behind him stood Meri and the old Larsson, both with clasped hands, and raised their beseeching eyes to the stern old man, with the same words:

"Father, here is thy son; give him thy blessing!"

For a moment Bertila seemed to struggle with himself; his lips trembled slightly, and his hand was unconsciously stretched out, as if to lift up the youth at his feet. But soon his bald head rose still higher, his hand drew back, his sharp eyes flashed more darkly than ever, and his lips trembled no longer.

"Go!" said he, shortly and sternly; "go, you apostate boy, back to your brother noblemen, and your sisters, the fine ladies. What do you seek in the simple peasant's cottage, which you despise? Go! I have no longer any son!"

But the youth went not.

"Do not be angry, my father," said he, "if in my youthful ambition I have at any time trespassed against your commands. Who sent me out among the illustrious and great ones of earth, to win fame and honor? Who bade me go to the war, to ennoble my peasant name with chivalric deeds? Who exposed me to the temptation of all the brilliant examples which clustered round the king? You, and you, and again you, my father; and now you thrust away your son, who for your sake twice refused a title of nobility."

"You!" exclaimed the old man, with overflowing anger. "You renounce a title of nobility!— you, who have blushed for your peasant name and taken another more imposing? No, on your knees have you begged for a coat of arms. What do I know about its being offered to you?—what is that to me? I only know that since your earliest childhood I have striven to implant in your soul, recreant, that there are no rightful powers other than *king and people;* that all who push themselves between, whether they bear the name of aristocrats, ecclesiatics, or whatever else, are a monstrosity, a ruin, a curse to government and country . . . . All this I have tried to inculcate in you;

and the fruit of my teachings has been that you have smuggled yourself among this nobility, which I hate and despise; that you have coveted its empty titles, paraded its extravagant display, imbibed its prejudices, and now you stand here, in your father's house, with a lie on your lips and aristocratic vanity in your heart. Go, degenerate son! Aaron Bertila is what he has always been — a peasant! He rejects and curses you, apostate!"

With these words, the old man turned away, and went, with a firm step and a high head, into the little bedchamber, leaving Bertel still on his knees.

"Hear me, father!" cried Bertel after him, as he quickly unbuttoned his coat and took out a folded paper; "this paper I had meant to tear in pieces at your feet!"

But the old man did not hear him; the paper fell to the floor, and when Larsson, a moment later, unfolded and read it, it was found to contain a diploma from the Regency in Stockholm, made at the solicitation of Duke Bernhard of Weimar, conferring upon Gustaf Bertel, captain of horse in the life-guards, a patent of nobility, and a coat of arms with the name of *Bertelsköld*.

While all in the house were still bewildered by the old Bertila's inflexibility, three of Lady Märtha's soldiers from Korsholm entered in great haste.

"Halloa, boys!" exclaimed they to the laborers. "Have you seen her? Here is something that pays. Two hundred silver dollars reward to him who seizes and brings back, dead or alive, Lady Regina von Emmeritz, state-prisoner at Korsholm."

At the sound of this name Bertel was roused

from his stupefying grief; he sprang up, and seized the speaker by the collar.

"Wretch! what do you say?" he exclaimed.

"Well, well; be a little more careful when you speak to the servants of his royal majesty and the crown. .I tell you that the German traitor—the Papistical witch, Lady von Emmeritz, succeeded in escaping last night from Korsholm castle, and that he who does not help to catch her is a traitor and a . . ."

The man had not time to end his sentence before a blow from Bertel's strong arm laid him at full length on the floor.

"Ha, my father, you have so wished!" exclaimed the youth; and in a flash he was outside the door, and in his sleigh, which the next instant was heard driving away through the raging storm.

CHAPTER VIII.

THE FUGITIVE.

LET us now direct our attention to the whereabouts of Lady Regina, and see what has led her to exchange the tender care of Lady Märtha for the adventurous experiment of fleeing, in mid-winter, through a strange region filled with desert tracts, where she was entirely ignorant of the roads, and was not able even to make herself understood in the language of the country.

We should not lose sight of the fact that our story is laid in a time when Catholicism and Lutheranism were engaged in the sharpest conflict; when Lutheranism, excited by the violence of the struggle, was as little inclined to religious tolerance as Catholicism itself. Lady Märtha was now thoroughly possessed of the idea that she was in duty bound to convert Lady Regina to the Lutheran faith; and from this well-meant but futile endeavor, no one could dissuade her. She therefore continued, in season and out of season, to torment the poor girl with her pertinacity;—sometimes with books, sometimes with exhortations, sometimes with persuasions and threats, or promises of freedom; and when Regina refused to read the books or listen to the preaching, the zealous old lady had prayers read in her prisoner's room morning and evening, and had services held there on Sundays. All these means were wasted on what Lady Märtha called Regina's stubbornness. The more the former exerted herself, the calmer, colder, and more impassive became her prisoner. Regina regarded herself as a martyr to her faith, and endured, with apparent indifference, all humiliations, for the sake of the holy cause.

But within the young girl of nineteen years fermented the hot Southern blood, and it was with great difficulty that she could subdue it into apparent calm. There were moments when Regina would have blown up Korsholm, had it been in her power. But the old gray walls defied her silent rage, and flight became finally her only means of salvation. Days and years she brooded upon it; at last she found a means of eluding Lady Märtha's vigilance.

In Kajana castle was confined at that time the celebrated and unfortunate Johannes Messenius, who in his youth had been educated by the Jesuits in Braunsberg, and chosen by them to become the apostle of Catholicism in heretic Sweden. Imprisoned for his libels and conspiracies in the interest of Sigismund's party, he had now for nineteen years, subjected to the harshest treatments, sat there like a mole in his hole, when rumors of his learning, his misfortunes, and his papistical sentiments, reached Lady Regina in her prison. From this moment, bold plans began to agitate the young girl's mind.

One day, about New Year's time, an itinerant German quack came to Korsholm with his medicine-chest on his back, like Jewish peddlers at a later period. A doctor and apothecary thus combined in one person did a lucrative business at the expense of the credulous people, and was frequently consulted even by the upper classes; for in the whole country there was not a single regular physician, and only one drug-store in Åbo—and even this one not especially well furnished. No wonder, then, that the man found plenty to do, even at Korsholm, with pains, stomach-aches, and gout; nay, Lady Märtha, who, every time she had thrashed her male servants, complained of colic and shortness of breath, received the foreign doctor with particular cordiality. In a few days the latter had become perfectly at home in the castle; and thus it happened that he was called in to Lady Regina, who was suffering from an obstinate headache.

Lady Märtha's usual craftiness this time failed her. On a fine morning, two days later, the young Regina, her old Dorthe, and the quack doctor, were all missing. A window grating, which had been broken off from the outside, and a rope-ladder, left no doubt possible that the quack had been instrumental in procuring the prisoner a free passage over wall and ramparts. Lady Märtha, in her amazement and rage, forgot both her colic and her shortness of breath; she stirred up the castle and town, and immediately sent out her soldiers in all directions to catch the fugitives. It will soon be seen how far she succeeded.

We return for a moment to Bertel, whom we find with his heart full of the most conflicting emotions, hurrying through the stormy night, and attended by his faithful Pekka. The honest soul could not comprehend a folly so great as that of leaving the cheerful fireside and the boiling porridge-kettle, where they had but just arrived, for snow-drifts and wolves in the wild woods. And Bertel did not comprehend it himself. While the army lay in winter quarters in Germany, he had obtained a furlough, and passed northward through Sweden to Torneå, and thence hurried south through Storkyro to Wasa, which was his secret destination. And now he met in one place a father's anger, and in the other the empty walls where she had been and was no more. Regina had disappeared, leaving no trace.

"Where shall I drive?" asked Pekka, monotonously and gruffly, when they came out on the broad highway, after leaving the farm of the old peasant-king.

"Wherever you please," answered his master, as gruffly.

Pekka turned his horses toward Wasa, about twenty miles distant; Bertel noticed this.

"Ass!" cried he, "have I not ordered you to drive north?"

"North!" repeated Pekka, shortly; and with a sigh he turned his horses toward Ny-Karleby, full forty miles away. At that period they had no regular inns, with horses provided for the accom-
S

modation of travellers. But there were farms at intervals, where all who travelled on government business could count on finding horses, while other travellers were obliged to bargain as best they could.

The parsonages were the general stopping-places for the night, and always had a room in order, where beds of straw and a table with cold food stood hospitably prepared for acquaintances and strangers.

It was therefore quite natural that Pekka, with his thoughts still on the porridge-kettle, ventured to ask a further question: Would they spend the night at Wörå parsonage?

"Drive to Ylihärmä," answered the captain, petulantly, and wrapped himself in his long sheepskin cloak, for the night wind blew icy cold.

"The devil take me if I understand such whims!" muttered Pekka to himself, as he turned off into the narrow village road leading northward from Storkyro toward Lappo parish.

Here the snow had drifted several feet high between the fences, and the travelers could only advance step by step. After an hour's struggling the horses were completely tired out and stopped every few steps.

Bertel, absorbed in his reveries, was scarcely aware of the situation. They had left Kyro's wide plains behind them, and were now in the forest of Lappo. The silence of the wilderness, broken only by the howling of the storm, surrounded the travellers on all sides; and as far as the eye could reach, there was no trace of human habitation.

Pekka had been walking at the side of the sleigh, raising it with his broad shoulders when it sank so deep in the snow that the horses could not pull it. At last even his sinewy arms were unequal to the task; the sleigh stopped in the midst of a mountain of snow.

"Well!" exclaimed Bertel, impatiently; "what is the matter?"

"Nothing," replied Pekka, calmly, "except that we need neither undertaker nor priest to find a grave!"

"How far is it from here to the nearest farm?"

"Six or seven miles, I think."

"Do you not see something that resembles a light, far away there in the woods?"

"Yes, yes, it looks like it . . ."

"Unharness the horses, and let us ride there."

"No, dear master, these woods are horribly haunted, as I know of old, ever since the peasants here beat their steward to death, during the Club War, and burned his house and his innocent children."

"Nonsense! I tell you we will ride there."

"Well, it is all the same to me."

In a few minutes the horses were taken out of the traces, and the two travellers mounted and pushed on in the direction of the light, which sometimes disappeared and then shone again between the snow-drifts.

"But tell me, Pekka," resumed Bertel, "how does the story run about this wilderness? I recollect that I often heard them speak of it in my childhood."

"Yes, my mother was born here."

"Was there not once a large settlement in this wood?"

"Yes, indeed, it was many hundred acres in extent. The steward had laid it all out for miles, as far back as King Gustaf's time; and here grew many hundred tons of grain, so father has told me ; and the steward had built a large house here and lived like a prince in the wilderness; and then, as I told you, the peasants came and set fire to the place in the night-time, destroying not only the cattle, but all the people with the exception of the young lady whom your father saved and afterward took for his wife. It is very certain that he had a finger in that pie."

"And so the place was never built up again?"

"You can imagine the fields were a fat prize, and so there were plenty of people who undertook to move here in defiance of the devil. But the devil was too smart for them; he began to stir up such a state of things here, with ghosts haunting about, night and day, that nobody was sure of his life, far less of his sinful soul. When people sat in their homes, the chairs were pulled from under them; the porridge-bowl rolled of itself down on the floor; the stones were torn from the walls and hailed down around people's ears. If they went out in the woods, they were no better off; they had to look out sharp that the trees did not tumble over their heads, although the weather was perfectly quiet, and that the ground did not open under their feet and draw them down into a bottomless pit. And when I think that we are now travelling through the same woods . . . oh, oh, I am sinking!"

"You simpleton, it is the pure snow!—and then you say the people could not stand it any longer?"

"Then they all moved away, so that there was not even a cat left, except one old laborer; but I suppose he is dead long ago. The whole settlement was deserted again; the ditches became filled up, the meadows became morasses, and the pine-woods spread over the former grain-fields. It is now forty years since that time . . ."

Pekka, who was not in the habit of making long speeches, seemed astonished at his unusual talkativeness, and suddenly checked his flow of words, as he reined in his horse.

"What is it now?" asked Bertel, impatiently.

"I don't see the light any more."

"Neither do I. It is hidden by the trees."

"No, dear master, it is not hidden by the trees; it has sunk into the earth, after decoying us here into the wildest woods. Didn't I tell you that it would be so? We will never get away from here alive."

"For the devil's sake, ride on, and don't stop here, or both man and beast will stiffen with the cold. It seems to me I see something like a hut over there."

"Hut indeed! it is nothing but a big rock with gray sides, from which the wind has blown away the snow. It is all over with us."

"Hold your tongue, and ride on! Here we come to a glade with young woods . . . I see something there between the snow-drifts."

"Saints protect us! We are now on the very spot where the house stood. Don't you see the old chimney sticking out through the snow? Not a step farther, master!"

"I am not mistaken . . . it is the hut."

Bertel and his companion found themselves on extremely uncomfortable ground, where the horses stumbled at every step over large stones, or sank into deep hollows covered with snow. High snow-drifts and felled trees made it still worse, and obstructed the passage to a dilapidated hut, which, either by chance or intention, was hidden behind two spreading firs, with branches hanging to the ground. The only window of the hut had a shutter which was at one moment blown open by the wind and then closed again, thus causing the light within to show itself and disappear by turns.

Bertel dismounted from his horse, tied it to a branch of the fir, and approached the window to glance inside. A secret hope gave wings to his feet. He took it for granted that if the fugitives had gone in a northerly direction, they could not have followed the main highway, but had sought to escape their pursuers by taking side roads. But in this part of East Bothnia hundreds of small roads at that time crossed each other, all leading to the new settlements further east. What was it that told him the fugitives would have chosen just this road?

His heart beat when he approached the window. Of the four small panes, two were of horn—a substance formerly used instead of glass; one of them was broken and stopped up with moss; only the fourth was of glass, but so covered with ice and snow that at first nothing could be seen through it. Bertel breathed on the glass, but found to his vexation that the frost on the inside defied his curiosity. Just then his horse neighed.

It seemed ridiculous to Bertel to stand spying into a poor peasant's hut. He was already on the point of knocking at the door, when at that instant a shadow obscured the light, and the frost on the inside of the glass was quickly melted by the breath of a human being, as curious to look out as he to look in. Bertel was soon able to discern a face with burning eyes, which, close to the window, stared out, as if to discover the cause of the horse's neighing.

The sight of this face had the effect of an electric shock upon the nocturnal cavalier. Thinking of the beautiful Regina, Bertel had expected a sight of a more agreeable kind. But instead he beheld a corpse-like face surrounded by a black tight-fitting leather calotte; and this dark frame made the pale face seem still paler.

Bertel had seen those features before, and when he collected his thoughts, the memory of a terrible night in the Bavarian woods rose within his soul. Involuntarily he drew back, and stopped a moment irresolute. This motion was observed by Pekka, who had remained on his horse in order to have retreat open.

"Quick! away from here!" cried he. "I have said that nobody but the devil himself lives in these woods."

"Yes, you are right," answered Bertel, smiling at his own fears and what he considered to be the product of his excited imagination. "If ever the prince of darkness has taken human form, then he lives in this hut. But that is just the reason why we will look the worthy gentleman in the face, and force him to give us lodgings for the night. Halloa there! open to some travellers!"

These words were accompanied by some violent blows upon the door.

CHAPTER IX.

DON QUIXOTE IN THE NORTH.

AFTER a long delay, the door of the hut was opened from the inside, and an old man, bowed with age, and with a snow-white beard, appeared at the entrance. Accustomed by the right of war to *take* what was needed, when it was not given voluntarily, Bertel pushed the old man aside and entered the miserable hut without ceremony. To his great astonishment, he found it empty. A half burnt pine-torch, placed between the stones of the fire-place, threw a flickering light around this abode of poverty. No door was seen except the entrance; not a living being was discovered, besides the old man and a large shaggy dog which lay stretched on the hearth and showed his teeth to the uninvited guest.

"Where is the man in the black leather hood, who was here a moment ago?" asked Bertel, sharply.

"God bless your grace!" answered the old man, humbly and evasively, "who could be here but your grace?"

"Out with the truth! Somebody must be hidden here. Under the bed . . . no. Behind the oven . . . no. And yet you have just had a large fire in the fire-place. What? I believe it is put out with water! Answer!"

"It is so cold, your grace, and the hut is full of cracks . . ."

Bertel's suspicions, once aroused, were not

easily dispelled. His eyes flew searchingly around the room, and discovered a little object which had fallen under a bench. It was a lady's glove, fine and soft, lined with hare-skin.

"Will you confess, old wretch?" burst out the youth, excitedly.

The old man seemed dismayed, but only for a moment. He suddenly changed his manner, nodded slyly, and pointed to the corner nearest the fire-place. Bertel followed his hint; but he had taken only a few steps, when the floor gave way under his feet. He had stepped into the open hole of a cellar, whose entrance had been hidden by the heavy shadow of the fire-place. Instantly a trap-door was closed over the opening, and he heard the rattling of a firm iron hasp, which made it quite impossible for him to raise the trap-door from below.

Bertel had fallen into one of those holes under the floor where poor people keep roots and ale. The hole was not deep, neither was his fall very dangerous; but nevertheless Bertel was furious. The little glove had told him the whole story.

She must be here; she, the beautiful, proud, unfortunate princess, whom he had so long adored in secret. How did he know but she had fallen into the hands of cruel robbers? And just now, when he, after years of longing, was so near her, just now when she perhaps needed his help and protection, he had been caught in a miserable trap, imprisoned in a rat-hole, more wretched than the hut itself, of which the floor served him for a ceiling. In vain did he try to raise the planks of the floor by the strength of his shoulders; they were as unyielding as the fate which had so long mocked his dearest hopes.

12*

Meanwhile he could distinguish from the room above him a low noise, as though several persons were passing over the floor. Then all became silent.

Bertel's only hope now was Pekka, who had not dared to enter the hut. But nothing was heard of him; and three or four hours passed in a deathly suspense, which was increased by the prospect of perishing from hunger and cold.

Then steps were again heard overhead; the iron hasp was unfastened and the trap-door raised. Half-frozen, Bertel crawled up from the damp hole, in the firm belief that Pekka had at last discovered his prison. He was met instead by the old man with the snow-white beard, who, humble and obsequious as before, offered his hand to help him up.

Enraged, the young soldier seized the old man by his bony shoulder, and prepared to question him thoroughly.

"Wretch!" he exclaimed, "are you tired of life, or do you not know what you are doing, madman! What should hinder me from crushing your pitiful frame against the walls of your own house?"

The old man looked at him with unmoved mien.

"Do so, Bertila's grandson," replied he. "Kill, if you choose, your grandmother's faithful old servant! What use is it for him to live any longer?"

"My grandmother's old servant, do you say?"

"I am the last survivor of all those who formerly inhabited this fertile region, now a wilderness. It was I who said to Aaron Bertila, when my master's house was devastated with fire and blood: 'Save my lady!' and Bertila did it;—cursed be he and blessed at the same time! He carried my fair and noble lady from the flames; and she, an aristocratic maiden, became the arrogant peasant's humble wife."

"But are you crazy, old man? If you are what you say, why then have you shut me up in this cursed hole? You must own that your friendship is of a strange kind."

"Kill me, sir; I am ninety years of age! Kill me; I am . . . a Catholic."

"You! Well, by my sword; now I begin to understand you."

"I am the last Catholic in this country. I am of the time of King Johan and King Sigismund. I was one of the four who buried the last nun in Nådenda cloister. For twenty years I have not heard mass or been sprinkled with holy water. But all the saints be praised! one hour before you came I had eaten of the holy wafer."

"A monk has been in your hut?"

"Yes, sir; one of ours."

"And with him was a young girl and her old duenna? Answer."

"Yes, they accompanied him."

"And at my arrival you hid them . . ."

"In the loft. Yes, your grace."

"Then you decoyed me into your miserable rat-hole, while you let the women and the monk flee?"

"I do not deny that it is so."

"And what do you think will be your reward for all this?"

"Anything — death, perhaps."

"I shall spare your life, but only on one condition. You must show me the way of the fugitives."

"My life! I have told you I am ninety."

"And you do not fear . . . the rack?"

"The saints grant I might be worthy so great an honor!"

"But if I should burn you alive in your own hut!"

"The holy martyrs have been burned at the stake."

"No, old man, I am no executioner; I have learned in the service of my king to revere faithfulness;" and Bertel pressed the old man's hand with emotion. "But one thing I will tell you," continued he. "You think perhaps that I have come to take the fugitives back to prison. It is not so. I swear upon my knightly honor to defend Lady Regina's freedom with my life, and to do all in my power to assist her flight. Will you now tell me what way she took?"

"No, your grace." said the old man calmly. "The young lady is under the protection of the saints and a prudent man. You are young and of hot blood; you would only plunge them all into ruin. Turn back, therefore; you will not find a trace of the fugitives."

"Bull-head!" muttered Bertel, indignantly. "Farewell; I shall get along without your help."

"Remain here quietly till to-morrow, your grace. To-day you have the liberty to walk, if you choose, six miles through the high snow-drifts, to the nearest farm. To-morrow you can ride comfortably."

"Wretch! you have sent the horses away?"

"Yes, your grace. . . . You must be hungry now. Here is a kettle of boiled turnips; may they suit your taste."

"Ah!" thought Bertel to himself, as he paced the scanty floor with hasty steps: "Not for ten bottles of Rhine wine would I have Larsson see me at this moment. He would compare me to the wandering Knight of Mancha, who on the way to his Dulcinea fell into the most prosaic adventures. How shall I get away from here through these terrible snow-drifts?"

"But," added he aloud, "I have an idea; I will try if one of the greatest amusements of my childhood cannot serve me a good turn now. Old man, where do you keep your snow-shoes?"

"My snow-shoes?" replied the old man, in confusion. "I have none."

"You have; I see it in your face. No Finn in the wilderness is without snow-shoes. Here with them, quick!"

And without heeding the old man's excuses, Bertel pushed open the trap-door which led to the garret, and drew out a splendid pair of snow-shoes.

"Well, old friend," exclaimed the young officer. "What do you think of my new horses? . . . I call them mine, for I wager you will sell them to me for these hard silver dollars. Nimbler steeds have seldom hurried over high snow-drifts. If you have any greeting to send to the monk and Lady Regina, I will take it with pleasure."

"Do not venture alone into the wilderness," said the old man. "There is neither track nor path; the woods are many miles wide, and filled with wolves. It will be your certain death."

"You are wrong, my friend," replied Bertel. "If I am not mistaken, there are traces in two directions: one after my horse, the other after the fugitives. Tell me, did they go in a sleigh or on horseback?"

"I think they went on horseback."

"Then I am sure they drove. You are a finished rogue. But I forgive you for the sake of your excellent snow-shoes. Farewell. In a couple of hours I will have found those whom I seek."

With these words, Bertel hurried away.

It was yet early in the morning, at least two or three hours before sunrise. But fortunately the storm had ceased; the sky had cleared, and the winter stars twinkled brightly in the blue arch of heaven. The cold had increased; a heavy frost had covered all the branches and snow-drifts with those diamonds of ice which at once dazzle and charm the wanderer's eye. The sight of woods and snow in a star-lit winter morning gives the Northerner a peculiar and exhilarating feeling. There is in this scene a grandeur, a splendor, a purity, a freshness, which carries him back to the impressions of childhood and the brilliant illusions of youth. There is nothing to oppress the heart or clip the soaring wings of fancy; all is there so vast, so solemn, so free. One might say that nature, in this deep silence of winter and night, is dead; and yet she lives, warm and rich, in the wanderer's breast. It is as though she had compressed into this little spot, this solitary heart in the wilderness, all her budding life, that it might be all the more beautiful amidst the surrounding crystallization, the stillness, and the radiance of stars.

Bertel experienced this feeling of freshness and life. He was still young, and open to all impressions. As he hurried along, lightly as the wind, between the trees and snow-drifts, he felt like a child. It seemed to him that he was again the boy who flew over the snow on Storkyro plains to spread his snares for the heathcock in the woods. It is true he was a little unsteady in the beginning, from lack of practice, when the snow-shoes glided down the icy slopes; he occasionally pushed unsteadily, and sometimes stumbled. But soon he had regained his former skill, and stood as firm as ever on the uneven surface.

His task was now to find the track of the fugitives; but this was no easy matter. He had wandered around an hour in the direction of Ylihärmä, and yet had not discovered the slightest clue. The last flurry of the storm had obliterated all traces of travellers; he could see only the fresh track of the wolf, where it had trotted through the snow, and now and then a frightened ptarmigan flew between the snow-covered branches. Want of sleep, hunger and fatigue began to exhaust the youth's strength; the cold increased as sunrise approached, and sprinkled his dark mustache and plumed hat with frost.

Then at last he saw, on a forest road which the broad pines had shielded from the blast, the fresh traces of runners and horses' feet. Bertel followed with renewed strength; at times the tracks were lost in the snow, and then appeared again where the road was sheltered.

The yellowish-red sun rose over the tree-tops in the south-east. The day was cold and clear. In all directions nothing was to be seen but forests and snow-drifts. But far away in the north a little column of smoke rose toward the clear morning sky. Bertel strove for this point. The snow-shoes regained their speed, the way seemed smoother, and at last the weary adventurer reached a solitary farm-house by the side of the highway.

The first person he met was Pekka, going to feed his horses.

"Scoundrel!" cried Bertel, with glad surprise. "Who sent you here?"

"Who?" repeated Pekka, equally delighted and astonished. "Well, I should say that the devil did it. I waited and waited outside that cursed old shanty in the woods, until my eyelids became heavy and dropped together, as I sat in the snow-drift. After a little while I was awakened by the neighing of horses; and what did I see? A sleigh just like ours, harnessed with two horses, dashing away upon the road. It is either my master or the devil, said I to myself, but anyway I will follow him. Then I climbed upon the horse's back again, and although I was horribly hungry I followed. Finally the horses became tired; I lost the sleigh from sight, and thanked all the saints, both Catholic and Lutheran, when at last I came here to this farm, and got a good bowl of porridge. For if it was hot at Lützen and Nördlingen, then it was cursedly cold in Ylihärmä, that is sure."

"Good!" said Bertel, "they will not escape us. But do you know one thing, Pekka: there are times when hunger and sleepiness are stronger than love itself. Come, let us go in!"

And Bertel entered, drank a bowl of boiled milk, and, overcome with fatigue, threw himself on a straw bed. There for a couple of hours we will leave our wandering knight in peace.

CHAPTER X.

KAJANA CASTLE.

FAR away in the North, where the waters of the vast and mighty seas roar in their icy caverns; where the foam of the cataracts never freezes; where the green of the pines never withers; where the gray and unyielding rocks compress the foaming rivers into narrow gorges,—here, for thousands of years, the powers of nature have waged their ceaseless strife, without rest, without reconciliation: the river never tires of beating against the rocks; the rocks never tire of beating back the stream; the mountain-crags never grow old; the immense morasses defy cultivation; the frosty-clear winter sky quivers forever in the northern light, and looks down with serene and majestic calm upon the scattered huts along the river-banks.

Here is the home of night and terror; here is the shadow in the golden pictures of Finnish poetry. Here sorcery, shunning the light, weaves its nets around human faith; here were the graves of heroes; here was the Mount of Plagues; here the mythic giants wasted their rude strength in mountain wilds; here stood Hiisi's Castle, with its massy steps. Here the spirit of the Past brooded its gloomiest thoughts; here it retreated, step by step, before the light of a newer time; and here it has bled to death in its impotent rage: heathenism, fallen from its greatness, and banished from more cultivated fields, steals around in the sheep's clothing of Christianity, haunting nightly churchyards with its ghastly rites.

Before the waters of the great Northern streams, maddened by their struggle in a hundred cataracts, seek a brief repose in Uleå lake, they pour out their concentrated anger in two immense falls, Koivukoski and Ämmä, close by the little village of Kajana. Like the breaking crests of mighty advancing ocean waves, the watery masses plunge headlong down the narrow gorge; so violent is their fall that human daring, accustomed as it is to wrestling with nature and being victorious at last, pauses here in amazement and admits its feebleness. Even in our day the numerous boats which have steered their course down the river to Uleåborg have here been forced to take to the land and be drawn by horses through the streets of Kajana.

Between the two falls of Koivukoski and Ämmä, in the stream, lies a flat ledge of rock, accessible from both sides by bridges. Here rise the gray walls of an ancient fortress, now in ruins, and constantly bathed by the waves of the stream. This fortress is Kajana Castle, built in 1607, during the time of Charles IX, as a bulwark against Russian invasion. Its history is brief, and has only one bright point—its fall. Mayhap the time will come in our story when we shall speak of it again.

We are now in the year 1635, and the castle stands in its youthful strength. Its form resembles an arrow with the point toward the current. It is considered to be impregnable, unless from famine, or from heavy artillery trained upon it from the surrounding heights. But how could a hostile army reach Kajana castle? All around in the immense wilderness there is no road where a wheel can advance. In summer, the traveller follows the narrow bridle-trail through the forest, or climbs the rock-hewn path; in winter, he hurries with his reindeer and sledge over the ice of the lakes.

It is winter; a thick crust of ice at the river shores and upon the walls of the castle shows that the cold has been severe, though it has not been able to freeze over the restless stream in its rapid course. Some soldiers, clad in jackets of sheepskin, with the woolly side turned in, are busy drawing home wood from the forest near by. There is peace in the land; the drawbridge is down, and horses' hoofs thunder over the bridge of the river. A violent altercation arises in the castle-yard. An old woman, tall in stature, with sharp and disagreeable features, has taken possession of one of the loads of wood, and pushed away the soldiers, while she gathers in her arms as many sticks as she is able to carry, and commands a younger woman to do the same. The soldiers pour out a volley of coarse words, to which the sharp-eyed woman is not slow to respond. An under officer, drawn there by the noise, inquires the cause, addresses the woman with hard words, and orders her to return the wood she has taken. The woman refuses to obey; the under officer orders the wood to be forcibly taken from her; the woman plants herself by a wall, raises a stick of wood in the air, and threatens to crush the skull of the first man who approaches her. The soldiers swear and laugh; the under officer hesitates; the woman's energy takes them by surprise.

Now an elderly man appears on the steps, and all respectfully give way before him. It is the governor, Wernstedt. As soon as the woman catches sight of him, she leaves her belligerent position, and with a stream of words relates all the injustice she has suffered.

"Yes, your excellency," said she, "that is the way they dare to treat a man who is the pride and ornament of Sweden! Not only do they shut him up in this miserable place, beyond reach of all justice and honor, but they let him freeze to death besides. What wood have they given us! Great God! nothing but soggy and rotten chunks, which fill the room with smoke, and don't give heat enough to thaw the ink on his table. But I tell you, that I, Lucia Grothusen, do not mean to be imposed upon any longer. This wood here is good, and I take it, as you see, right under the nose of these vagabonds, who every one of them deserve to hang on the highest pine in the Paldamo forest. Pack yourselves off, you lazy, good-for-nothing fellows, and mind how you behave before me and the master. The wood is mine; that is all there is about it."

The governor smiles.

"Let her keep the wood," said he to the soldiers, "else not a soul in the castle will have any peace. And you, Lucia, I tell you that you must hold your wicked tongue, which has done so much harm; otherwise it might happen that I should again put you and your husband in that dungeon you know of, where Erik Hare kept you, and where the stream runs right under the floor. Is this the thanks I get for the mild treatment I have shown you, that you are constantly stirring up quarrels here in the castle? Day before yesterday you scolded because you did not receive soap enough for your washing; yesterday you took a leg of mutton, by force, from my kitchen; and to-day you make a fuss about the wood. Take care, Lucia; my patience may come to an end."

The woman looks the governor straight in the face.

"Your patience!" repeats she. "How long do you think mine will last? It is now almost nineteen years that I have stayed here in this wolf-den. For nineteen long years has Sweden suffered the stain of having her greatest man confined here like a malefactor! . . . Mark what I say: Sweden's *greatest* man; for the day will come when you, and I, and all these greasy souls, all these wandering ale-jugs, shall be food for worms, and remembered no more than the hog you slaughter to-day; but the name of Johannes Messenius shall shine with glory in all times. Your patience! Have I, then, not had patience,—I, who all these eternal years have been fighting with you for a bit of bread, for firewood, for a pillow for this great man, whom you abuse? I, the only one who has kept his frail body alive, and strengthened his soul for the great work which he is now completing? Do you know what it means to suffer as I have suffered; to forsake all, as I have done; to be snatched away from one's children; to go with despair in the heart and a smile on the lips, seeming to have hope when none remains? . . . Do you know, governor, what all that means? And you come here and speak of your patience!"

The soldiers' loud laughter interrupts the old woman's volubility. She now perceives, for the first time, that the governor has taken the wisest course under the circumstances, and gone his way. It is not the first time that Lucia Grothusen has put the commander of a fortress to flight. She was quite able to drive a whole garrison to the woods.

But it vexes her that she cannot fully relieve her mind. She throws a stick of wood at the nearest and worst of her deriders, and then hurries, with the wood in her arms, to reach a low back door. The soldier, struck in the leg, seizes the stick, with an oath, and in his turn flings it after the old woman. Lucia, hit in the heel, utters a cry of pain and anger; then she disappears through the door, followed by the soldiers' mocking laughter.

During the scene of self-sacrifice on one side and rudeness on both sides, a group of strangers have arrived over the western bridge to the castle, and ask to be conducted to the commander.

The soldiers regard them with curiosity. They wear the humble garb of peasants, but their whole manner betrays a foreign country. At their head is an old man with dark, squinting eyes and sallow complexion; his face is scarcely seen under a hairy cap of dog-skin, which covers with its earflaps the greater part of his head. After him comes a young women in a striped homespun woolen skirt, and a close-fitting jacket of new and fine white calf-skin. Her face also is almost entirely hidden under a hood of coarse felt, bordered with squirrel-skin, the fine fur of which is covered with frost. Yet there can be seen a pair of beautiful dark eyes of unusual brilliancy, which look forth from the hood. The third in the company is a little old woman, so wrapped up in furs, doubled in countless folds, that her short figure has broadened out into the form of a well-stuffed walking bolster.

All these persons are brought before the governor. The man with the dog-skin cap shows a paper, according to which he, Albertus Simonis, of his royal majesty's service, is appointed army physician for the troops which are to go to Germany the next spring, and is now, with his wife and daughter, on a journey from Dantzic to Stockholm, by way of the north road through Wiborg and Kajana. The governor examines closely both the document and the man, and seems to approve them. Then he conducts the travellers to a room in the east wing of the castle, and orders that they be provided with the refreshments necessary after a long journey at that severe season.

CHAPTER XI.

THE PRISONER OF STATE.

WE now enter a room situated in the southern turret of the castle. It is not very inviting. It is large and dark, and although having a sunny exposure, the narrow window, with its thick iron gratings, only admits a few sunbeams of the winter days. A large open fire-place with a gray stone hearth occupies one corner of the room; a rough unpainted bedstead, a couple of benches, a few chairs, a clothes-chest, a large table under the window, and a high cupboard next to it, comprise the furniture of the room. All these things have an appearance of newness, which in some measure reconciles the eye to their coarseness.

But the room is a singular combination of kitchen and study. At the upper end, nearest the window, learning has established its abode. The table is covered with ink-spots, and loaded with old yellow manuscripts and large folios in parchment covers. The door of the cupboard is open, disclosing that it is used as a library. The lower part of the room, near the fire-place, has a different appearance. Here stands the washtub beside a barrel of flour; a kettle is waiting for some dried fish and bits of salt pork, which struggle for a place with a bucket of water and a shelf filled with stone dishes.

Such is the abode which Governor Wernstedt granted to the state-prisoner, Johannes Messenius, his wife and servant, in exchange for the horrible place where Messenius' tormentor, the old Erik Hare, for so many years confined the unfortunate man. This room is at least high and dry above the ground. Its furniture is likewise a friendly gift from the governor. Messenius occupies the upper part of the room and the women of the household the lower.

By the large ink-spotted table sits a bent and gray-haired man, with his body wrapped in furs, his feet in high reindeer boots, and his head covered with a thick woolen cap. One who had seen this man in the days of his prosperity, when he imperiously addressed Upsala Consistory, or, proud as a king on his throne, ruled over all the historical treasures of the Swedish state archives, could scarcely have recognized in this withered form, bent by age and misfortune, the man with the arrogant mind, the opponent of Rudbeck and Tegel, the learned, gifted, haughty Jesuit apostle and conspirator, Johannes Messenius. But if one looked deeper into those sharp, restless eyes, which seemed constantly trying to penetrate the future as they had done the past, and read the words which his trembling hand had just penned—words full of egotism, even to presumption,—then one could divine that within this wasted tenement toiled a soul unbroken by time and events, proud as it had always been, ambitious as it could never cease to be.

The old man's gaze was fixed upon the paper long after he had laid down his pen.

"Yes," said he, thoughtfully and reflectively, "so shall it be. During my lifetime they have trampled me like a worm in the dust; when I am once dead, they will understand upon whom they have trampled. *Gloria, gloria in excelsis!* The day will come, even if it be a hundred years hence, when the miserable prisoner who now, forgotten by the whole world, pines away in the wilderness, shall with admiration and respect be called the father of Swedish history. Then," continued he, with a bitter smile, "then they can do nothing more for me. Then I shall be dead. . . . How strange! The dead man, whose bones have long mouldered in the grave, lives in his works; his spirit goes revivifying and ennobling through the centuries. All that he has suffered while he lived, all the ignominy, all the persecutions, all the prison bars, shall be forgotten, shall exist no more; only his name shall still shine like a star through the night of time, and posterity, with its short memory and its long list of human ingratitudes, shall say, in thoughtless admiration, 'He was a great man!'"

During these words, the old woman whose acquaintance we made in the castle yard entered the room. She opened the door carefully, and walked on tiptoe, as if afraid of waking a sleeping babe. Then she put down, slowly and quietly, the wood she carried in her arms. A little noise was unavoidable; the old man at the table, startled from his thoughts, began to upbraid the intruder:

"Woman!" said he, "how dare you disturb me! Have I not told you, *iterum iterumque*, that you shall take away your *penates procul a parnasso?* Do you understand it . . . *lupa?*"

"Dear Messenius, I am only bringing you a little wood. You have been so cold all these days. Don't be angry, now. I will make the room nice and warm for you; it is splendid wood . . ."

"*Quid mihi tecum.* Go away! You vex me. You weary me. You are, as the late king Gustaf always said, Messenii *mala herba;* my wormwood, my nettle."

Lucia Grothusen was a very quick-tempered woman, angry and quarrelsome with the whole world; but now she kept quite still. How strangely had her domestic position changed! She had always idolized her husband, but so long as he was in the full strength of his manhood and his prosperity, her sturdy strength had bent his unquiet and vacillating spirit like a reed under her will. All that time the learned and feared Messenius had been completely under her thumb. Now, the *rôles* were changed. In the same measure as his physical strength declined, indicating more and more that he approached the end of his life, his wife's idolatrous love overcame her domineering disposition, and brought about the incredible result of curbing this disposition to humble submission. She nursed him as a mother nurses her sick child, for fear of losing him. She bore everything patiently, endeavoring by kindness to soften his querulous disposition, and had never an angry word to reply to his ill-natured remarks. Even on the present occasion, only a slight trembling of the lips gave evidence of the effort it cost her to check her anger.

"Never mind," said she, kindly, as she went a few steps nearer, "don't feel bad about it, my dear; you know it injures your health. I will not do so again; next time I will lay a mat under the wood, so that it will not disturb you. Now I will cook you a splendid leg of mutton for supper . . . Believe me, I had trouble enough to get it. I almost had to take it by force from the governor's kitchen."

"What, woman! have you dared to beg *beneficia* of the dainty food of tyrants! By Zeus! do you consider me a dog, that I should eat the crumbs from their tables? And you limp. Why do you do that? answer me; why do you limp? I suppose you have been running around the castle like a gossipping old woman, and tripped on the stairs."

"Do I limp?" repeated Lucia, with a forced smile. "I really believe . . . I have hurt my foot. . . . Ungrateful!" added she, silently, to herself; "it is for your sake that I suffer."

"Go your way, and let me finish my epitaph."

But Lucia did not go; she stepped nearer to him. Her eyes filled with tears, and she folded both arms around the old man's neck.

"Your epitaph!" repeated she, in a voice so mild that one would never have expected it from these withered lips, which seemed made only for hard words and invectives.

"Oh my God!" continued she, in a low tone, "shall, then, all that is great and glorious on earth finally become dust? But that day is still far distant, my friend; yes, it must be so. Let me see the epitaph of the great Johannes Messenius!"

"Certainly," said the old man, reconciled by her flattery, which was, however, uttered with the most perfect sincerity; "you, Lucia, are decidedly the true *persona executrix* who ought to read my *epitaphium*, as you are also the one who will have it engraved on my tombstone. Look, my dear; what do you think of this?

"'*Here lie the bones of Doctoris Johannes Messenius. The soul is in God's kingdom, but his fame is all over the world.*'"

"Never," said Lucia, weeping, "never were truer words carved over a great man's tomb. But let us say no more about it. Let us speak of your great work, your *Scondia*. Do you know, I have a feeling that its glory will in a short time prepare freedom for you."

"Freedom!" repeated Johannes Messenius, in a melancholy tone. "Yes, you are right; the freedom of the grave, to moulder wherever one chooses."

"No," replied Lucia, with eagerness and enthusiasm; "your eyes shall yet see the honor that is due you. Your great *Scondia illustrata* will be read; it will be printed . . . with your name in gilded letters on the title-page; . . . the whole world, full of admiration, will say, 'Never has its equal existed in the North!'"

"And never will exist again!" added Messenius, with confidence. "Oh! who will restore me my freedom?—freedom that I may behold my work, and triumph over my enemies. *Exaudi me, Domine, porrigo manus meas coram facie tua! Libera me a miseris; etenim dixisti: prosternam inimicos tuos calcondos pedibus tuis.** Who will

---

* Hear me, Lord, I stretch out my hands before Thy face. Save me from misery, for Thou hast said: I will prostrate thine enemies, to be trampled under thy feet.

give me freedom—freedom and ten years of life to witness the fruit of my labor?"

"I!" answered a hollow voice from the lower end of the room.

At the sound of this voice, Messenius and his wife turned around with superstitious terror.* The loneliness of the prison, and the impression of the wild nature surrounding them, which in all times will be the fruitful soil of superstition, had increased the belief of both in supernatural things to perfect conviction. More than once had Messenius' brooding spirit been at the point of plunging into the enticing labyrinth of Kabala and the black art, but his zealous work and his wife's religious exhortations held him back. Now came an unexpected answer to his question . . from heaven or the infernal abyss, it mattered not which; it was an answer—a straw for his drowning hope.

The short winter day drew to a close, and twilight already spread its shadows over that part of the prison room which lay nearest the door. From this obscurity advanced a man, in whose sallow features could be recognized the same person who a few hours before had gained an entrance in the castle, under the name of Albertus Simonis. He had probably, in his capacity of physician, obtained permission to see the prisoner; for the whole medical faculty of the castle consisted only of a barber, who practiced chirurgery, and an old soldier's widow, whose skill in curing internal diseases was highly commended, especially when it was assisted by incantations, which, forbidden by the church, were still used in the bath-room as a powerful form of sorcery.

"*Pax vobiscum!*" said the stranger, with great solemnity, and approaching the window.

"*Et tecum sit Dominus!*" answered Messenius, quite as solemnly, and with mingled curiosity and inquietude.

"*Procul sit a concilio lingua mulieris!*" continued the stranger, in the same tone.

Lucia, in whose youth the daughters of learned men read Latin better than those of the nineteenth century read French, did not wait for a further admonition, but left the room, with a scrutinizing glance at the mysterious stranger.

Messenius made a sign to his guest to take a seat at his side. The whole of their conversation was carried on in Latin.

"Receive my greeting, great man, whom misfortune has been able only to elevate!" began the stranger, craftily touching Messenius' weakest side.

"Welcome, you who do not disdain to visit the forsaken!" replied Messenius, with unusual courtesy.

"Johannes Messenius, do you recognize me?" continued the stranger, letting the light fall on his pale features.

"It seems to me that I have seen your face before," answered the prisoner, hesitatingly; "but it must have been long, long ago."

"Do you remember a boy in Braunsberg, some years younger than you, who was educated with you in the school of the holy fathers, and afterwards in your company visited Rome and Ingoldstadt?"

"Yes, I remember . . . a boy who gave great promise of one day becoming a pillar of the church . . . Hieronymus Mathiæ."

"This Hieronymus Mathiæ am I."

Messenius felt a shiver run through his frame.

How had not the tooth of time, the experiences of years, and the soul-destroying doctrines of Jesuitism, changed the features of the once blooming boy! Father Hieronymus, for it was he, observed this impression, and hastened to add:

"Yes, my revered friend, five and thirty years' struggle for the welfare of the only saving church has withered the roses forever in these cheeks. I have toiled, I have suffered, in these evil times. Like you, great man, but with a smaller measure of genius, have I wrought in the vineyard, without any recompense for my trouble save the holy martyr's crown in Paradise. You have in my youth shown me much friendship; now I will repay it, so far as is in my power. I will restore you to freedom and to life."

"Ah, reverend father," answered the old man, with a deep sigh, "I am not worthy that you, the faithful son of the holy church, should extend to me, poor apostate, your hand. You do not know, then, that I have renounced our faith; that I, with my own hand and mouth, have embraced the accursed Lutheran religion, which in my heart I abhor; nay, that I have even sometimes persecuted your holy order with all kinds of godless libels?"

"Do I not know all this, my honored friend? Have not the great Messenius' work and deeds flown on the wings of fame even to Germany? But what you have done, you have done only as on outer show, in order to work in secret for the welfare of our holy Roman church. Do not the holy Scriptures teach us to meet craft with craft in these godless times?—*perinde ac serpentes estote:* 'ye shall be wily as serpents.' The Holy Virgin will give you absolution for all you have done for her sake. Yes, revered man, even have you seven times abjured your faith, and seventy-seven times sinned against all the saints and the dogmas of the church, it shall be accounted to you for glory and not for condemnation, provided you have done it with a mental reservation and to serve the good cause. Even if your tongue has lied and your hand slain, it shall be deemed a pious and holy work, when it was for the purpose of bringing back stray sheep. Courage, great man; I give you absolution in the name of the church."

"Yes, pious father, those teachings which the worthy Jesuits in Braunsberg so eloquently implanted in my young soul, I have faithfully followed. But now, in my old age, it sometimes seems to me as if my conscience had many objections to . . . ."

"Temptations of the devil!—nothing else. Drive them away!"

"That may all be, pious father! Yet, to quiet my conscience, I have written a formal confession, in which I openly explain my adoption of the Lutheran faith to be a hypocritical act, and as openly proclaim my adherence to the Catholic church."

"Hide this confession—show it not to any mortal eye!" interrupted the Jesuit, quickly. "Its time will yet come."

"I do not understand your reasons, pious father!"

"Listen attentively to what I have to say. Do you think, old man, that I, without important reasons, have ventured up here in the wilderness hundreds of miles, daily exposed to hunger, cold, wild beasts, and the still wilder people, who would burn me alive if they knew who I was and what were my designs? Do you think that I would have forsaken the field in my own country, too wide for my feeble energies, had I not hoped to accomplish more here? Then will I briefly explain the matter. . . . Can anybody hear us? Are there any secret passages in these walls?"

"Be composed; no mortal ear can hear us."

"Know then," continued the Jesuit, in a low voice, "that again we have taken up the never-abandoned plan of restoring heretic Sweden to the bosom of the Roman church. There are only two powers which can still resist us; and, the saints be praised, these powers become day by day more harmless. The house of Stuart, in England, is enmeshed in our nets, and secretly does everything for our cause. Sweden still lies stunned by the terrible blow at Nördlingen, and cannot, without some new miracle, retain its arrogant position in Germany. The time has come; our plans are matured; we must avail ourselves of our enemies' powerlessness. In a few years, England will fall into our hands like a ripe apple. Sweden, still proud of former victories, will be forced to do the same. The means to this end will be a change of dynasty."

"Christina, King Gustaf's daughter . . . "

"Is a nine-year-old child, and besides, a girl! We are not without allies in Sweden, who still remember the exiled royal family. The weak Sigismund is dead; Vladislaus, his son, stretches out his hands, with all the impatience of youth, for the crown of his fathers. It shall be his."

CHAPTER XII.

THE TEMPTER.

"Vladislaus on the throne of Sweden? I doubt if we shall live to see that day," interrupted Messenius dubiously.

"Hear me to the end," continued the Jesuit, inspirited by the far-reaching plan his artful head had woven. "You yourself, great Messenius, are the one who shall perform this miracle."

"I . . . a miserable prisoner! Impossible."

"To the saints and genius, nothing is impossible. The Swede is loyal. He follows his king, for good or evil. He has especially a great reverence for old King Gustaf Vasa. If it could now be proved that the said king, in death-bed repentance, declared the Lutheran doctrine to be false, that he abjured and condemned the reformation, that he charged his youngest son, the papistical Johan, to atone for his great errors . . ."

"What do you dare to say?" burst out Messenius, with undisguised surprise. "A lie so evident, which is in direct opposition to Gustaf Vasa's last words and death, all of which has been so faithfully recorded . . ."

"Calm yourself, revered friend," interrupted the Jesuit, coolly. "If it further could be proved that the second founder and bulwark of Lutheranism, Charles IX, likewise on his death-bed declared the reformation a misfortune and a blasphemy . . ."

Messenius regarded the Jesuit with dismay.

"And if it finally can be proved that King Gustaf Adolf himself, before breathing his last on the battle-field of Lützen, was seized by a sudden inspiration, and died a heretic's death, in unavailing repentance and anguish of soul . . ."

Messenius' pale cheeks flushed.

"Then," continued the Jesuit, with the same imperturbable boldness, "then there remains of the Wasa dynasty only the foolish Erik XIV, the acknowledged papist Johan III, and the professed Catholic Sigismund, with none of whom do we need to trouble ourselves. Once convinced that their greatest kings, all of them in fact, either have been papistical or have become so in their last moments, the veil will finally fall from the eyes of the Swedish people; they will penitently confess their guilt, and at last fall back into the bosom of the only saving Roman church."

"And how will you, reverend father, in the face of all the facts, convince the Swedes of the apostacy of their kings?"

"I have already said," replied the Jesuit, flatteringly, "that such a great and meritorious mission can be accomplished only by the gifted Johannes Messenius. All know that you are the most learned man and the greatest historian of Sweden. They know that you have possessed, and still hold in your hands, more historical documents and secrets than any one else in the whole kingdom. Use these advantages skillfully and judiciously; fabricate documents that never existed; imagine events which never took place . . ."

"What do you dare to say?" exclaimed Messenius, with flaming cheeks.

The Jesuit misunderstood his emotion.

"Yes," continued the father, "the undertaking

is a bold one, but far from impossible. A hasty flight to Poland will, besides, place you in security."

"And it is to me—to me—you propose this?"

"Yes," added Hieronymus, in the same tone. "I realize that Gustaf Adolf would cause you the greatest trouble, and therefore I take that part of the task. You have thus only Gustaf I and Charles IX as your share, to portray them in such a light as will best serve our cause and that of the holy church."

"*Abi a me, male spiritus!*" cried Messenius, in an outburst of rage, which the Jesuit, in spite of his sagacity, was far from expecting. "You vile calumniator! you liar! you wretch, who profane with your touch the holiest things!—do you believe that I, Johannes Messenius, have worked so many long years to become Sweden's greatest historian, in order suddenly, in so infamous, so unheard-of a way, to violate the historical truth which I have re-established with such protracted toil? Pack yourself off this instant! quick . . . away, *in Gehennam!*" . . . and with these words the old man, beside himself with anger, flung at the Jesuit's head everything that he could get hold of—books, papers, inkstand, sandbox—with such violence that the bold monk started. The father's sallow face became for a moment still paler . . . then he took a few steps backwards, rose to his full height, and opened the plaited Spanish doublet of velvet, which covered his breast. A crucifix, set with flashing diamonds, and surrounded by a crown of thorns composed of rubies, glittered unexpectedly in the gathering twilight.

This ornament seemed to have a magic effect upon Messenius. His excited voice suddenly became silent; his anger changed almost instantly to unmistakable fear . . . his knees trembled; he staggered, and was on the point of falling, but supported himself with difficulty against the high-backed chair by the writing-table.

The Jesuit, advancing slowly, pierced the prisoner with those indescribable eyes which have been compared to the rattlesnake's. "Have you forgotten, old man," said he, with a measured and commanding tone, letting each crushing word be followed by a pause calculated to increase its sharp effect, "have you forgotten the penalty which the church and the laws of our holy order ordain for sins like yours? For apostacy, death . . . and you have seven times apostatized! For blasphemy, death . . . and you have seven times blasphemed! For disobedience, death. . . . and you have seven times disobeyed! For sin against the Holy Ghost, damnation . . . and who has sinned like you! For heresy, the stake . . . and who has merited it like you! For offense and disrespect against the holy ones of the Lord, eternal fire . . . and who has offended like you?"

"Grace, holy father, grace!" exclaimed Messenius, while he writhed like a worm under the Jesuit's terrible threats.

But Father Hieronymus continued:

"Nicolaus Pragensis, the celebrated man, went over to Calvin's false doctrines, and dared defy the head of our order. He fled to the remotest corner of Bohemia; but revenge found him. The dogs tore his body, and the spirits of hell tear his soul . . ."

"Grace! mercy!" sighed the prisoner, annihilated.

"Well," continued the Jesuit, haughtily, "I have given you the choice between glory and perdition; I will present it to you once more, although you do not deserve it. Do you believe, miserable apostate, that I, the head of the German and Northern Jesuits, who do not acknowledge any one above me except the holy father at Rome—do you believe that I, who have defied a thousand dangers to seek you here in your wretched corner, will allow you with your disobedience and irresolution to deter me, the invisible ruler of the whole North? I ask you once more, in the name of our holy order, if you, Johannes Messenius, will be faithful to the oath you swore in your youth, and passively obey the behests and commands which I, your superior and your judge, enjoin upon you?"

"Yes, holy father," answered the prisoner, trembling; "I will."

"Listen, then, to the penalty I impose. You say that you have through your whole life striven for a single aim: to gain the name of the greatest historian in the North; and you think that you have at last attained your aim?"

"Yes, holy father, this has been my aim, and I have attained it."

"Your aim is false!" exclaimed the Jesuit, in crushing tones. "Your aim is of sin and the devil; for you have worked for your own glory, and not for that of the holy church, as you have sworn. Therefore I inflict upon you the punishment that you destroy, with your own hands, the idol of your life—your great fame with posterity—by perverting history, and writing it, not as it is, but as it ought to be. I bid you cast away fame and posterity, in order to serve the cause of the present, which is the victory of the Roman church in the North. I bid you write the history of the kings Gustaf I and Charles IX in such a way that all they have done for the Reformation may redound as a ruin and a curse to them and their kingdom. And I bid you base this new history on documents so plausible that in the eyes of the people they may defy any proofs to the contrary . . . documents which do not exist, I know it full well, but which you shall manufacture . . . documents whose spuriousness may possibly be discovered in a coming generation, but which for the present shall serve the desired purpose."

"And thus," said Messenius, in a voice which trembled with the most varied emotions—fear, anger, humiliation, "thus I shall stand before posterity as a base falsifier, an infamous defamer of history's holiest truth . . ."

"Yes; and what then?" resumed the Jesuit, with a mocking smile; "what matters it if you, miserable tool, sacrifice your name, provided the church gains its great victory? Of what benefit to you is the praise of men, if your soul burns in the fire of hell? and what harm can human contempt do you, if through this sacrifice you have gained the martyr's crown in heaven?"

"But the cause of truth—the inexorable judgment of history?"

"Bah! what is historical truth? Is it anything more than the obedient slave who follows at the heels of human errors . . . the parrot which thoughtlessly repeats human follies? Or is it not rather reality such as it *ought to be,* purified from error, freed from crime and folly . . . God's kingdom on earth, as wise as it is almighty, as good as it is holy and wise?"

"But is it then we who dictate to God what is good and wise? Has he not himself told us this, through reality *as it is?*"

"Ha! vacillating apostate! you still dare to

argue with your superior about right and wrong! Choose and obey! Choose on one side temporal and eternal death; on the other the joys of Paradise and the glory of the saints. One word more; and upon this depends your weal or woe: Will you obey my commands?"

"Yes, I will obey," answered the prisoner, trembling and crushed. And the Jesuit strode away, silent and cold, with a ruler's nod that the slave had his good grace.

CHAPTER XIII.

ABI, MALE SPIRITUS.

A WEEK or so had passed since we listened to the secret conference. During this time, the Jesuit had not lost sight of the prisoner. He was daily seen to smuggle himself, under the pretext of medical attendance, into Messenius' room, and spend several hours with him. He was too prudent to rely upon the vacillating promise of the prisoner. What they did together, no one in the castle knew, and the governor had no suspicions. The situation of Kajana Castle, remote from the world, had lulled Wernstedt into a feeling of security; he rather found pleasure in the society of the foreign doctor, who gave evidence of great learning joined to great worldly experience.

There was one, however, who, with a vigilant eye, followed the stranger's steps; and this was Lucia Grothusen, Messenius' wife. A Catholic by education and conviction, she had always strengthened her husband in his papistical trickeries; the Jesuit knew this quite well, and therefore felt sure of her co-operation, although he cautiously avoided trusting his plans to the tireless female tongue. But the subtlest plans are often stranded upon these hidden impulses of the human heart, especially woman's heart, which work in quite a different direction from the one which cold reason marks out. The Jesuit, with all his shrewdness, had been mistaken in Lucia. He had not calculated that when fanaticism in her head cried, "Push on!" love cried still louder in her heart, "Hold back!" And with women, love always gains the mastery.

Lucia was an uncommonly sharp-sighted woman; she had seen through the Jesuit before he could suspect it. She saw the destructive inward strife which raged in Messenius' breast—a strife of life and death between fanaticism on the one hand, which bade him sacrifice fame and posterity for the victory of the church, and on the other ambition, which continually pleaded in his ears: "Will you, then, yourself, break down your whole life's work? Will you, then, blindly desecrate the sanctuary of history? Will you expose to contempt the brilliant name which still, in the night of captivity, is your wealth and your pride?"

All this, Lucia saw with the sharp eye of love; she saw that the man she loved, and for whom she had sacrificed an entire life in patience and self-denial, might sink under this terrible inward strife; and she resolved to save him by one bold and decisive step.

Late one evening, the lamp still burned on Messenius' writing-table, where he and the Jesuit had been working together since morning. Lucia had received permission to retire to her bed, which stood at the other end of the long room, near the door; and she pretended to be asleep. The men at the table had finished their work, and were conversing in a low voice, now, as always, in Latin, which language Lucia understood very well.

"I am content with you, my friend," said the Jesuit, with apparent satisfaction. "These documents, which bear the stamp of truth, will be sufficient to prove the conversion of King Gustaf Wasa and King Charles; and this introduction, signed by you, will further strengthen their validity. I will now return to Germany through Sweden, in order to have these documents printed, either through our adherents in Stockholm, or, if found possible, in Lübeck or Leyden."

Messenius stretched out his hand involuntarily, as if to snatch back a precious treasure from a robber's hands.

"Holy father," exclaimed he, with visible consternation, "is there then no reprieve? My name . . . my reputation . . . Have mercy upon me, holy father!—give me back my name!"

The Jesuit smiled.

"Do I not give you a name," said he, "far greater and more glorious than the one you lose—a name in the chronicles of our holy order—a name among the martyrs and benefactors of the church—a name which may one day be counted among the saints?"

"But with all this, a name without honor—a liar's, a falsifier's name!" burst out Messenius, with the despair of a condemned man who is shown the glory of heaven shining through the clouds of the scaffold.

"Weak, vain man, who do not know that great

ends are never won by the fear or praise of humanity!" said the Jesuit, in a contemptuous tone. "You might still be able to recall your word and forfeit your claims to the gratitude of all christendom. But happily it is now impossible. These documents"—and with this he extended his hand triumphantly with the papers—" are now in a hand which knows how to keep them, and, against your will, to use them for the glory of the church, the victory of faith, and your own soul's eternal welfare."

Father Hieronymus had scarcely uttered these words, before a hand behind him swiftly and unexpectedly seized the papers, which he had raised so triumphantly, snatched them from his hand, crumpled them together, tore them in a hundred pieces, and strewed the fragments over the floor of the prison. This movement was so unlooked for, the Jesuit was so far from expecting anything of the kind, that he for a moment lost his usual resoluteness, and with amazement which overcame his presence of mind, gave the daring hand time to finish its work of destruction. When the fragments lying around convinced him of the reality of his loss, he compressed his lips with rage, he raised his arms, and with the ferocity of a tiger fell upon the presumptuous being who had dared to annihilate his plans in the very moment of victory

Lucia—for the daring hand was hers—met the outbreak of the monk's fury with the energetic courage which distinguishes woman when she struggles for her holiest possessions. In her youth she had been able to take a man by the collar, and this scarcely womanly strength of arm had more than once been exercised during the constant quarrels with the rude soldiers of the castle.

She hastily clasped her sinewy fingers around the monk's outstretched arms, and held them as in a vise.

"Well," said she, in a mocking tone, "keep your distance from me, sir; what is it you wish?"

"Mad woman!" roared the Jesuit, foaming with rage. "You know not what you have done! Miserable thief! you have stolen a kingdom from your church and a paradise from your husband!"

"And from you I have stolen your booty—from the wolf his secure prey; is it not so?" answered Lucia, in a tone which in its turn began to rise with the fire of her violent temper. "Monk," continued she, with increasing anger, as she violently shook the mighty man, who in vain tried to get loose, "I know a thief who, in the sheep's clothing of the church, comes to steal from a great man his honor, from a whole nation its history, from a poor forsaken woman her sole pride—her husband's peace, fame, and life. Tell me, pious and holy monk, what punishment does such a thief deserve? Would not Ämmä falls be too shallow for his body, and the eternal fire too cool for his soul?"

The Jesuit glanced quickly toward the window, outside which the mighty torrent descended gloomily in the winter night.

"Ha!" exclaimed Lucia, with a bitter smile, "you fear me—you, the powerful one who rules kingdoms and consciences! You fear that under my gray dress might be concealed a man's arm, which could hurl you down into the cataract's abyss. Be calm . . . I am only a woman, and therefore I fight with a woman's weapons. You see . . . I do not throw you out of the window . . . I content myself with placing the wild beast behind bolts and bars. Tremble, monk! I know who you are!

Lucia Grothusen has followed your steps; you are betrayed, and it is she who has betrayed you."

"Betrayed!" repeated the Jesuit, who realized but too well what this word involved. In a time so full of hatreds, when two religions fought together for temporal and spiritual supremacy, when the Jesuits' plots irritated the Swedes in the highest degree, a member of this order, detected in disguise within the borders of the kingdom, was lost beyond rescue. But the threatening peril restored to this dangerous character all its elasticity.

"Betrayed by you, my daughter," repeated he, as his arms dropped, and his features assumed an expression of doubt and mild grief. "That is impossible!"

Lucia regarded him with hate and distrust.

"I your daughter!" exclaimed she, pushing the monk from her with aversion. "Falsehood is your daughter, and deceit your mother. These are your relatives!"

"Lucia Grothusen," said the Jesuit, very gently, "when you were a child, and followed your father, Arnold Grothusen, who was expelled with King Sigismund, you came one day, a distressed fugitive, and surrounded by persecutors, to a peasant's cot. They refused you refuge; they threatened to deliver you to your enemies. Then your childish eyes discovered in a corner of the hut an image of the Virgin, a relic from former times, profaned as a plaything for ignorant children. You took this image, you kissed it, you held it up before the hard-hearted inmates of the cot, and said to them: 'See, the Virgin Mary is here; she will protect us!'"

"Well, what then?" said Lucia, with an involuntary softness in her voice.

"Your childish trust . . . no; what do I say?—

the Holy Virgin—moved the hard peasants; they gave you shelter, they placed you in security. Still more, they gave you the image, which you have ever since preserved as your guardian saint; and there it hangs yet upon your wall. What you once said, I say now: 'The Virgin Mary is here; she will protect me.'"

Lucia tried in vain to struggle against an inner emotion. She bit her lip and made no reply.

"You are right," continued the monk, with shrewd calculation, "I am a Catholic like you, persecuted like you; if my disguise is known, they will kill me. My life is in your hands; betray me; I flee not; I die for my faith, and I forgive you my death."

"Fly!" said Lucia, half conquered; "I give you till to-morrow. But only on the condition that you do not see my husband again."

"Well, then," said the Jesuit, sadly, "I fly, but I leave here my beautiful dream of a better future. Ah, I had imagined the great Messenius and his noble wife as those who would reinstate the Catholic church in the North; I had imagined the time when millions of people would say: 'We wandered in darkness and blindness, but the light of history has dawned for us; the great Messenius has revealed to us the falseness of the Reformation.'"

"If it could be done without infringing upon the truth!" exclaimed Lucia, whose fiery soul was more and more transported by the future which the Jesuit so skillfully placed before her view.

"The truth!" repeated the Jesuit, with mild persuasion. "Oh, my friend, truth is our faith—falseness is the heretics' faith. If you become convinced that I ask of your husband only the truth itself, will you then, instead of tearing down your church, help to rebuild it?"

"Yes, I will!" answered Lucia, warmly and earnestly.

"Then listen . . ." continued the Jesuit; but he was just then interrupted by Messenius, who, hitherto stunned and crestfallen, now seemed to waken from a horrible dream.

"*Abi, male spiritus!*" exclaimed he, with frantic violence, as though he feared the Jesuit's serpent tongue would once more conquer. "*Abi, Abi!* you are not a human being, you are the prince of lies himself, you are the very serpent of paradise! *Abi, abi in æternam ignem, sabitaculum tuum, in regnum mendacii, imperium tuum!*" And with this he pushed the Jesuit before him toward the door, while Lucia made not the least effort to hinder.

"*Insanit miser!*" muttered the Jesuit, as he disappeared.

"Thanks, my friend!" said Lucia, with a relieved heart, as though freed from a dangerous spell.

"Thanks, Lucia!" answered Messenius, more mildly than usual with him for a long time in addressing his wife.

CHAPTER XIV.

THE JUDGMENT OF THE SAINTS.

VERY early the following morning, Father Hieronymus entered the room occupied by Lady Regina von Emmeritz and old Dorthe. Pale from vigils and grief, the beautiful girl sat by the bedside of her faithful servant. At the entrance of the Jesuit, Regina hastily rose.

"Save Dorthe, my father!" she exclaimed impetuously. . . . "I have looked for you everywhere, and you have abandoned me!"

"Hush!" said the Jesuit in a whisper. "Speak low; the walls have ears. So . . . indeed! . . . Dorthe is sick? Poor old woman! it is too bad; I cannot help her. They have found out our disguise. They suspect us. We must flee this day—this moment."

"Not before you have made Dorthe well. I beseech you, my father; you are wise, you know all remedies; give Dorthe a restorative, immediate in its effect, and we will follow you wherever you choose."

"Impossible!—we have not a moment to lose. Come!"

"Not without Dorthe, my father! Holy Virgin! should I abandon her, my nurse, my motherly friend?"

The Jesuit stepped to the bed, took the old woman's hand, touched her brow, and pointed to it in silence, with a mien of which Regina but too well understood the significance.

"She is dead!" exclaimed the young girl, in dismay.

"Yes; what matters it?" continued the Jesuit; and a strangely sinister smile struggled with the air of regret which he tried to assume. "You see, my child," added he, "that the saints have wished to spare our faithful friend a toilsome road, and have taken her instead up to the heavenly glory. There is nothing more to be done here. Come!"

But, in the midst of her tears, Regina had perceived the peculiar smile, and it struck her with an indescribable terror. She seemed to divine a dark secret.

"Come!" repeated he, hastily. "I will give Messenius' wife, who is a Catholic, the charge of burying our friend."

Regina's dark eyes stared at the monk in horror.

"Last evening, at seven o'clock," said she, "Dorthe was in good health. Then she drank the potion of strengthening herbs which you have prepared for her each evening. At eight o'clock she was taken ill . . . ten hours afterward she has ceased to live."

"The fatigue of the long journey . . . a cold . . . an *inflammation* . . . nothing more is wanted. Come!" said the Jesuit, uneasily.

But Regina did not go.

"Monk!" said she, in a voice that trembled with horror and loathing, "you have given her poison."

"My child, my daughter, what are you thinking of? Grief has unsettled your reason; come, I forgive you."

"She was a burden to you . . . I saw your impatience on our journey here. And now you wish me to place myself in your power without protection. Holy Virgin, save me! I will not go with you!"

The Jesuit's mobile features hastily changed their expression, and assumed that commanding severity with which he had made Messenius yield.

"Child," said he, "do not draw upon yourself the anger of the saints by listening to the suggestions of the tempter. Remember *where* you are, unfortunate, and *who* you are. One moment's further hesitation, and I leave you here, a prey to want, captivity, death; a target for the heretics' scorn, a lost sheep which the Holy Virgin has abandoned. Here, perdition and misery . . . there, in your fatherland, freedom, fortune, the comforts of religion, the favor of the saints. Choose, but choose quickly, for the sleigh stands waiting; the morning dawns, and day must not find us in this heretic den."

Regina hesitated.

"Swear," said she, "that you are innocent of Dorthe's death!"

"I swear it," exclaimed the Jesuit, "by this cross and by the holy Loyola's bones. May the firm ground open under my feet, and the abyss swallow me alive, if I have ever given this woman any other drink than that of health and healing."

"Well," said Regina, "the saints have heard your oath and written it down in the book of judgment. Farewell, Dorthe, my friend, my mother! Come, let us go!"

Both hurried out!

It was still dark. A pale streak of light appeared over the dusky firs at the borders of Koivukoski fall. The horses stood harnessed to the sleigh. The sleepy guard at the castle gates gave free passage to the physician, whose familiar intercourse with the commander was known to all.

The Jesuit believed himself already in safety, when a sleigh from the mainland met the fugitives on the narrow bridge, and drove close up to them in the darkness. The monk's sleigh turned partly upon its side, and was hindered only by the half-rotten and rickety railing of the bridge from upsetting into the depths below.

Regina gave a cry of affright.

At the sound, a man sprang from the other sleigh and approached the fugitives.

"Regina!" cried a well-known voice, which trembled from surprise.

"You are mistaken, my friend," the Jesuit hurried to say, in a disguised voice. "Give way to Doctor Albertus Simonis, army physician in the service of his royal majesty."

"Ha! it is you, miserable Jesuit!" cried the stranger. "Guard, to arms! To arms, and seize the greatest villain on earth!" And so saying, he grasped the monk by his fur cloak.

For an instant Hieronymus tried to disengage the sleigh and escape by the speed of his horses. But when he found that this was impossible, he left his fur cloak behind him, squirmed from his enemy's grasp, and, throwing himself quickly over the railing of the bridge, jumped down on the ice, which, in the unusually intense cold, had formed between the castle island and the mainland. In a short time he had disappeared in the twilight.

The guardsman at the castle gates, attracted by the cry, discharged his gun after the fugitive, but without hitting him. Some of the soldiers were inclined to pursue him on the ice.

"Don't do that, boys!" cried a bearded sergeant; "it has thawed during the night, the stream has cut the ice underneath; I think it will break up to-day."

"But he jumped down there!" cried some.

"The devil will get him," answered the sergeant, calmly, lighting his morning pipe. "I think by this time he has reached Ämmä."

"What do you say?" exclaimed the man from the other sleigh, in horror.

"I say that the old woman * has got her breakfast to-day," answered the sergeant, with undisturbed composure. "Listen! she barks like a chained dog; now she is satisfied."

All listened, appalled, to the din of the waters. It seemed to them that the mighty fall roared more wildly, more terribly than before, in the gray winter twilight. The sergeant was right; it was like the howl of an angry dog that has secured its prey.

CHAPTER XV.

BERTEL AND REGINA.

OUR wandering Don Quixote, whom we left, worn out by the fatigue of his adventures, sleeping in a peasant's cottage at Ylihärmä, re-appeared at Kajana castle, engaged in the vain attempt to secure the feared and hated Jesuit, whom he had recognized through the window-pane of the miserable forest hut. Bertel's circuitous course during the ten or twelve days interim can easily be imagined. Led by false traces in his chase after

* The Finnish word *Ämmä* means *old woman*.

the fugitives, he had scoured all the roads in East Bothnia, as far even as Uleåborg; and it was only when he there lost all track of them that he resolved, as a last resort, to seek the fugitives far away in the wilderness of Kajana. Why the young knight pursued them with such an indefatigable perseverance, will soon be shown.

Some hours after the scene on the bridge, we find Bertel in the new apartment which the governor had assigned to Lady Regina, and where she was under the protection of one of his female relatives. More than three years had elapsed since these two young people last met, under such different circumstances, in Frankfort-on-the-Main, in the presence of the great king. Bertel was then an inexperienced youth of twenty, Regina an equally inexperienced girl of sixteen. Both had since then endured many trials; with both had the first burning enthusiasm of youth been cooled by trials and by suffering. The distance between the prince's daughter and the humble lieutenant had been diminished through Bertel's military fame and lately acquired coat of arms; nay, at this moment, she, an abandoned prisoner, might consider herself honored by the attentions of a nobleman. But the distance between their convictions, their sympathies, their hearts—had this been diminished through these trials, which generally strengthen a conviction instead of breaking it?

Bertel approached the young lady with all the stately courtesy which the etiquette of his time had retained as an inheritance from the chivalry of past centuries.

"My lady," said he, in a slightly trembling voice, "since my hope of finding you at Korsholm failed, I have pursued you through forest and wilderness, as one pursues a criminal. Perhaps you divine the cause that prompted me to do so?"

Regina's long black eyelashes were slowly lifted, and she regarded Bertel with an inquiring glance.

"Sir," answered she, "whatever has prompted you, I am convinced that your reasons have been noble and chivalrous. You cannot have meant to take an unhappy young girl back to her prison; you have only wished to snatch her away from a man whom the poor deceived one has regarded ever since childhood as a holy and pious person, and whose deeply concealed wickedness she has now for the first time learned to know and detest."

"You are mistaken," said Bertel, with warmth and animation. "It is true I shuddered when I saw you in the company of this man, whose real character I perceived before you, and I then redoubled my efforts to rescue you from his hands. But before I imagined any danger from that direction, I hastened to find you with the glad tidings of a deed of justice . . . late, but I hope not too late."

"A deed of justice, you say?" repeated Regina, with a surprise which drove the blood to her cheeks.

"Yes, my lady," continued Bertel, regarding in amazement this picture of dazzling beauty, "at last, after several years of vain effort, I have succeeded in obtaining this deed of justice toward an innocent sufferer. You are free; you can now, under the protection of the Swedish arms, return to your fatherland; and here—" at these words Bertel bent his knee and handed Regina a paper with the regency's seal—"here is the document which insures your freedom."

Regina had overcome her first emotion, and received the precious document with cool dignity.

"Sir," said she, in short and measured tones, "I know that you do not ask my thanks for having, beyond any of your countrymen, acted like a man of honor."

Bertel arose, a little surprised at this pride, which however he ought to have expected.

"What I have done," said he, with a touch of coldness in his turn, "I have done only to efface an act of injustice which might have thrown a shadow upon the memory of a great king. Each one of my countrymen would have done the same as I, had not the exigencies of war made him forget the reparation you had a right to demand. First of all would the noble-minded King Gustaf Adolf have sought to make amends for the hasty deed of a moment's indiscretion, had not Providence so suddenly cut short his days. . . . But," said Bertel, interrupting himself, "I forget that the king whom I love and admire, you hate!"

At these words the bright and beautiful color again rose to Regina's cheeks. Without knowing it, Bertel had touched one of the most sensitive chords in this ardent heart. A new discovery—a wonderful resemblance in figure, voice, gesture, nay, in thought, a resemblance which she had never before observed, and which these three years had developed in Bertel's whole personality—made an indescribable impression upon the young Southerner's soul. It seemed to her that she saw him himself, the greatest of mortals, the pride of her dreams, her life's happiness and misery; him, the beloved and feared, the conqueror of her country, her faith, and her heart . . . and that he himself said to her, in the well-known tones: "Regina you hate me."

This impression came so swiftly, so strongly, and with such a surprising power, that Regina suddenly grew pale, staggered, and was compelled to lean on Bertel's outstretched arm.

"Holy Virgin!" whispered she, bewildered, and not knowing what she said, "should I hate you . . . you whom I . . ."

Bertel caught this half-unspoken word, incomprehensible and yet so full of meaning, with a surprise as sudden and unexpected as Regina's. Beside himself with amazement, fear, and hope, he was still too chivalric to avail himself of so involuntary a confession. Mute and respectful, he led the young girl to her protector, in whose care she soon recovered from her sudden faintness—an effect of long-suppressed emotions, which now sought relief.

Bertel had obtained the commission to escort Lady Regina von Emmeritz to Stockholm, from whence she could, at the opening of navigation, return to her fatherland. He was therefore at liberty to remain at Kajana Castle until his charge should be ready for the journey; and this event was again delayed through the unforeseen lack of a fitting female companion for the high-born prisoner.

Weeks passed in the waiting, and during this time entirely new relations were formed, which one could scarcely have surmised from Regina's proud coldness toward her deliverer. Ah! this coldness was the ice over a glowing volcano; every day it grew thinner, and melted; every day Regina's pride became haughtier, while its foundations gradually gave way; and at last there remained only one barrier—the strongest one of all, it is true—the bitter struggle of religious convictions. Vain wall! It, too, finally crumbled before the fire of a Southern passion; and ere three weeks were ended, the girl of nineteen and the youth of twenty-three had forgotten all differences of faith and rank, and sworn each other fidelity for life. Did Bertel know that he had to thank the memory of Gustaf Adolf for his beautiful, his proud, his black-eyed bride?

A singular destiny waited to seal this union in an unexpected and wonderful manner. With a secret anxiety for his happiness, Bertel had in vain tried to discover the fate of the Jesuit. Since the morning when the monk jumped over the railing of the bridge, no one had heard or seen anything of him, until, three weeks afterwards, a peasant reported that on opening the ice a little below Ämmä fall, they had found the body of a man without ears, clothed in foreign garments, which the peasant brought with him, and which were recognized as those of Father Hieronymus. In addition, the honest Paldamo peasant produced a little copper ring which had been found hanging by a cord around the dead man's neck.

Bertel looked at this ring with amazement and joy.

"At last I have you!" exclaimed he, "this ring which I have so long lost . . . and with you the certainty of the death of this formidable man."

"The judgment of the saints upon the perjurer!" exclaimed Regina, awe-stricken.

"The judgment of the saints, which confirms our happiness!" rejoined Bertel, and placed on Regina's finger the *King's Ring*.

CHAPTER XVI.

THE KING'S RING.—THE SWORD AND THE PLOUGH.
—FIRE AND WATER.

ONCE more we return to Storkyro, to Bertila's farm, and to the old peasant-king.

It is a wintry day in March, 1635. The snow already feels the influence of the spring sun, and drips from the roofs upon the sunny side; the icy crust upon the northern slope of the hills is firm and unyielding, but breaks on the southern side. Aaron Bertila is just returning from church, with all his people; his gray head is bowed; he leans on Meri's arm. At his side walk two precious looking thick-set figures—the old Larsson, and his lately returned son, the brave and learned captain of the same name, the faithful image of his little father, except in years. Walking beside him is his young wife, a pretty and light-hearted little creature, whose features we recognize. She is none other than Kätchen, the plucky and merry girl, whose soft hand once made the noble captain lose his wits. After that day he swore by all the Greek and Roman authors, whom he formerly read in Åbo Cathedral School—*sic unde ubi apud unquam post*, as the ancients used to express themselves—that the soft-handed novice among the Würtzburg sisters of charity should one day become his. And when the vicissitudes of war again brought them together, when Kätchen was without protection, and, besides, had nothing against an honest and jovial soldier, this cheerful and contented pair were wedded in due form in the autumn, at Stralsund, and then went to visit their round-bodied goodhearted father in Storkyro, where they were warmly welcomed, and received as children.

It must be added that Larsson had quit the service, and after much higgling obtained his discharge, but without promotion. He complained that he had not a farthing left from the spoils of Germany, though so many of his fellow-soldiers had. All that he had earned—and if we can believe him, it must have been millions—had taken wings; where? At Nördlingen, he says. Certainly: in revels and sprees with jolly fellows of the same calibre as himself. But now he meant to be as regular and steady as a gate-post; to succeed his father as overseer of Bertila's large farms; to plough, sow, harvest, and *pro modulo virium prolem copiosam in lucem proferre*, as the ancients so truly expressed themselves.

Old Bertila treats him with apparent favor. Significant words have escaped the old man, and he has just delivered his will into the hands of the judge.

As for Meri, she has withered like a flower without roots, and clings to life only by her feeble heart-thread—the banished and rejected Gustaf Bertel, now ennobled to *Bertelsköld*.

This domestic circle, composed of such different elements, both shadowy and bright, is now gathered in the large room, surrounded by the numerous laborers; and old Larsson still tries, in secret alliance with Meri, to soften the mind of the stern peasant-king toward Bertel. All their prayers and reasons are stranded against the unbending firmness of the old man. Larsson turns away angrily;

Meri conceals her tears in the darkest shadows of the room.

Then is heard again the tinkling of sleigh-bells outside, as on Epiphany evening; a large sleigh stops in the yard, and two persons alight from it: an officer in his large cloak, and a young beautiful woman in a magnificent mantle of black velvet lined with costly fur. Meri and old Larsson turn pale at this sight; Larsson hastens out, but it is too late. Bertel and Regina enter the room.

Both the Larssons and Meri surround Bertel, with warm although apparently embarrassed greetings. Kätchen jumps up, and, without thinking of the difference between her burgher dress and the costly velvet cloak, throws herself into Regina's arms, who, with emotion, clasps to her heart the faithful friend of her childhood.

Bertel frees himself gently from Meri's embrace, and goes with a firm step straight up to old Bertila, who, mute and cold in his high-backed chair at the end of the table, does not honor him with a word or a glance.

All present await with dismayed looks the result of this meeting, which they all know must be decisive. The young officer has removed his cloak and hat; his long fair hair falls in beautiful curls around his open brow; his cheeks are very pale, but the blue and expressive eyes regard the iron-hard features of the gray-haired man with a firm and steadfast gaze.

Bertel now, as before, bends his knee, and says, in a voice at once humble and steady:

"My father!"

"Who are you? I know you not; I have no son!" interrupted the old man, in chilling tones.

"My father!" continued Bertel, without allowing himself to be discomfited, "I come once more, and for the last time, to ask your forgiveness and blessing. Do not repulse me! I leave my fatherland, to fight and perhaps die on German soil. It depends upon you whether I ever return. Remember, my father, that your blessing restores to you a son; that your curse drives him into exile forever."

The old man in the high-backed chair does not change a feature, but his voice betrays an inward struggle.

"My answer is brief," said he. "I had a son; he became unworthy of me and all the principles which have governed my life. He abandoned the cause of the people, for that of the pernicious power of the nobility, which I hate and detest. I have no longer a son. I have to-day disinherited him."

The faces of the hearers turn pale at these words. But Bertel colors slightly, and says:

"My father, I do not ask your property. Give it to whomsoever you consider more worthy than I. I ask only your forgiveness . . . your blessing, my father."

All except Regina surround the old man, fall on their knees, and exclaim: "Grace for Bertel! Grace for your son!"

"And if I had a son, do you believe he would for my sake give up his false ambition for the distinctions of nobility? Do you believe that he would become a peasant like me, a man of the people like me, ready to live and die for their cause? Do you believe that he, with his fine gloved hands, would plough the earth and would choose a wife from my station, a simple and honest

woman, as becomes a true man, without parade
and boasting?"

"My father," says Bertel, in a voice more tremulous than before, "what you ask has been made impossible by the education you yourself have given me. I will honor and respect your station; but I have been bred to the career of a soldier, and that I will not, I cannot abandon. To choose a wife according to your mind, is equally impossible. Here stands my mate; she is a prince's daughter, my father, but she has not blushed to choose a peasant's son for her husband; let this be a proof that she will not blush to call you father."

At these words, Regina approaches humbly, as if to kiss the old man's hand; and all except Bertel and his father rise. But the fiery temper of Bertila, the peasant king, flames forth in anger.

"Did I not say so!" exclaims he, in thundering tones. "There stands the renegade who was born a free peasant and became a servant of lords! Ha! by God! I have in my day seen much strife and much defiance between the sword and the plough; but a defiance like this I have never seen. The boy who calls himself my son dares to bring before my eyes his high-born harlot and call her his wife."

Bertel springs up and supports Regina, who at these words almost sinks to the floor.

"Old man," says he, in a voice trembling with anger, "thank your name of father and your gray head that you have been allowed to utter what no one else could have uttered, and lived an hour thereafter. Here is the ring I placed on the hand of my lawfully wedded wife,"—at these words he takes from Regina's finger the king's ring—"and I swear that her hand is as pure and as worthy as that of any mortal to wear this ring, which for so many years has been worn upon the finger of the greatest king."

Meri's eyes stare at the ring; her pale cheeks are colored by a deep flush; she struggles violently with herself. Finally she steps nearer, presses the ring with ecstacy to her lips, and says, in a broken voice, and with an emotion so strong that it dries every tear in her eyes:

"My ring which *he* has worn . . . my ring which has protected *him* . . . thou art innocent of his death; he gave thee away, and then came the bullets, then came death. Do you know, Gustaf Bertel, and you, his wife, the real power of this ring? In my youth I went one day into the wilderness, and found there a dying man, who was languishing from thirst. I gave him drink from the spring; I refreshed his tongue with the juice of berries. He thanked me, and said: 'My friend, I am dying, and have no other reward to offer you than this ring. I found it on an image of the Holy Virgin, which alone was left uninjured in the midst of the broken emblems of Popish rites, in Storkyro church; and when I took the ring from the finger of the Virgin, the image fell to dust. This ring has at once the power of the saints and of magic, for with me the ancient greatness of sorcery descends into the grave.' He who wears this ring is secure against fire, water, steel, and all kinds of dangers, on the sole condition that he never swears a false oath, for that annuls the power of the ring; with this ring goes happiness in peace, and victory in war: love, honor, and fortune; and when it is worn by three generations successively from father to son, then from that family shall come brilliant generals and statesmen . . ."

Here Meri paused; all listened with intense expectation.

"But," continued she, "if the ring is worn by six succeeding generations, then shall spring from that family a powerful dynasty. 'But,' said the old man to me, 'you ought to know that great gifts are accompanied by great dangers. False oaths and family enmity will constantly tempt the possessor of the ring, and seek to neutralize its power; pride and inordinate ambition will continually work within his breast to prepare his fall; and a great steadfastness of soul will be required, joined with a meek and humble heart, to overcome these temptations. He who possesses and wears this ring shall enjoy all happiness in this world, and only have to conquer himself; but he will also be the most formidable enemy of his own happiness. All this is signified by the three letters, *R. R. R.*, which are engraved on the inside of the ring, and interpreted by these words: *Rex Regi Rebellis*—the king rebels against the king; the happiest, the mightiest among men, has to fear the greatest danger within his own breast.'"

"And this ring, O Regina, is ours!" exclaimed Bertel, with mingled fear and joy. "What a wealth and what a responsibility go with this ring!"

"Beware, my daughter!" said Meri, sadly. "Behind these words lurks the greatest danger of the ring."

The old Bertila regarded the ring and the young people with a contemptuous smile:

"False gold!" said he. "Vanity! Useless ornament! False ambition! This is a gift worthy to descend from generation to generation among the nobility. Come, young Larsson, you, who are also of peasant origin and who wish to return to your station, although you have been a soldier,—I will give you something which is neither gold nor useless ornament, but which will perhaps bring you more blessings than all the kings' rings in the world. Take my old axe with the oak handle from the wall there; yes, fear not, there is no magic in that; my father forged it with his own hand, in Gustaf Wasa's time. With it, my father and I have done great deeds in the forests, and cleared many a field. May it descend through your family; and I promise you that he who possesses my axe shall be blessed with happiness and contentment in his honest labor."

"Thanks, Father Bertila," answered the captain gleefully, as with an air of importance he tried the edge of the old axe. "If we took a fancy to engrave any inscription on it, I should propose *R. R. R., Ruris Rusticus Robustus*, which is to say briefly. 'The devil cannot disturb such a powerful chopper!' a very beautiful and thoughtful saying among the ancients."

The elder Larsson now thought the opportunity at hand to give the bitter contest a more placable turn. He stepped up to old Bertila, leading by the hand the two newly married couples, and said:

"Dear old friend, let us not meddle in the Lord's business. Your boy and mine are both great rascals, that is granted; but are they to blame that our Lord created one of them of fire and the other of water? Bertel is like a flame—burning hot, high-soaring, brilliant, transitory, and I wager that his little wife is of the same sort. My boy, here is of the purest water . . ."

"Stop!" cried the captain. "Water has never been my weak point!"

"Hold your tongue; my boy is clear water—flowing and unstable, contentedly keeping itself to the ground, and created especially to put out the other youngster's poetic blaze with its prosaic philosophy. As for his wife, she is of the same stuff. Do you not see, Bertila, that our Lord has intended the boys to be friends?—the fire to warm the water, and the water to quench the fire; and you would make them enemies by taking from one and giving to the other. No, my friend, do not do it, that is my advice; give your son what belongs to him; my son shall not want it."

Old Bertila remained silent a moment. Then he said, vehemently:

"Do not teach me the meaning of the Lord! Can you believe that he, the newly-baked nobleman, whom you compare to the fire, could be induced to give away the ring and take the axe in its stead?"

"Never!" exclaimed Bertel, excitedly.

Meri seized his hand, and looked at him beseechingly. "Give away the ring," said she. "You know some of its dangers; but there is still one which I have feared to mention. All who wear this ring shall die a violent death."

"What matters it?" exclaimed Bertel. "The death of the soldier on the battle-field is beautiful and glorious. I ask no better."

"Listen to him!" said old Bertila, contemptuously. "I expected it: he runs after fame, even to the grave. A peaceful death, like a peaceful life, is to him an abomination; but you, Larsson, tell me, have you a desire to give away the axe and take the ring?"

"Hm!" replied the captain, thoughtfully, "if the ring were of gold, I might sell it in town and get a good cask of ale for it. But as it is only of copper ... pshaw, I let it go and keep the axe, which is at least good to cut wood with."

"Good!" continued Bertila; "it is, as your father said, to sprinkle water on fire. It is not I who have made fire and water eternal enemies to each other. Come, Larsson—you, the man of sound common-sense, the man of tangible things,—come, be my son, and some day take my goods when I am no longer among the living. My blessing be with you and your descendants. May they multiply, and work like ants in the soil, and may there be an eternal enmity between them and those in high places, the nobility, the people with the fiery dispositions. May there be war and no peace between them and you, until this useless glitter disappears from human society. May the axe and the ring live in open feud until both are melted in the same heat. When this occurs, after a hundred years, or more, then it will be time to say, class distinctions have seen their last days, and a man's merit is his only coat of arms."

"But, my father," exclaimed Bertel once more, in an entreating voice, "have you then no blessing to give me and my posterity, at the moment when we separate forever?"

"You!" repeated the old man, still in the tones of anger. "Go, you lost, vain, worm-eaten branches of the people's great trunk, go in your pitiful parade to your certain ruin. Until the day when, as I said, the axe and the ring, the false gold and the honest steel, melt together. ... until then I give you my curse as an inheritance, even unto the tenth generation; and with it shall follow dissension, hatred, strife, and finally a pitiful fall."

"Stop a little, Father Bertila!" cried young Larsson. "Grace for Bertel!"

"No grace for nobility!" answered the peasant-king.

"Beware, unnatural father!" cried old Larsson. "The doom may fall upon your own head."

"I no longer ask any grace," said Bertel, pale, but calm. "Farewell, you who were once my father! Farewell, my fatherland! I go, never to see you again!"

"One moment more," interrupted Meri, who with great effort and in violent emotion placed herself in his way. "You go! Yes, go . . . my heart's darling, my hope, my life, my all . . . go, I shall no longer stand in your way. But before you leave me, you shall take with you the secret which has been at once my life's highest bliss and greatest agony . . ."

"Hear her not!" cried old Bertila, with a changed voice and in evident alarm. "Listen not to her; madness speaks from her lips! . . . Think of your honor and mine!" whispered he, sternly, in the pale daughter's ear.

"What do I care for your honor and mine!" burst out Meri, with an impetuosity never before shown. "Do you not see that he goes . . . my life's joy leaves me, never more to return? He goes; and you, hard, inhuman father, wish me to let him depart with a curse to foreign lands. But thus he shall not go. For every curse you fling upon his head, I will give him a hundred blessings; and we shall see which will avail the most before the throne of the Highest—your hatred or my love, the curse of the grandfather, or the blessing of the mother . . ."

"My mother!" exclaimed Bertel, beside himself with surprise. Duke Bernhard's enigmatical words now suddenly became clear to him.

"Believe her not; she knows not what she says!" exclaimed old Bertila, vainly trying to appear calm.

Meri had sunk in Bertel's arms.

"It is now said," whispered she, in a failing voice. "Gustaf . . . my son. Ah! it is so strange and so sweet to call you this. Now you know the secret of my life; . . . and I have not long to blush over it. Do you love me? . . . Yes, yes! now I go from life gladly . . . the veil is lifted . . . light comes. . . . My father . . . I forgive you . . . that you have hated and cursed your daughter's son. . . . Forgive me . . . that I . . . love . . . bless . . . my son!"

"My mother!" exclaimed Bertel, "hear me, my mother! I thank you . . . I love you! . . . You shall go with me, and I will never leave you. Oh, you do not hear me. You are so pale . . . Great God . . . she is dead!"

"My daughter! my only child!" exclaimed Bertila, the iron-hearted peasant-king, annihilated.

"Judge not, lest ye be judged!" said old Larsson, with clasped hands. "And you, our children, go out into life with peaceful hearts. Curse and blessing struggle for your future, and not only for yours, but for that of your posterity, unto the tenth generation. Pray to Heaven that the blessing may conquer!"

"Amen!" said young Larsson and Kätchen.

"Amen!" said Bertel and Regina.

END OF FIRST CYCLE.

Selections from the Publications

OF

JANSEN, McCLURG & CO.

GOLDEN POEMS. By British and American Authors. Edited by FRANCIS F. BROWNE. Crown 8vo. Richly bound, Cloth, Full Gilt. Price, $2.50. Morocco Antique—Price, $5.00.

GOLDEN THOUGHTS. From the Words of Leading Orators, Divines, Philosophers, Statesmen and Poets. By Rev. S. P. LINN. Crown 8vo. Richly bound, Cloth, Full Gilt. Price, $2.50. Morocco Antique—Price, $5.00.

LIFE OF MOZART. From the German of Louis Nohl. By JOHN J. LALOR. With Portrait. Price, $1.25.

LIFE OF BEETHOVEN. From the German of Louis Nohl. By JOHN J. LALOR. With Portrait. Price, $1.25.

LIFE OF HAYDN. From the German of Louis Nohl. By GEORGE P. UPTON. With Portrait. Price, $1.25.

MUSIC-STUDY IN GERMANY. By Miss AMY FAY. Price, $1.25.

A SUMMER IN NORWAY. By Hon. J. D. CATON. Portrait and Illustrations. Price, $1.75.

TRUTHS FOR TO-DAY. (Sermons.) By Prof. DAVID SWING. 1st Series—Price, $1.50. 2d Series—Price, $1.50.

MOTIVES OF LIFE. By Professor DAVID SWING. Price, $1.00.

CLUB ESSAYS. By Prof. DAVID SWING. Price, $1.00.

PUBLISHED BY JANSEN, McCLURG, & CO.

MEMORIES: A Story of German Love. From the German of Max Muller. Full Gilt. Price, $1.25.

GRAZIELLA: A Story of Italian Love. From the French of Lamartine. Full Gilt. Price, $1.25.

MARIE: A Story of Russian Love. From the Russian of Alex. Pushkin. Full Gilt. Price, $1.25.

MADELEINE: A Story of French Love. From the French of Sandeau. Full Gilt. Price, $1.25.

FAMILIAR TALK ON ENGLISH LITERATURE. A Manual embracing the Great Epochs of English Literature, from the English conquest of Britain, 449, to the death of Walter Scott, 1832. By ABBY SAGE RICHARDSON. Price, $2.00.

CHOICE READINGS; For Public and Private Entertainments. By Prof. R. L. CUMNOCK. Price, $1.75.

SKETCH OF EDWARD COLES, Second Governor of Illinois, and of the Slavery Struggle of 1823-24. By Hon. E. B. WASHBURNE. With Portrait and Fac-Simile Letters. Price, $1.75.

LIFE OF BENEDICT ARNOLD; His Patriotism and his Treason. By Hon. ISAAC N. ARNOLD, author of "Life of Abraham Lincoln." Price, $2.50.

SEWER-GAS AND ITS DANGERS. With an Exposition of Common Defects in House Drainage, and Practical Information relating to their Remedy. By G. P. BROWN. Price, $1.25.

TALES OF ANCIENT GREECE. By the Rev. Sir G. W. Cox, Bart., M.A., Trinity College, Oxford. Price, $1.50.

SHORT HISTORY OF FRANCE; For Young People. By Miss E. S. KIRKLAND. Price, $1.50.

TALES OF THE CARAVAN, INN AND PALACE. From the German of William Hauff. By E. L. STOWELL. Illustrated. Price, $1.25.

Mailed, Pre-paid, on receipt of price, by the publishers,
JANSEN, McCLURG, & CO., 117 & 119 State Street, CHICAGO.

www.ingramcontent.com/pod-product-compliance
Lightning Source LLC
Chambersburg PA
CBHW031851220426
43663CB00006B/574